Promised Land

Inside the Mike Harris Revolution

John Ibbitson

Canadian Cataloguing in Publication Data

Ibbitson, John
      Promised land : inside the Mike Harris revolution

Includes index.
ISBN 0-13-673864-8

1. Ontario - Politics and government - 1995-
I. Title.

FC3077.2.I22 1997   971.3'04   C97-931685-5
F1058.I22 1997

 © 1997 John Ibbitson

Prentice Hall Canada Inc.
Scarborough, Ontario
A Division of Simon & Schuster/A Viacom Company

Prentice-Hall, Inc., Upper Saddle River, New Jersey
Prentice-Hall International (UK) Limited, London
Prentice-Hall of Australia, Pty. Limited, Sydney
Prentice-Hall Hispanoamericana, S.A., Mexico City
Prentice-Hall of India Private Limited, New Delhi
Prentice-Hall of Japan, Inc., Tokyo
Simon & Schuster Southeast Asia Private Limited, Singapore
Editora Prentice-Hall do Brasil, Ltda., Rio de Janeiro

ISBN 0-13-673864-8

Managing Editor: Robert Harris
Acquisitions Editor: Sara Borins
Editor: Rick Archbold
Copy Editor: Wendy Thomas
Editorial Assistant: Joan Whitman
Creative Director: Mary Opper
Production Coordinator: Julie Preston
Photo Researcher: Joan Whitman
Cover Photographs: Portrait of Mike Harris/Peter Bregg, OPSEU strikers/Phill Snell
Cover and Interior Design: Kevin Connolly Design
Page Layout: B.J. Weckerle

1 2 3 4 5   RRD   01 00 99 98 97

Printed and bound in the United States of America

Visit the Prentice Hall Canada Web site! Send us your comments, browse our
catalogues, and more. www.phcanada.com

For Andy and Doug.
We go back.

Contents

Preface

Richard Brennan, a compact, fierce-tempered reporter who had been around the Park longer than most, barrelled in the bureau, incredulous.

"Now they've done it," he exclaimed. "Now they've really shot themselves in the foot."

"They've done what?" someone asked.

"Boot camps." He shook his head. "They want to open boot camps."

Well, that was it—the inevitable misstep that everyone had been waiting for. The Progressive Conservative Party under leader Mike Harris had been showing astonishing strength in the last half of the 1995 election campaign. Recent polls suggested they were in a tight race with the Liberals under Lyn McLeod, who was supposed to have taken this election in a walk. Every Tory policy that should have been laughed off by the voters, from workfare to tax cuts, seemed instead to improve the party's standing. But this was the limit. Boot camps for young offenders. Where did they think they were, Alabama?

Four days later a poll showed the Tories headed for a majority government.

Journalists tend to describe as astonishing anything that astonishes them. And we were certainly flummoxed by the victory of Mike Harris on June 8. Ontario politics was supposed to be all about conciliating conflicting interests, establishing broad coalitions, winning over the middle ground. But the ground had shifted, and no one but the Tories had noticed. Their Common Sense Revolution had tapped a well-spring of discontent, impatience, and longing for change that other political observers and political parties had failed to detect. The Tories' electoral strategy was a modern masterpiece of voter divination.

But the election of 1995 was only the first surprise. The second was the discovery that Mike Harris had meant what he said. Never in the province's history has a government moved so emphatically to keep its promises and advanced simultaneously on so many fronts: slashing welfare benefits and government jobs; launching enormous reforms in education, health care, and social services; rewriting the province's environmental and planning laws; reconstructing its jails and its courts; redefining the very relationship between the municipal and provincial governments. No one could find a precedent of any government anywhere cutting its tax rate by 30 per cent while balancing its budget and taking a knife to spending, in the process reshaping how it delivered every major program. In the fall of 1995, when Columbia University economist Roberto Perotti was told about Ontario's intentions, he responded, "Well, it's a [long pause] *brave* plan."

Once the Tories assumed power, it became hard to keep track, from day to day, of what was going on, of what they were doing to whom. If there was a breathlessness to the reporting coming out of Queen's Park, it was only because the reporters were out of breath, as were opposition politicians, labour leaders, social activists, doctors and lawyers, and all the others who struggled to define a response to Mike Harris's radical reshaping of the province. There was a crying need to step back, to take a deep breath and examine the whys and wherefores of the government's agenda. But there just wasn't the time.

There was also a need to know more about the people behind this revolution. Who was this Mike Harris, who had been derisively dismissed as a golf pro from North Bay without a hope of becoming premier? The former golf pro was now running the country's most important economy and doing it with a greater sense of urgency than had been seen in the province since the days of World War Two. What's more, he had surrounded himself with a band of advisers who seemed fearsomely young, and whom no one seemed to know very much about.

Though the Harris government is only halfway through its first term, and the agenda of the Common Sense Revolution is not yet complete, the time has come for an accounting of the most tumultuous two years in the province's modern history. We need to understand how this band of radicals rose from the ashes of a once-great political party to seize power, why the people of the province were ready to entrust them with that power, and why and how the Tories enacted the agenda that has dominated the lives of Ontario's citizens from the day the new government took office.

These are the themes of this book.

More than do most authors, I have debts to acknowledge. The people at Prentice Hall have shown firm and uncompromising support for this book from the moment I first proposed it. Despite these valued efforts, however, *Promised Land* would not be in print but for the overriding contribution of Rick Archbold, its editor. Rick took an impossible project with a hair-raising schedule and prodded, cajoled, and guided me and everyone else through it. He understood the book's potential, and its potential traps, better than any of us. Always encouraging, never quite satisfied, he pushed me farther than I thought, as a writer and a journalist, I could go. I am deeply grateful for his wisdom, insight, and forbearance, and forever in his debt.

I was also fortunate that first Jim Travers at the *Ottawa Citizen* and then Kirk Lapointe at Southam News offered the resources needed to pursue my beat and the time needed to write my book. It has been a joy to work for both organizations.

The material for this book was largely compiled through interviews. Statistics were obtained from the relevant ministries or from the Legislative Library, whose staff were most helpful. Quotations are derived from interviews or from remarks widely reported in the media or found in the provincial *Hansard*.

Premier Harris declined to be interviewed, which is regrettable but not surprising, given his personal reserve. However, I obtained extensive co-operation from staff within the premier's office, from ministers and their staff, and from public servants. Not all wished their contribution to be publicly acknowledged, and that wish has been respected. The government's opponents, from Leah Casselman to John Sewell, were equally helpful; their contributions have enriched the book.

Certain published works also provided information and quotations. Christina Blizzard's *Right Turn: How the Tories Took Ontario* is a valuable accounting of the election of 1995. University of Toronto political scientists David Cameron and Graham White graciously provided a copy of *Cycling Into Saigon*, their examination of the transition between the NDP and Conservative governments. Profiles by Richard Brennan of the *Windsor Star* and Michael Hanlon of the *Toronto Star* offered important insights into Harris's early years. *Toronto Star* reporter Susan Kastner contributed a perceptive portrait of John Snobelen. Greg Crone, of the *Kitchener-Waterloo Record*, provided two valuable academic essays he wrote on events surrounding the legislative stand-off over Bill 26 and the Bill 103 filibuster.

And I received much help from other colleagues. Jim Coyle, Queen's Park columnist for the *Ottawa Citizen*, listened to the Tories playing Bruce Springsteen's "Promised Land" at the Hamilton policy convention and instantly decided he had the title for my book. I instantly agreed. Jim's wisdom was a great asset during my time at the Southam Queen's Park Bureau. I stole shamelessly both from him and my other compatriots in the bureau, for which much thanks. And I drew as well on the collective wisdom of the press gallery, through both the daily press clippings and many informal conversations.

Finally, my friend Stephen Northfield ran me around a squash court every Thursday and then listened patiently afterward to my anguish and exhilaration. He was the book's sounding board.

For any errors or misinterpretations that remain, I alone must bear responsibility.

1
Getting There

CHAPTER 1

Mike

Beneath him, to his right, lay the silver glint of Lake Nipissing, which he'd grown up beside. Early that morning, the win—what it meant—had reached inside and put an end to sleep. The flight south to Toronto would take an hour and this might have been a chance for a nap, but for the thick, black briefing binders that had been handed to him, outlining issues and decisions he would have to confront during the transition. He settled into a seat at the back of the plane and set to work, every now and then lifting his head to look out the window at the province below.

For more than a decade Mike Harris had driven the 200 miles from Toronto to North Bay most weekends—four hours, unless the traffic was bad coming out of the city, or the highways north to Muskoka were clogged with cottagers, or he lingered at that place just south of Gravenhurst with the chicken sandwiches he liked so much. Bill King was usually the only one with him in the car. King liked to talk—it was hard to get him to shut up—but his many opinions were congenial and he had been there since the first days, back in 1981, when Harris had run as a long shot against an entrenched Liberal MPP and won. "Davis and Harris: What a Team" the signs had read.

After the 1981 win, King, who had just quit his job as a *North Bay Nugget* reporter, had asked to become Harris's new constituency assistant.

"Are you here for the long haul?" Harris asked him.

"What do you mean?" King replied.

"There's no question I'd like to be in cabinet some day," Harris had answered. "And I could see a situation within the next twelve or fifteen years where I might take a shot at becoming premier."

It had taken fourteen years, two months, and twenty days, but now the Member for Nipissing, the leader of what used to be called the Progressive Conservative Party of Ontario, but was now called simply the Mike Harris Team, was premier-designate, headed from his home town of North Bay back to the capital in a chartered airplane. The years of endless car rides with Billy King were over.

The night before, the night of Thursday June 8, 1995, Harris had stood before several hundred ecstatic party supporters at his local campaign headquarters, a former North Bay carpet store, and celebrated the victory—82 of 130 seats, a strong majority government—by reciting poetry. Robert Frost, to be exact:

Two roads diverged in a wood and I —
I took the one less traveled by,
And that has made all the difference.

Apt, except Harris wasn't a reader of Robert Frost, or of any poetry, or of much else beyond papers and briefing notes. But David Lindsay, his principal secretary, had a sentimental fondness for the American poet, could quote him at length. The idea was his.

After the celebration Harris, his wife Janet, and their two sons had gone back to their suburban family home on the outskirts of North Bay, along with a few friends and aides. Lindsay and his wife, Charmine, were there, old friends Peter and Barb Minogue, aides Peter Hickey and Debbie Hutton. The adults were exhausted, but not the kids. Jeffrey Harris, all of three years old, was on a high, sitting in the driver's seat of the campaign bus, opening and closing the swinging doors. It took forever to get him and his brother, Mike Jr., to bed.

No one really got much sleep. Lindsay was in the air at 7:30 the next morning, to organize the first meetings of the transition team. Back in North Bay, Harris struggled through a morning press conference, showing little grace for the defeated candidates—"I believe they were gone in some measure because they didn't do what they said they were going to do"—and offering a warning: "We are going to implement changes. Some people may not want those changes." Even as he spoke, Lindsay and Bill Farlinger—a Bay Street executive, friend, and co-chair of the transition committee—were meeting with David Agnew, outgoing premier Bob Rae's secretary of cabinet. One crucial appointment needed to be arranged: the obligatory meeting between Harris and Rae. The men visibly disliked each other, but they were politicians and would assume the mask.

As the plane droned towards that meeting, the premier-designate gazed at the hilly pinelands that spread beneath him. It had been, for almost every Ontario Conservative except him, a humiliating decade. But it was over. Not since the United Farmers of Ontario had stormed into power in the election of 1919 had a political party that wasn't even the official opposition won an election. His aides liked to repeat the statistic among themselves, savour it. And why not? But no one, not those aides, not the flabbergasted media, not his many political enemies, could deny that the victory belonged to Michael Deane Harris. He had shown them all. He'd fulfilled his fourteen-year-old boast to Bill King. And he had finally erased, forever, the failures and frustrations of his youth.

Mike Harris was only a year old in 1946 when his parents, Deane and Hope, moved him and his older brother, Sid, from Toronto to North Bay. A younger sister, Mary, was born later. Deane, who sold welding supplies, had been transferred north by his employer. But Deane Harris was and is a determined, independent-minded man. He wanted to work for himself. Before long, he had set up his own welding-supply company in North Bay. He did well by it.

The Harrises' youngest son was rambunctious, more interested in sports and parties than school and responsibilities. Younger brothers are often the difficult ones. Sid was a serious kid, determined even in high school to get his business degree and take over the family firm. Mike just wanted to torment his little sister and have fun. But he could also show fierce determination. When he was eleven, for example, Mike became seriously worried about his physique. Though Deane was six-foot-two, Deane's younger brother, Neale, had struggled to reach five-six. Mike, who was a small child, looked at his uncle in alarm and concluded that second sons were the runts of each generation's litter.

Michael—as his mother, Hope, still calls him—was not prepared to bow to fate. He sent away for a chest expander he saw advertised in the back of a comic book, and when it arrived he went to work. Deane figured the obsession would last for a week. It lasted for years. By the time he was in high school, Mike Harris was a strapping, good-looking adolescent.

Peter Minogue first met Mike Harris when they were both around ten, playing pee-wee hockey on opposite teams. Minogue's coach warned him to watch the kid named Harris on the other team. "You had to be careful not to let him get loose," Minogue recalls. It was not that Harris was a particularly gifted player, so much as a dangerously determined one. By high school, Minogue and Harris were fast friends.

Harris was a popular student at Algonquin Composite School. He played hockey and baseball, water-skied, golfed a bit. Unlike the typical jock, he also belonged to the high school drama club, appearing as the wise old farmer in *The Rainmaker* by N. Richard Nash. In his graduating high school yearbook, Harris listed his ambition as "becoming prime minister." He says now it was a joke. It certainly seemed like one at the time.

For at age nineteen Michael Deane Harris was a frustratingly rudderless young man. His lack of direction worried his parents, "but what could you do?" shrugs Deane. In 1964, after completing Grade 13, Mike went to Waterloo Lutheran University[1] to study science. But the academic life didn't take, and he decided

[1] Now Wilfrid Laurier University.

not to return for his second year. "He was at that age where he didn't know what direction he wanted to go in," recalls Hope. "He had no interest at all in school," says Minogue. Now water-skiing, partying—that was different.

By this time, Deane had sold his welding business and bought Wasi Falls Resort, a collection of cabins, restaurant, and marina in Callander, a village wrapped around the east shore of Lake Nipissing, not far from North Bay. When Mike gave up on college, he joined Deane and Sid in helping run the business. Mike looked after the marina, Sid the restaurant, "and I was the boss," Deane adds, with emphasis.

Sidney Deane Harris is a strong-willed man of pronounced conservative views. He bestowed his first name on his first son and his second name on his second son. He says the three of them were able to work together by keeping relatively far apart. Though it was clear Mike wasn't planning to run a marina for the rest of his life, he worked hard at the job. "I don't think there was another marina in North America that had a daily report as thorough as ours, where they could tell you how many minnows you'd sold," claims Deane. But more than punctiliousness motivated Mike Harris. "Mike had a very dominant father," Minogue recalls. "We were all a little bit afraid of him. He could get angry at you." Harris came to work at Wasi Falls, Minogue believes, "because he felt he had to please his dad."

Mike Harris was drifting. In 1967 he wed Mary Alyce Coward. He was twenty-two; she was twenty-one. They had started going out not that long before. "He was just lonely," Minogue believes. "She was about the only girl he had ever met." Coward was an avid curler, enjoyed golf and skiing. "I understood his sports, and we partied, and we had the same friends and so on," Coward remembers. "There were reasons there for the attraction." The decision to marry was sudden. Deane Harris had added a ski hike to the family's operations and Mike wanted to go to Quebec, to learn how to be a ski instructor. The sexual revolution had not reached North Bay. The only way Coward could go with him to Quebec was as his wife. "At that young age, you don't know what goes into a marriage," she says now.

By the following summer, the marriage was already in trouble. Harris had decided to go to the teachers' college in North Bay, to which he and his wife had returned to live after their time in Quebec. He made the decision, says Minogue, because it offered "free tuition, free books, no dress code, and there were 500 people there and 400 of them were women." When Harris described teachers' college to Minogue, his friend also decided "That's the place for me." As exam period approached, Harris moved into Minogue's house, so the two could study together. He never returned to live with his wife. The following summer, Harris sent Coward a letter from northern Ontario, where he was working with the Ontario Northland Railway. The marriage was over. "The only thing that still bothers me to this day is that after we separated I asked him if he could help me [financially] when I went back to college but he said no. That's life, I guess," she says. Harris will only say about the marriage that it was a mistake "for both of us."

Teaching was also a mistake. Neither Harris nor Minogue lasted very long at it. Harris spent a couple of years drilling math and science into Grades 7 and 8 kids, but it wasn't for him. He resented, in particular, the seniority system that ensured older teachers would get promoted ahead of younger ones. Harris wasn't prepared to wait for his reward. He went back to work for his dad. Minogue ended up in real estate.

By the mid-1970s, as well as helping run the resort and the ski hill, Harris was managing a nearby golf course owned by a friend of the family. He hadn't golfed much up until now, but he took the necessary courses and was certified. The press would later dismissively dub him a golf pro, as though he'd spent all his early years swinging clubs and drinking at the nineteenth hole. In truth, Harris had established himself as a successful business manager.

As his twenties turned into his thirties, it looked as though Mike Harris was finally settling down. In the early seventies, he had met Janet Harrison at a local water-ski club where he was giving lessons. In 1974, they were married, and this marriage took. "I've attempted to make Mike a little bit more romantic, a bit more compassionate," she has said. ". . . I've always said politics is really good for him in getting him to mature. But some of that has come from me, too. I'm more sensitive."[2]

Rougher edges still showed, however. For example, in 1973 Harris sent an angry letter to the editor of the *North Bay Nugget*. Residents of a new suburb outside of town were agitating for municipal services. Harris thought it was outrageous. "I have absolutely no sympathy whatsoever for the residents of the Hill," he wrote indignantly. "They moved there for a reason—the land was cheap . . . . I believe it is their right to ask for anything, but it is not the duty of the majority to grant it when the request is unreasonable and stupid."[3] This was how Harris sounded when there was no one to edit him or calm him down. "They expect us to provide them with services prematurely so their land will be worth much more money," he fumed. "I respect and indeed even admire those industrious individuals who buy and develop land, or any other business for that matter, but when they dupe the public into assisting the development to come about prematurely, then I call it greed."

Harris still displays a visceral antagonism to any form of what he feels is exploitation by the undeserving, be they grasping suburban home owners, over-protected unionized public servants, or welfare recipients with under-the-table incomes. It is rooted both in political belief and in personality. Harris has a flash temper, a temper that he has increasingly learned to curb over the years, though it can still flare up, such as the time he brought reporters into his office and a television cameraman tried to focus on papers on his desk—a clear breach of the unwritten rules of photo-ops. "Use your fucking head," the premier snapped. In the early days as a backbencher at Queen's Park, his

---

[2] Christina Blizzard, *Right Turn: How the Tories Took Ontario* (Toronto: Dundurn, 1995).

[3] *North Bay Nugget*, December 13, 1973, page number unknown.

fits of pique were more frequent. During his time as opposition leader, rumours floated through the office door of petulant tirades, especially when things seemed to be going wrong.

"He has a temper," Bill King acknowledges. "It's kind of like mine—it's quick to flare up and a few minutes later you're not quite sure why you were upset." King claims special privileges in this area, based on all those years, all those commutes between North Bay and Toronto. "He snaps at me, I snap back at him."

By the mid-1970s, Harris's political opinions were pushing him beyond the letters-to-the-editor stage. In 1974, he ran for trustee on the Nipissing Board of Education. Peter Minogue's wife, Barbara, was on the board (Peter and Barbara had met at teachers' college) and had encouraged him to take a shot. It was a long shot—Harris wasn't all that well known—but he won nonetheless. Two years later, in 1977, his fellow board members elected him chair. By 1980, at 35, he was president of the Northern Ontario Trustees Association.

Friends and relations, accounting for Harris's meteoric rise in local politics, put it down to his ability to get along, to forge a consensus. They remind us that he has always worked passionately at whatever he has committed himself to. And they point out Harris has always wanted to be the leader of whatever team he's on. "In whatever capacity he has been involved," observes King, "he's had a tendency to assume a leadership role." Michael Harris is neither a solitary man nor a man comfortable as part of a crowd. He wants to belong, but he also wants to control that to which he belongs.

Reporters interviewing Harris often discover he likes to begin any conversation with a joke—usually a bad one, and often off-colour. His surface friendliness is one of Harris's most important political assets. He's a hard man not to like. Ronald Reagan was another conservative politician famous for his affability. Henry Kissinger once said of Reagan, "He was both congenial and remote, full of good cheer but, in the end, aloof. The bonhomie was his way of establishing distance between himself and others. If he treated everyone with equal friendliness—and regaled them all with the same stories—no one would have a special claim on him."[4] The words apply equally well to the premier of Ontario. Colleagues speak, not only of Harris's ability to connect with strangers, but of his personal reserve. He is not a man given to intimacy.

Six years on a school board—debating property tax increases, teachers' contracts, funding for a French-language school—were enough for Mike Harris. Fifteen years of working at tourist operations were also enough. The restlessness was still there, the frustration with the limits of his life. His success at the school board pointed to a way out: a way out of town, a way out of a provincial, restricted life. He would run as the Progressive Conservative candidate for the Ontario legislature in the 1981 election.

The choice of party was never in doubt. Harris was a card-carrying Tory. His antipathy to Pierre Trudeau, to the Liberals' obsession with the Constitution and their casual contempt for a deteriorating economy, was typical of Harris's time and of the small-town, small-business voters he associated with. "I thought he was ruining the country," Harris once claimed. But as a former school board chair, Harris's expertise was in education, a provincial responsibility. Most of his concerns were with local issues such as development and resource management. It made sense to run provincially rather than federally.

In the early eighties, to run provincially as a Conservative in North Bay was a chancy thing. The riding had been Liberal for twenty-one years. The incumbent, Mike Bolan, had taken the riding by a comfortable 1,626 votes in 1977. Unseating the Liberals in North Bay would be a formidable task. But before he could take it on, Harris faced another, greater, challenge: his health.

In 1980, as Harris was preparing for the election expected within the year, he contracted Guillain-Barré syndrome, a very rare disease, afflicting only one or two out of every 100,000 people. It appears after a bad flu or cold and may be caused by an

---

[4] Henry Kissinger, *Diplomacy* (New York: Simon & Schuster), p. 766.

immune system that goes haywire and begins attacking healthy nerve tissue. The tissue becomes inflamed, leading to temporary paralysis, starting in the feet and legs and working its way up. In some cases, the patient may be forced onto a respirator. About half of those who come down with the disease fully recover. The others become mildly or severely disabled. Up to 5 per cent of those who contract Guillain-Barré die from its complications.

The disease put Harris in the hospital for two months. "He was very scared," says Minogue. "For a long time they didn't know what it was. It was the scariest time in his life." The episode "brought my wife and I [sic] a lot closer together," Harris has said. But it did not appear to change his view of the world in any way. He was fully recovered and ready to run by the time the writ was dropped.

In the 1981 election, Harris won Nipissing by almost 5,000 votes—15,795 to Bolan's 10,924—in part by capitalizing on the organization he had built up while on the school board, in part thanks to the coattails effect of the last, autumnal victory of the popular Brampton Billy Davis. As a rookie MPP from an unsafe riding with little political experience and a mediocre résumé, Harris might have been intimidated by the legislature, might have listened to the oft-given advice for new members: Watch and wait respectfully. "More people talk their way out of this legislature than talk their way into it,"[5] one veteran repeatedly told newcomers. But Harris had no intention of languishing on the back bench. He let it be known that he was available for any job that needed to be done, any committee with an available seat.

Premier Davis was only half-listening. Following a cabinet shuffle in 1983, he promoted the new member from Nipissing to the rank of parliamentary assistant to the Environment minister. Parliamentary assistantships are given to young MPPs in need of seasoning, or as a sop to veteran also-rans. They may quarterback

[5] Carolyn Thomson, "'This Place': The Culture of Queen's Park," *Inside the Pink Palace: Ontario Legislature Internship Essays* (Toronto: University of Toronto Press, 1993), p. 5.

some ministry initiative, or even fill in for the minister in the House on quiet days. Harris was lucky to land the job so early in his legislative career. But the new Environment minister, Andy Brandt, was himself a rookie MPP, and Harris resented being left behind. To make matters worse, another first-timer, Susan Fish, won Citizenship and Culture.

The usual excuses were given—cabinet making was a delicate art, geographical and gender balances had to be considered, patience would be rewarded next time—but it put Harris in a temporary funk. "There were two or three in the class of '81 who got into cabinet in '83–'84 and that actually pissed him off, because they were his same generation: Susan Fish, Andy Brandt," explains Bill King. "He was quite competitive with those two."

Part of the reason Harris was passed over may have been his identification with the conservative wing of the party at a time when moderate, or Red, Toryism was in the ascendant. Harris may have despised Pierre Trudeau, but Bill Davis got along with the prime minister just fine. Ideologically, there was little to choose between the federal Liberals and provincial Conservatives of the early 1980s. Harris was further to the right. His conservatism didn't spring from any deep analysis of society, from any coherent political philosophy. It was instilled in him by the place from which he came and is as natural to him as it is alien and contemptible to his urban, southern critics. It is in his bones.

North Bay's economy rests on the timber and minerals extracted from the surrounding Precambrian Shield, and on the agencies that governments have placed there. It was the Canadian headquarters for the North American Aerospace Defence Command (NORAD), and everyone in town lived with the unpleasant certainty that, if nuclear war came, North Bay would be one of the first to go. But though the military and other government workers buttressed the local economy, North Bay was, and is, an outpost on the edge of the bush, a town of harsh hotels with strippers in the bars that Harris and his buddies liked to frequent on a Friday afternoon, a place bisected by railway tracks and highways, where pickup trucks fill the parking lots outside the liquor stores and teen-age boys take off from school in November to hunt deer with their dads. North Bay is also the northern terminus of what remains of Ontario's rural English Canadian settler culture.

For more than a century and a half, from the arrival of the first Loyalists in the late 1700s, to the great influxes that followed the Second World War, Ontario's politics were dominated by a contest between two groups of settlers. The first was a Toronto-based Tory elite, the descendants of United Empire Loyalists and the better class of British émigrés who came to this province in the early years of the nineteenth century. "[Later arrivals] found the political life of the colony a comfortable monopoly of the privileged," observed John Kenneth Galbraith, whose family emigrated to southwestern Ontario in the 1800s. "At the apex was the Lieutenant-Governor, an appointee of the Crown, and almost invariably a retired general (or some lesser officer) of Wellington's armies. Surrounding him and advising him were Anglican bishops, businessmen and minor members of the aristocracy who had 'come out' from England to make good and were starting in at the top. There have been, one imagines, more wicked oligarchies than the Family Compact as it was called. But, undeniably, it ruled in its own behalf."[6]

These Tories favoured the British connection, high tariffs to protect their businesses, strong banks, and as little democracy as possible. Ranged against them were the English, Scottish, Irish, German, Polish, and other immigrants who cleared and farmed the land—good in the south, poor in the centre and north—that lay beneath the forests. They hated the Tories, called themselves Reform, or Grits, or Liberals. They were pro-American, anti-tariff (for the tariff raised the cost of growing their grain and blocked business opportunities in Buffalo and Detroit), and suspicious of "the money interest." "Most of the Scotch simply kept on voting against the Family Compact and handed the habit on to their children," Galbraith writes. "These

[6] John Kenneth Galbraith, *The Scotch* (Baltimore: Penguin, 1964), p. 70.

were the predictable mass, the solid rank and file of the Liberal party."

After the Second World War, more immigrants flooded into the province: from southern and eastern Europe, then from Asia, the Caribbean, and Africa. Southern Ontario became a multicultural, urban place, typified by the endless string of identity-less suburbs that stretch from Oshawa in the east to Burlington in the west, surrounding the old cities and increasingly bleeding them of their identity. But in the counties and districts of central Ontario, from Renfrew to Parry Sound, from the Severn River to North Bay, the sinews of the old settler culture remain. In Renfrew and Lanark counties, the sixth generation of founding families still farm the same 200 acres—though the land here is rocky and thin—making do with eighty-five head of dairy cattle and the wife's income as a secretary in town. In the upper Ottawa Valley, Polish accents are still thick around Wilno, generations after settler-refugees arrived from Poland. A few miles down the road, the Irish of Barry's Bay still speak with a lilt.

North Bay keeps one foot amid the old settler culture of Renfrew, Lanark, Haliburton, Muskoka, and Parry Sound, and another in the more itinerant, isolated true Ontario north. Harris calls himself a northerner, but he isn't. True northerners look on southern Ontario as a remote and distant land—in Thunder Bay they call it "down east." Northerners' dependence on the Crown for lumbering and mining rights and the fragility of their economy make them more amenable to big government. Harris—in his beliefs, his attitudes, his prejudices—reflects the traditional culture of the southern and central Ontario pioneers, whose descendants he grew up among. His natural political enemy is the high-tax, high-tariff, arrogant and snobbish town Tory. In the nineteenth century, Harris would have seen himself as a Grit. In the twentieth, he has become leader of a party that is Tory in name only. Many of his political enemies call themselves Liberals, because political nomenclature is sometimes contradictory, because political parties sometimes evolve into the opposite of what they once were. But during his first term at Queen's Park,

Harris found himself on the ideological fringe of a party of the comfortable centre, ruled by an urban Tory elite.

As the premier-elect's plane taxied to a private terminal at Pearson International Airport, several men in ill-fitting suits were waiting. The rotating six-person premier's escort of the Ontario Provincial Police had already detached itself from Bob Rae and, from this point on, would accompany Harris everywhere he went. In an unhappy coincidence, Liberal leader Lyn McLeod's chartered plane arrived at the same terminal at almost exactly the same time. The two leaders were within sight of each other as they walked to their respective cars. McLeod knew what meeting Harris must be on his way to. Until two weeks earlier, when the Liberal's election campaign had gone horribly wrong, almost everyone had assumed Rae would be meeting with her. The sight was a cruel reminder of everything the Liberals had lost.

An inconspicuous cavalcade of grey Ford Crown Victorias whisked Harris from the top of the city down to Queen's Park, where Premier Bob Rae waited in his offices on the second floor of the legislative building. Two more disparate men could not have been chosen, back to back, as premiers of Ontario. Rae is a fine writer, a careful thinker, always articulate and often eloquent in conversation, address, and debate. The most one can say for Harris when he speaks is that much of the time he is grammatically correct. Harris looks uncomfortable in his suits, which may be expensive but appear ill-fitting and inappropriate—he's a bulky sweater kind of guy. Rae, by contrast, gives the impression of having loosened the tie over his oxford-cloth shirt just so.

Though Rae had, in the past, displayed a suspicion of Harris's depth of intellect, had dubbed Harris Mike the Knife, and had been the victim, he felt, of "a vicious campaign that appealed to public fear and emotion"[7] from the Conservatives, as the two sat down to discuss the transition, he offered the incoming premier

---

[7] Bob Rae, *From Protest to Power: Personal Reflections on a Life in Politics* (Toronto: Viking, 1996), p. 263.

some sincere advice. Keep the cabinet small, he warned. Former Saskatchewan premier Allan Blakeney had given Rae the same advice when he was about to select his cabinet, but Rae had ignored it. The results had been a disaster. "Too soon old, too late smart," he later ruefully observed. His second piece of advice was to delegate authority. Rae felt, in retrospect, he had taken on too much of the decision-making process, despite a welter of cabinet committees and advisory groups. The premier must guide, not decide, he warned. His final words of counsel were more personal. The new premier should move his family from North Bay to Toronto. Until now, Harris had made do with a downtown apartment and the weekend commute. "You can't govern the province and keep your family life by living in North Bay," Rae told Harris.

All this advice was well-meant and unnecessary. Harris had already committed to keeping his cabinet small. It would, in the end, be the smallest cabinet in twenty-eight years. The decision making structure for the new government had already been thought out. The new premier would tightly control both his office and his cabinet. And he had already decided to move the family south.

Harris wanted only one thing from Rae: his agreement to a swearing-in date of June 26, which would require one of the shortest transitions between an election and a change of power in the history of the province. But the date meant a lot to the Conservatives. It would mark the tenth anniversary of their loss of power to David Peterson and his hated Liberals. The outgoing premier readily agreed. Harris thanked Rae, and they parted cordially.

There were other meetings to attend, with Bill King, and with David Lindsay and Bill Farlinger, who were in charge of the transition. And there was a party to go to. The Tories had decided to celebrate their win at the Albany Club, favoured Toronto home to Conservative elites for generations. Yet the choice concealed a fundamental shift in the party of Leslie Frost and William Davis. This election hadn't been won by any Big Blue Tory Machine. The small crowd that had helped make Mike Harris the next premier was a collection of young outsiders who hated the old party establishment almost as much as they hated the Liberals and NDP. One Tory adviser had told Harris months before the election, "The day you win a majority is the day they let jeans into the Albany Club."[8] And so the Tory team booked their victory party at the Albany, and came in jeans and T-shirts, and invited the campaign bus driver, and drank beer rather than scotch.

Harris settled on khaki trousers and a denim shirt, and offered a speech more heartfelt than the one the night before. There were tears in Janet's eyes, and some say his own glistened, as the premier-designate thanked the young group of passionate supporters who had brought him to this night. He also had some advice: "Remember, we're in the Albany club," he quipped. "So don't do anything Sir John A. Macdonald wouldn't do."

It was late in the day when Mike and Janet Harris retreated to the leader's apartment in the midtown Manulife Centre, a favourite address for Queen's Park politicos, where Harris could finally take off his shoes and pour himself a last glass of white wine. Harris likes his beer, but at fifty the paunch was a continuous problem, and he tried to stick to what he calls his "white wine diet." The first day of the rest of his life was over. It had been a long, winding ten-year road that had brought him here, from defeat, to recovery, to victory. And now, to the brink of revolution. There were decisions to make, positions to fill—in the bureaucracy, in cabinet. Most important of all were the positions in his own office, the staff who would advise him, run herd on the new ministers, help him keep the raft of promises he had made. There was no question from where he would pick them. The new premier would surround himself with the same people he'd thanked at the Albany Club that night. They had worked miracles, including the greatest miracle of all: the election of the day before.

[8] "Harris revolution storms Tory bastions," *Toronto Star,* June 11, 1995, p. A1.

18

True Believers

Before 1995, the party that took Toronto in an election typically took the province. In 1990, for example, the NDP won six of nine City of Toronto seats and formed a majority government; in 1987, the Liberals won seven of nine seats and formed a majority; in 1981, the Tories won five of the ten seats, and a majority.[1] Toronto was important, not because of the number of seats it represented, but because it mirrored the rest of what is now called the Greater Toronto Area (GTA) in voting intentions. The party that took Toronto was also likely to take Scarborough and North York and the other suburban cities in Metropolitan Toronto. In Metro Toronto, with the City of Toronto excluded, the Conservatives took thirteen out of nineteen available seats in 1981; the Liberals took seventeen out of twenty-one in 1987; and the NDP took eleven out of twenty-one in 1990.[2] And the party that took Metro Toronto also did well in Mississauga and Oakville and Burlington and Pickering and Ajax. In the Greater Toronto Area, excluding Metro Toronto, the

---

[1] No theory, however, is without its wobbles. In 1985, the Conservatives took four Toronto seats, the NDP four, and the Liberals only two. In the GTA as a whole the Conservatives grabbed nine seats, the Liberals four, and the NDP one. But though the Tories had a plurality of seats across the province, the Liberals formed the government, with the help of the NDP. In 1990, when the NDP won its majority, the Liberals dominated with eight seats, while the Tories and the New Democrats each took five.

[2] In 1985, the Liberals took seven seats in Metro, the PCs six, and the NDP six.

Conservatives took twelve of fourteen seats in 1981, while the Liberals took fourteen of nineteen seats in 1987. Suburban voters, in other words, were likely to see the world in the same light as their downtown cousins. There was a perceived community of interest between the needs of the core and the needs of the periphery.

In 1995, all that changed. The suburban ridings split away from their downtown counterparts. In the City of Toronto itself the Tories did poorly, winning only four of nine available seats. Once the suburban ridings of Metropolitan Toronto were added in, the situation improved, with the Tories winning sixteen of thirty seats. It was in the edge cities surrounding Toronto and Hamilton, however, that the Conservatives found their majority government, winning all nineteen seats. Nor was the pattern unique to Toronto. The Liberals and the NDP also did well in other urban cores, winning two of four seats in Hamilton and four of five seats in Ottawa (though only one of three seats in London). The Tory gains in those areas also came in suburbs, such as the wins for John Baird in Nepean, an Ottawa suburb; Bruce Smith in Middlesex, which surrounds London; and Ed Doyle in Wentworth East, outside Hamilton.

The Conservatives weren't strong only in the suburbs. They swept the rural parts of the province, taking virtually every riding outside the major cities. The Conservatives, it has been said, are creatures of 905, the new telephone area code created in 1993 to encompass everything in the Golden Horseshoe outside of Toronto. It would be truer to say the Tories were the party of 905, 519, 613, and 705. In one non-urban part of the province, however, the Conservatives were completely shut out: northern Ontario. In the ridings north of North Bay, the NDP garnered seven seats, while the Liberals took six. The north's close ties to, not to say dependence on, provincial subsidies pushed voters away from the party that wanted to cut programs and slash spending.

The Mike Harris Conservatives, it appeared, had forged a coalition between the rural descendants of Ontario's settler farmers and middle-class suburbia. Harris's appeal to the traditional values of Ontario's settler culture—self-reliance, low taxes, minimal interference from big-city politicians—struck chords both with the hinterlands and with the edge cities, including many of the most recent settlers who had moved to Canada from Asia and elsewhere. Harris had tapped the root values of a culture many more sophisticated critics thought no longer existed.

This writer, wandering across southern Ontario in the wake of the 1995 election in search of answers to the unexpected Conservative victory, was surprised to hear the re-assertion of Old Ontario coming from every crossroad and shopping mall. It found its most eloquent expression in the gentle, implacable warnings of Father Gilbert Simard, forty-four, an accountant turned priest who cared for the 317 souls in the village of St. Joachim, east of Windsor. "To me, there is a longing in the heart of the people of the province to find what held our communities together thirty or forty years ago, and is not there now," he mused, one warm July morning. "There has been, in government, in the past ten, fifteen, even twenty years, a shift away from the Judaeo–Christian values that have always been the basis of our legislation, our conduct with each other, and our conduct with the community. We have lost the sense of that. We have lost the sense of values that our predecessors gave to us." And so, he believed, the people "elected somebody they envisioned came from an environment where there were values. Not from the big city."[3]

Such sentiments were echoed by shopkeepers, farmers, commuters waiting for their bus. Angela Loranger, the twenty-one-year-old tour guide at the Beachville Museum, near Woodstock, maintained, "I don't know that they're planning to cut a lot of welfare, they're just asking people to work for the money they're getting." House-husband David Covel in Ajax explained, "There are all these white-collar workers who commute into Toronto, here, and we're pretty conservative." Royal Brunet, an unemployed worker who owned a house just fifty paces from the

[3] "The view from Highway Two," *Ottawa Citizen*, August 19, 1995, p. B1.

Quebec border, refused to be cast in the stereotype of the unemployed. "You could think I'd say, 'Well, I want the unemployment [insurance] to be high, or I want the welfare to be high,'" he asserted. "But no, I'm not a believer in that. I don't believe in laziness. I don't believe in people getting handouts. That's why I am a supporter of this government."

This was the will of the people.

It was not, however, the will of those who lived in downtowns. Here the reaction to the election of Harris was one of dismay and indignation. How could people have voted these barbarians into office? Steve Borisenko, who helped unionize the employees at the Queen Street West guitar store where he worked, fumed at the Tories' promise to repeal the NDP's labour legislation and worried about the effect their cuts would have on the poor. He worried, too, about the isolation of Toronto, confronted by a political union of suburb and country. "There's going to be a big division. I was talking with my union representative yesterday, and he used the term 'riots in the streets.' I don't think it will go that far. But I don't know."

It wouldn't go that far, but it would get close. And the coalition of opposition to the Conservatives that would emerge and grow over the next two years would be centred in the urban cores, among the professionals who had moved back into the cities in the seventies, the social-interest groups representing the poor and disadvantaged, the public-sector unions who staffed Toronto's provincial and municipal bureaucracies, and the elites of education, the arts, media, and government, who find civilization in cities, recreation in the hinterlands, and who consider suburbs something one averts one's gaze from while getting from town to country.

Soon after the election, former Toronto mayor John Sewell could be found prowling the corridors of the legislature. A large, round-shouldered, fearsomely intense man, he was lobbying to preserve some remnant of the planning act the NDP had passed in response to a commission he had headed. These Tory MPPs are all alike, Sewell fumed one late summer afternoon. They have the same middle-class values and the same suburban fear of diversity that marks the typical resident of Burlington or Ajax. "They commute from their homes in the suburbs down the Don Valley Parkway to their offices downtown, and at the end of the day they drive back, and they never see the city, they never walk on its streets, or ride on a streetcar, and confront the mix of people and classes and races that make up this place." It infuriated him that such blinkered people, simply because they were in the majority, could dictate policy to the rest of the province, including the people of the downtowns.

The ancient contest between the Family Compact and the Reformers was about to be rejoined in Ontario. Except the Reformers now inhabited the former party of the Family Compact, while the successors of the Family Compact—academics and public servants, teachers and city politicians, artists and activists—would ally themselves with labour and the poor. In the early years, at least, they would lose every battle.

The three weeks from the election to the swearing-in of the Mike Harris government passed in a June blizzard of decisions. The Conservatives were determined to seize control of both the government and the political agenda. They had, they figured, two years to implement their many promises and reforms before inertia, resistance, and an approaching election began to slow them down. Harris did not intend to wait for the swearing-in before taking power. More than a year before the election, in the winter of 1994, he had formed a secret committee to plan the logistics of the transition. At the time, the Tories were so far from first in the polls that word of a transition committee would have invited derision. The two men who headed the committee brought complementary attributes to their joint role. David Lindsay, Harris's longtime principal aide, was the consummate party insider and problem solver. Bill Farlinger, a tough-nosed Bay Street executive, who was the former chair of the accounting firm of Ernst & Young, brought the experience of a successful career in the private sector.

Lindsay was a logical choice to co-head this crucial working group. Small, thin, bald, as outwardly affable as his boss, Lindsay had been Harris's principal secretary since the member for Nipissing was elected party leader in 1990. The son of northern Irish immigrants, Lindsay loves to tell or hear a story. Though his temper can flare quickly—especially if someone criticizes his boss—he has the crucial ability to lead from the background, to co-ordinate and encourage, to ride gentle herd on the big egos around him while remaining relatively inconspicuous himself. "I'm the conciliator, the balm on the emotions," he says. "I love to work with strong personalities. I'm the grease on the wheel." He is also passionately loyal. Lindsay believes Harris to be the most intelligent, insightful, inspiring, and underestimated political leader of our times. The premier's principal secretary doesn't just work for Mike Harris; he idolizes him.

Farlinger, on the other hand, is the picture of a strong-willed corporate executive. He is also the uncle of Bill King, Harris's oldest-serving subordinate. It was King who arranged for Harris and Farlinger to meet in 1987 at, of course, a fishing tournament, while Harris was planning his run at the Conservative leadership. Farlinger and the future premier hit it off, and the Bay Street executive became a major Harris supporter and fund raiser. Now, Harris wanted to put his friend's business acumen to work at shaping the new government.

The morning after the election, Lindsay and Farlinger met with David Agnew, Bob Rae's cabinet secretary, in Agnew's office on the fourth floor of the Whitney Block, across the street from Queen's Park. It should have been a pro forma gathering, the type where people shake hands, offer congratulations and condolences, and agree on a date for a more serious discussion. Instead, Agnew produced a collection of carefully prepared briefing binders for the new team.

Rae and his advisers had been traumatized by the transition of 1990, later dubbing it "the transition from hell." The NDP victory in 1990 had caught everyone by surprise. Confusion, coupled with an innate suspicion by the New Democrats of what they considered a hostile public service, had led to disarray. The bureaucracy, not having studied the NDP election platform, scrambled to put together policy backgrounders and briefing notes. The NDP leadership, not having studied their election platform either, waited for guidance they desperately needed but would never receive. David Peterson, wounded and depressed by his own defeat, offered little counsel. In an act of rare political altruism, Rae and Agnew were determined to make things easier for whomever came after. In 1995, with a change of government a distinct probability, Agnew had created a multi-ministry contact group to co-ordinate a possible transfer of power. Each ministry was also ordered to have its own transition team, with backgrounders and briefing notes at the ready.

After offering the briefing binders and settling the details of that day's meeting between Harris and Rae, Agnew took Lindsay and Farlinger on a tour of the fourth floor of Whitney. Usually the cavernous rooms of the old office building served as the nerve centre of the provincial government. Today the place was eerily empty. Agnew showed the two Tories the area that had been set aside for the transition team; for the next few weeks, Tories and socialists would work together. Before leaving, Lindsay and Farlinger made their first request: would Agnew telephone the following deputy ministers, asking them to present themselves Saturday morning for interviews with the transition team and the premier-designate? Agnew readily agreed.

The next morning, six senior deputy ministers of the Ontario government arrived at the Park Plaza Hotel, just up the street from Queen's Park: Rita Burak (of Agriculture and Food), Richard Dicerni (of Environment and Energy), Michelle Noble (of the Solicitor General), Larry Taman (of the Attorney General), Margaret Mottershead (of Health), and Judith Wolfson (of Consumer and Commercial Relations). None of them had any inkling of why they'd been summoned.

As each deputy minister arrived at the hotel suite, he or she was greeted by the members of the still-unofficial Conservative transition team. Besides Farlinger and Lindsay, there were government consultant and longtime Tory George Boddington, Barbara Cowieson, a party administrator, Graham Scott, a former high-ranking provincial public servant, Tom Campbell, once deputy treasurer and chair of Ontario Hydro, and Stanley Hartt, Brian Mulroney's former chief of staff. Since the Ontario Tories had gone to great lengths to avoid any connections with the unpopular Mulroney government, Hartt was a very interesting choice. They simply needed his experience at this delicate time. Even so, he would stay behind the scenes throughout the transition.

To the enormous relief of the six deputy ministers, they quickly discovered that the news was, at least for them, reassuring; they had already been identified by the Tories as competent and willing to work with the new regime. The meeting was intended both to inform them of this, and to interview three of the six—Burak, Dicerni, and Wolfson—for the post of cabinet secretary, the head of the provincial bureaucracy. Agnew might be co-operative, but he was a die-hard NDPer—he would be gone before the week was out—and the Tories wanted to pick his successor immediately.

After meeting with the transition team, each of the three candidates for cabinet secretary was shown into a separate room for a private conversation with Harris and Lindsay. In the wake of his election win, the incoming premier exuded confidence and calm. And he delivered two messages. First, after purging the upper ranks of recent NDP appointments, he hoped to establish a co-operative working relationship with the senior administrators of the public service. The government had a great deal to do in the next few years; trying to do it without the help of the mandarinate would only make the job harder. But—and it was a crucial but—the government had an agenda it planned to carry out. Harris told each of the three what he later told a meeting of all the deputy ministers of the Ontario government: he had promised the people of Ontario "to change the way government does business. This means gut-wrenching changes both inside and outside government."[4] How the government

---

[4] Text of address of Harris to deputy ministers, June 27, 1995.

imposed those changes was open to discussion. The changes themselves were not.

Mike Harris had got himself elected by presenting the
province with a blueprint for reform called *The Common Sense
Revolution*, the centrepiece of the Tory's astonishingly successful
election strategy and the cornerstone of the new government. It is
a remarkable creation, not simply because of the neo-conservative agenda contained within it, but because of its genesis. In the
act of its creation, the Tories fashioned both a political platform
and an electoral strategy that vaulted them from last to first in a
matter of months, to the bewilderment of all who thought they
knew better.

The seeds were there from the start. Harris was from a small
city in north-central Ontario. His core values were forged there;
his experience as a businessman and local politician tempered and
refined his prejudices and beliefs. He was by nature comfortable
opposing state intervention in the lives of ordinary citizens,
whether through legislation mandating whom a citizen could hire
or fire, or through taxes that robbed the citizen of wealth. He
would agree with the principle that the community should look
after those who've had bad luck or bad lives, but he would add it
should not comfort them with the delusion that they are victims
of other people's success. Most important, he would argue that
we should distinguish between those who, with few assets, struggle hard for a dignified life, and those who are simply too lazy to
work. This attitude was bred in the bone. Such convictions are
almost universally shared by the modern descendants of the old
settler culture.

But Harris lacked the intellectual rigour to translate his intuitions into a credible and successful political agenda. Had he been
left on his own, the small businessman from North Bay would
today most likely still be railing from the opposition benches at
his more sophisticated and successful opponents. Harris, however, had the smarts and good fortune to forge an alliance with a
small band of young ideologues who had taken control of the
provincial wing of the Progressive Conservative party in the late

1980s. An unlikely alliance at first glance, the middle-aged, good old boy from up north wed his instincts to the fervour of these university-bred neo-conservatives. They, in turn, became his most passionately loyal supporters. It would turn out to be a marriage made in political heaven.

On the university campuses of Ontario in the late 1970s and early 1980s, a small, strident group of radical students waged civil war against the Progressive Conservative Party. These young campus Tories were neo-conservatives, a doctrine utterly foreign and repugnant to both federal and provincial Conservatives at the time. Neo-conservatism arrived late in Ontario, having already made progress in other parts of the English-speaking world. In essence, it is classical liberalism revisited. Liberalism is the child of such eighteenth-century philosophers as Adam Smith and John Locke, who argued the state had no right to curtail the liberties of the individual, whether in the economic sphere through tariffs and taxes, or in the political sphere through restrictions to freedom of speech or assembly. In the course of the late nineteenth and early twentieth centuries, the word "liberal" gradually became transformed into an almost opposite meaning. Politicians who called themselves liberals increasingly emphasized that the greatest liberty for the greatest number could only be achieved by redistributing income from the more fortunate or successful to the less.

In the mid-twentieth century, some writers warned that modern liberalism was turning into exactly the coercive philosophy it had originally opposed. The Austrian political philosopher Friedrich August von Hayek in 1944 published a small text called *The Road to Serfdom* that served as a sort of bible for the new Right after the Second World War. Hayek warned that replacing the impartial discipline of the market with the intrusive hand of state intervention would lead the western democracies into an abyss almost as totalitarian as the Nazi chasm from which they had barely escaped. By the 1964 U.S. presidential campaign,

Republican candidate Barry Goldwater was carrying these warnings to a broad North American audience. His motto was "In your heart, you know he's right." In their hearts, however, most Americans thought he was a crank. Observers concluded that Goldwater's defeat proved the classical version of liberalism, which put unfettered individualism ahead of social engineering, was now dead. Society had become too complex, they argued, and the needs of its various groups too interdependent, for the simple brutalities of laissez-faire capitalism.

Nonetheless, a new wave of writers and politicians emerged in the 1970s who found their champions in Ronald Reagan in the United States and Margaret Thatcher in Great Britain. By the early eighties, both were in power, and classical liberalism, now dubbed "neo-conservatism"—yet another example of political nomenclature reversing itself—was back in vogue. And just as the neo-conservatives in the United States and England began making their first real gains in the late 1970s, capturing the leadership of their parties and preparing to take on the liberal establishment in elections, four young men who would play a pivotal role in the triumph of Mike Harris arrived at college.

Tom Long, a brash, baby-faced son of a Sarnia petrochemical worker, whose mother had taken him with her as she went campaigning door-to-door for the local Tories, arrived at the University of Western Ontario in 1977 as interested in becoming leader of the campus Conservatives as in getting a degree. He soon made friends with Mitch Patten, who had been active in the PC organization at Wilfrid Laurier University since he arrived there in 1976. Patten had even taken a year off school to work in the office of Premier Bill Davis. Meanwhile, at the University of Toronto, Alister Campbell, the eloquent, long-haired, guitar-playing son of two Queen's University professors—he had become "radicalized to the right" during a teachers' strike in Grade 13—formed an alliance with Tony Clement, an eager young worshipper of Margaret Thatcher and Ronald Reagan. Together they set about capturing control of the tiny campus Conservative club.

Clement, who was born Tony Panayi,[5] had come with his family from the Middle East by way of England in 1965, when he was four years old. In 1972, his parents newly separated, Tony found himself living in a high-rise apartment in suburban Toronto with his mother, Carol, who had found work as a secretary in the office of Tory MPP Bill Hodgson. In the election of 1975, to help his mom keep her job, Tony knocked on doors and handed out leaflets.

But Clement's political convictions were forged out of more than the pragmatic need to keep Mom employed. "What I saw on the front of *Time* magazine, which I read religiously every week, was this failure of the American democratic impulse," he remembers. "Around us was the fall of Vietnam, the emasculation of American power, Watergate . . . . What I remember was the frontal assault on American power, and the encroachment by communism all over the world. And in Canada, there were the failed experiments of Pierre Trudeau. His economic experiments were a shambles, his anti-Americanism wasn't getting us anywhere, the increasing role of the state in all aspects of our lives was, in my view, creating more problems than it was solving. And then in 1978 you had this woman named Margaret Thatcher, who proved you could turn back some of the awful things done by socialism and set things right again. And then in 1980 you had this guy Ronald Reagan. They showed you could have conservative principles and still win."

Clement arrived at the University of Toronto in 1979 filled with missionary zeal to bring the faith of Thatcher and Reagan to the Progressive Conservative Party of Ontario, but the audience for his ideas was small. Campus Conservatives were *outré* in the late 1970s; the young still gravitated to the left. And what Conservatives there were, were moderates. At the University of Toronto, Alister Campbell remembers, "everyone was a Red Tory: rock and roll, marijuana is okay in small doses."

---

[5] When Clement's mother, Carol, remarried, in 1979, to former attorney general John Clement, Tony took his step-father's name.

Campbell, Clement, and their peers were anything but moderate. They believed that governments needed to cut taxes in order to stimulate spending and increase individual choice, that they needed to balance their budgets in order to escape the trap of escalating deficits, that they needed to get out of most economic regulation in order to let the market reward winners, punish losers, and generate wealth for everyone. Most important, governments needed to abolish most of their social programs, which took money from people who earned it and gave it to people who hadn't. Such a doctrine was anathema to moderate Conservatives, who felt, as former federal leader Robert Stanfield argued, that the market should not be trusted more than was necessary.

After Campbell and Clement met and became friends, they quickly took control of the moribund U of T campus Conservative association. Before long, they had enlarged its numbers to 500, in part through aggressive marketing techniques that Campbell learned when he visited the Chicago Republican Convention in 1981. If you've got a display set up in the student centre, for example, you don't stand behind the table, cut off from the people passing; you stand in front, grabbing and shaking the hands of everyone you see. Do whatever it takes to get attention, even if that means walking around in a penguin costume. (Clement did.) Don't rely on the lib-left campus newspapers to cover your campaigns; distribute your own broadsheet.

Eventually the young PCs at the University of Toronto also decided to take on their left-wing enemies on campus, launching a campaign against a proposal to double the compulsory fees levied against each student in support of the Ontario Federation of Students. The Tories accused the federation of wasting money on a bloated administration, and of worrying more about helping the Sandinistas than representing student interests. (Among other things, the Tories put up a sign in an Engineering building proclaiming "Three dollars will get you the Ontario Federation of Students or seven beers at the Brunswick House. Take your pick.") They won a referendum on the issue in a landslide. Two years later, Clement helped force a referendum on whether the student body should continue to belong to the Canadian Federation of Students. They won that one, too.

By the early 1980s, as Mike Harris was first finding his feet as a young MPP, the neo-conservative youth were an increasing power within the provincial Conservatives. Long—a bit older than most of the others, passionate and uncompromising—led the troops. "There were huge fights over who was going to control the campus wing of the party," Long remembers. "That got settled in the late seventies, and for about ten years or so my faction controlled the campus wing." In 1982, Long managed the campaign that secured control for the neo-cons of the executive of the Progressive Conservative Youth Association. Both the campus and youth wings of the party were now firmly led by ideologues of the far Right. These wings were important to the party, both for the influence they wielded at leadership conventions, and for the legions of indefatigable volunteers they supplied during campaigns. And no one knew that better than these young PCs. They had demonstrated their power on university campuses. Now they planned to take on the party leadership.

There were few, if any, more moderate, entrenched, and successful liberal parties in the English-speaking world than the Progressive Conservative Party in Ontario. It had been in power for so long that when Chinese premier Zhao Ziyang visited Ontario in 1984, the *Globe and Mail* pointed out that the Tories had governed in Ontario longer than Communists in China. The party had run the province since 1943, and Premier Bill Davis had held the reins since 1971 by following the same consensual, centrist politics that had made the PCs so enduring. Advisers such as Hugh Segal, Norm Atkins, John Tory, and John Laschinger were more into taking over oil companies than slashing taxes and curtailing spending.

The party leadership was no more happy with the rising power of the neo-cons than the neo-cons were happy with the leadership. But some in the party welcomed the arrival of the young bucks. Many backbenchers, including the rookie member for Nipissing, were growing restive with the government's

Liberal-in-all-but-name approach. Certain members of the government, including Gordon Walker, Alan Pope, and senior cabinet minister Frank Miller, also believed the party had drifted too far to the left. They saw the young new arrivals as potential allies and shock troops for their own leadership bids. For everyone knew Davis was bound to resign soon.

The first clash came in 1982, at the Tory policy convention. Two years before, the government had introduced a new human-rights bill, which the young radicals loathed. They felt it gave the state excessive powers to enter an employer's premises and examine documents; they felt it strengthened the objectionable concept of reverse-onus, in which the accused must prove his innocence. Led by Tom Long, the young Tories tried to force a debate on the issue at a party policy convention. The senior guard warned the young rebels to tone it down; policy conventions were no place to debate policy. But the campaign continued, and faced with the prospect of an ugly public fight, the leadership compromised. Representatives of the youth wing were allowed to help draft the wording of the final resolution on amending the code at the convention. "It wasn't perfect," says Clement, "but it was something we could live with."

The campus radicals were also instrumental in the defeat of federal Conservative leader Joe Clark by corporate lawyer Brian Mulroney. "In 1981 to '83 there was a guerrilla campaign against the leadership of Joe Clark orchestrated by Brian Mulroney and the people who backed Mulroney," says Campbell. "In Ontario, the PC campus and youth associations were all hotbeds of anti-Clark activity and we were all on the anti-Clark side." The success of the right young Tories in helping force a leadership convention and in electing Mulroney over Clark strengthened their confidence. The wild bunch had won control of part of their party; they had demonstrated their ability to elect their own and bring down their opponents. But they were powerless to dislodge the elite that ran the provincial government. Nor was that elite prepared to let a bunch of whelps filled with what the leadership considered politically suicidal notions anywhere near the levers of power. As long as Brampton Billy Davis reigned, the youngsters would be in the cold. But on October 8, 1984, Thanksgiving Monday, Premier Davis announced to a packed and surprised roomful of reporters and supporters that he had decided to step down. There would be a new leader, a new premier, and new opportunities for those who backed the winner.

The young Tories split into several different camps during the leadership contest. Long and Mitch Patten campaigned for Miller. Clement and Campbell worked for cabinet minister Larry Grossman. They were joined by Leslie Noble, who had met Clement and Campbell at U of T when she was in her first year and they were in their fourth. Even that early in her political development, Noble was a strong-willed and formidably talented organizer. Though Grossman was further to the left than any of the young recruits liked, they believed he would be successful at opening the party up to new influences, especially theirs. Besides, Clement was dating a Grossman supporter. (It was worth it: Lynne Golding became his wife.)

In the 1984 leadership campaign, Mike Harris decided to support veteran cabinet minister Frank Miller for good and obvious reasons. The two had much in common. Miller was from Muskoka, not far south of Harris's Nipissing. He was a small businessman, even owned a resort, like Harris's dad. And Miller, like Harris, was on the right wing of the Progressive Conservative Party, a discontented rump that chafed at the Tories' increasingly interventionist approach to governing: the new human-rights code, the purchase of shares in the Suncor oil company, the decision to extend full funding to separate schools. Miller campaigned on a promise to emphasize his party's noun over its adjective. If Miller won, Harris knew, the cabinet post he had been denied would finally be his.

Harris chose wisely in picking Miller, who won a bitterly divisive leadership contest and became premier with the help of a grass-roots membership that has traditionally always been more conservative than the party leadership. As a reward for his support, Harris was elevated to the post of Minister of Natural

Resources and Energy. But Harris barely had time to order coffee before Miller called an election, which he lost.

The cause of the Conservative demise in 1985 has been much debated. It may have been that, in extending provincial funding of Catholic schools in his last, grand gesture as premier, Bill Davis had triggered the latent strain of anti-Catholicism that still underlay Ontario's Protestant ethos. It may have been that, in Miller, the Conservatives had nominated a leader whose small-town conservative manner alienated urban voters, especially at a time when Toronto was desperate to believe it was, per capita, the chicest place on earth. It may have been that, once elected leader, Miller allowed himself to be recast by the boys of the vaunted Big Blue Machine into a pin-striped nonentity, confusing his supporters but not convincing the electorate at large. It may have been that, in David Peterson, the Liberals had found a leader who seemed more in tune with the boom-time-for-yuppies eighties, especially after he dropped the horn-rimmed glasses and got rid of the page-boy cut. It may have been that, after forty-two years, it was time for the Tories to go.

Technically, Miller did not lose the election. The Conservatives took fifty-two seats to the Liberals' forty-eight, but came second in the popular vote: 37 per cent to the Liberals' 37.9. And NDP leader Bob Rae had no intention of letting the Tories govern with a minority, as Davis had in the 1970s by co-opting Stephen Lewis. Rae and Peterson negotiated an accord, in which the NDP would support a Liberal government in exchange for legislation sympathetic to the NDP agenda. On June 18, 1985, Miller's fledgling government was defeated in a motion of confidence. Eight days later, David Peterson was premier of Ontario. And the wilderness years had begun.

The Conservatives were in desperate straits. They had been in power so long, they assumed that their leadership contests were more crucial than elections. The leadership campaign had been bitter, and Miller had been unable to assuage the hurt pride of the losers. Now, blamed for sending his party into opposition for the first time in forty-two years, Miller was finished. On August 20,

1985, he stepped down, and the party plunged into yet another leadership campaign. With Miller gone, most of the young recruits joined Campbell, Clement, and Noble in supporting Larry Grossman's second leadership bid.

Contender Alan Pope, from Timmins, expected the support of the northern caucus, including the former Natural Resources minister, Mike Harris. Pope had known Harris since they were both young men and had urged Harris to run in 1981, but the member from Nipissing chose to remain neutral in the race of 1985. Harris's decision angered Pope, but it was a wise move. Though the Grossman campaign triumphed, the psychic wounds to the party were deep. "It was bad, really bad for the party," Clement remembers. The Tories were riven with faction and mistrust. And as if a bitter and divisive leadership campaign weren't enough, twenty-two months later there was another election.

The accord with the NDP had proved a gift from God for the Liberals. The agenda that Rae demanded was wildly popular with the electorate, and the Ontario economy—recovering nicely, it seemed, from the early eighties recession—was more than able to accommodate the necessary increase in government spending. Environmental laws were toughened, the scope of rent controls widened. Money was spent on child care and affordable housing. Equal rights for homosexuals were entrenched in the province's human rights code. First steps were taken towards pay equity for women. And most important, the Liberals moved to ban extra billing by doctors, an increasingly common practice across the province. The doctors reacted by going on a limited strike. The government stared them down. The strike collapsed.

Ontario was in the midst of the biggest boom since the oil shocks of the seventies; Peterson's high-spending, state-expanding agenda was enormously popular. The NDP got little credit for putting the Liberals' feet to the fire, while the Tories were not even in the argument. When Peterson dissolved the legislature and called for new elections in the summer of 1987, the outcome was predictable. The Liberals won a handsome majority, the NDP became the official opposition, and the Tories were reduced to sixteen seats, only four above the minimum needed for party status. Grossman, defeated in his own riding, stepped down.

Once again the party was leaderless. And it was broke. Two elections and two leadership conventions had sent it deeply into debt, and the Bay Street donations no longer flowed to a party that wasn't even close to the prospect of governing. Worst of all, the Bill Davis Tories were in a state of trauma.

Most of the mechanics of the defeated regime—Segal, Atkins, Tory, Laschinger—either headed into corporate life or headed up the 401 to Ottawa, where the Conservatives were still in control. "The grownups basically left—retired, quit, lost interest, or went to Ottawa," says Campbell. The only Tories left in the provincial party were either over fifty-five or under thirty. With the support of the latter, Long became party president. "It was horrible," he remembers. "If I had understood how much psychic damage had been done to the party through those two leadership conventions, I never would have run for president . . . . There were people who were not only angry with one another, they would not deal with one another. They were mindlessly vindictive and spiteful." No wonder the natural next leader decided not to run. Many in the party believed that the leadership was Dennis Timbrell's for the taking. His organization was intact, and no one could seriously have challenged him. But after losing two conventions, then resigning his seat before the 1987 election, Timbrell's heart wasn't in it. When he announced he would not be a candidate, the race suddenly looked wide open. It was an opening the young activists hoped to fill. Their efforts had helped push Grossman to the top, and their leader, Tom Long, held the party presidency. There might not have been much left of the Ontario Progressive Conservative Party, but it was theirs for the taking.

The first member of the crew to notice Harris was Leslie Noble, who had gone to work for Larry Grossman after he won the leadership. "I remember coming from a meeting with Larry, and he introduced me to Mike, and when we went into his office Larry said, 'You keep your eye on that guy. He's the next leader of the party. He's the smartest man in caucus, and he's going to go places,' " she recalls. "From that moment on, I started to pay attention to this guy."

Harris was also making an impression on one David Lindsay, Dennis Timbrell's former aide. Improbably, Lindsay came to Harris from the left wing of the party. Raised in Ajax, he had attended Queen's University and campaigned for Red Tory Flora MacDonald in her bid for the 1976 federal Conservative leadership. After four years as an accountant, he fled the life in 1984— "It makes your hair fall out"—taking a job with a Toronto-area MPP, and ending up as Timbrell's assistant as House Leader. Harris's neutrality in the second 1985 convention now paid off; when the smoke cleared, Harris inherited the job of House Leader. He also inherited Lindsay.

Lindsay's first and lasting impressions of the man who would be his boss for most of the next decade were forged in the meetings between the three House leaders during Peterson's majority government. Former Liberal leader Robert Nixon, David Peterson's treasurer, was government House Leader. Veteran MPP Ross McClellan, the member for the Toronto riding of Bellwoods, held the job for the NDP. Each week they would meet, exchange pleasantries, and get down to business. At such sessions, the government typically attempts to convince the opposition parties to allow it to proceed with its agenda with a minimum of fuss. The opposition parties are all about fuss. But they need the government's help, too, to agree to sufficient debate or public hearings. And oftentimes, a critic might be absent or the opposition unprepared, and a request will go in for a delay, to give the other side some time. Though the three parties may appear implacable enemies in the House, there can be considerable give and take behind the scenes. "If you ever wanted to see three good poker players, it was those three," Lindsay recalls. Behind his good-old-boy exterior, Harris struck Lindsay as a shrewd and skilled negotiator. His respect for and attachment to Harris had begun.

The party in 1987 was in no shape for yet another leadership convention. Sarnia MPP Andy Brandt and Alan Pope, still hungering for the leadership, both vied for the job of interim leader.

Brandt promised he wouldn't run for the permanent leader's job and promised Harris he could stay on as House Leader; when Pope refused to stay out of the leadership race, Harris threw his support behind Brandt, who won the caucus election. Pope was furious. "The rift never healed with Harris after that," says Clement. Pope would actively campaign against Harris's leadership bid in 1990.

The party was hollowed out, broke, leaderless. But for the young neo-cons, it was an opportunity waiting to be seized. They filled its powerless vacuum, taking the key positions on the executive and redrafting the party's constitution. Long, Patten, Clement, Campbell, Noble, and their compatriots were determined to break the hold of the Red Tory elites who had dominated the party for so long. They were also determined to reduce the influence of the youth wing, which they were convinced wielded too much power. They knew this better than anyone; they had wielded it. "It was a reasonably corrupt system in our view," says Campbell. No one should be allowed to do to them what they had done to their predecessors.

At the Ontario Tory convention in North York in February 1989, Tom Long and the rest of the leadership proposed that the Ontario Conservatives become the first party in English Canada to adopt the one-member-one-vote system. Rather than sending delegates to leadership conventions, a process guaranteed to encourage patronage, string-pulling, and lack of representative balance, every member of the party would vote for the next leader. The amendment to the constitution required two-thirds support from the delegates. "The Norm Atkinses of the world and the Hugh Segals of the world just hated it," remembers Clement, who chaired the committee that drafted the proposal. The one-member-one-vote system would place control of the party in the hands of the grass-roots membership, a far more conservative body than the former leadership. The old guard, says Clement, "actually ran a campaign against it with buttons: 'Tories look before they leap.' They lost 3 to 1."

By the spring of 1990, the Tories knew they simply had to have a new leader. The Liberals were showing increasing signs of wanting to go early to the polls, and someone had to be in place to carry the party standard into an election. During the interregnum, five names had been bandied about, three of which had now been discarded. Dennis Timbrell had returned to private life. Alan Pope, whose strong showing in the second 1985 convention had put him in contention for next time out, had fatally damaged his chances by going into a prolonged sulk over not being elected interim leader. And Tom Long, who had been touring the province, drawing crowds at party gatherings and more media attention than the party had enjoyed for a while, finally concluded that the leadership could not be his. In quiet conversations with party supporters the message came through: You're too young (Long was thirty-two at the time), and too brash. Besides, his obsession with politics had helped ruin his first marriage, which was ending. Reluctantly, he announced he wouldn't be a candidate.

That left only two serious contenders for a prize that to many seemed hardly worth having: Dianne Cunningham and Mike Harris. Cunningham, who had won a by-election in 1988 in the riding of London North, seemed like a natural step along the road that would return Big Blue to power. At a time when any Tory win was a blessing, the former chair of the London Board of Education looked awfully good—articulate, intelligent, energetic, and a Progressive Conservative. Cunningham instantly became a potential leadership candidate. On January 24, 1990, she became an official one. One day earlier, Mike Harris had announced he would be after the job as well. But in fact the lawn signs from the 1987 debacle had barely been burned before the Tory's House Leader had begun organizing a run at the leadership.

In the almost five years since the brief reign of Frank Miller, Harris had climbed steadily through the party ranks. Shortly after the 1987 defeat, he had met with Leslie Noble and his close friend Ernie Eves to chew over the notion of a leadership bid. Eves and Harris, who had known each other since school-board days, had arrived at Queen's Park together as rookie MPPs from adjoining ridings in 1981. (Eves represented the next-door riding of Parry Sound.) Both loved to golf, both loved their part of the country, both espoused similar political views. Eves had also become friends with Noble; they shared season's tickets to the Blue Jays. Harris was often a guest. For Noble, Harris's greatest strength was an acute mind hidden by a simple exterior. "When you sit down and talk to him, you think, 'This is a good old boy, this is a golf pro, this is a ski bum,' " she says. "You hear all that. And yet lurking behind that facade is probably one of the smartest policy minds in politics today. The guy is a wonk."

Noble thought Harris should run; Harris was already ahead of her. "Mike was definitely interested," says Noble. "It wasn't as though he hadn't thought about this before." By 1988, Harris was known within the party to be a potential candidate for the leadership; by early 1989, he and his supporters were hard at work. Eves and Noble wooed former Timbrell supporters while Harris worked on the caucus. As House Leader, Harris could grant favours to MPPs who wanted to raise issues in Question Period with the government. That helped bring many MPPs onside. By the time Harris made his official announcement, his organization was in place and his core support identified.

It was during the 1990 leadership campaign that the alliance between Mike Harris and the young neo-conservatives who dominated the party was forged. Noble and Alister Campbell, now a young insurance executive, had become best friends since working together on Larry Grossman's leadership, so it was natural that she would bring him on board. Mitch Patten, now a public relations consultant, also joined the team. Only one obvious name was absent: Tom Long. No longer party president, he had taken up a job as a corporate head-hunter on Bay Street. Long took little part in the leadership campaign or election of 1990. The wounds of his own failed leadership bid were too fresh for him to work heart and soul for another.[6]

The young neo-cons were attracted to Harris personally and ideologically. While their neo-conservatism was, at root, subtly

---

[6] As head of the leadership campaign's new election process, Tony Clement was required to stay neutral.

different from Harris's natural conservatism—Harris's opposition to big government is intuitive and limited by pragmatic considerations; their ideology is intellectual and, it would turn out, sometimes impractical—the two agreed on most fundamentals: the need to reduce taxes and spending; the need to get government out of areas the private sector could better manage; the need to curtail the numbers and power of the public service. Perhaps equally important, the young bucks liked Harris and he liked them. They were engaged by his affability, his ability to forge consensus, his social ease. Harris was energized by their youthful zeal and dedication. As they got to know one another during the campaigns of the 1990s, they found they liked and respected one another more than a middle-brow former businessman and a bunch of hot-headed intellectuals should have.

None of the young women and men who flocked to Harris in 1990 would have found themselves at home in the Cunningham camp. Dianne Cunningham was too much of the old Tory school. Her platform could have comfortably been read out by Bill Davis in 1971. Her campaign was organized, in part, by remnants of the Big Blue Machine, who came back to provincial life to block the election of Harris, whom they saw as dangerously right wing.

"In the final months of the campaign, it split ideologically," says Campbell. "It had not been ideological up until then, but when it shook out to just the two contenders, Tory and Segal and Gregg and all those guys threw their alleged heft behind Dianne Cunningham and began 'Mike's a right-winger, Mike's too far right.'" He grins. "We stomped on them." Harris won the contest 8,689 to 7,164.

But the new leader had won a dubious prize; had it been any more valuable, it might not have been his to win. The party that once bestrode the powerhouse of Canada was a rump of its former self, without money, a recognizable leader, or any real prospects of winning an election.

Which was one reason why David Peterson decided to call one.

CHAPTER 3

Writing a Revolution

The Tories had taken far too long to choose a new leader—so long, they almost went into the 1990 election with Andy Brandt as head of the party. In the months leading up to the convention, Brandt's allies had argued that a leadership campaign in the spring of 1990 was premature, that the party was broke and the Liberals only three years into their mandate. But by early 1990 there were storm warnings that the Liberals might not wait the full four years. Harris's allies were convinced that Brandt's supporters knew this as well as anyone and were trying to delay the convention to give Brandt, by default, the leadership he had vowed not to seek. But Brandt's people didn't have control of the party presidency and executive; these were in the hands of the neo-cons, who were determined to complete their take-over. The leadership campaign went ahead—as it turned out, at almost the last possible moment.

In Harris's victory speech May 12, before 200 Tory supporters at the CNE Coliseum (where the votes from across the province had been tabulated), the new leader practically pleaded with Peterson not to call an election. "The people of Ontario gave you a job to do," he maintained, "And halfway through your term you want to call an election instead of doing your job. You were given a five-year contract, and you haven't begun to live up to your end of the bargain." Media reports that weekend speculated that Peterson could call the election as early as the autumn. He would call it before the end of July.

As their rationale, the Liberals argued that the federal Conservative government had so fundamentally changed the shape of the federation—through free trade, the GST, and the failed Meech Lake Accord—that Peterson needed a new mandate to cope with the change. But pundits accused the Liberals of simply cashing in on their 50 per cent support while they still had it. The poll numbers were indeed tempting, but there were other reasons for calling an election, including the Liberals' difficulties during the past three years of majority rule. A series of scandals involving links between fund raiser Patti Starr, the Liberal Party, and certain prominent developers had tarnished Peterson's reputation. And, after the flurry of action in the minority years, the government appeared sluggish and complacent.

The promiscuous courting of special interests had also come back to haunt the party. Those interests had been valuable allies during the minority years. The government had discovered that bringing gay-rights groups in on human-rights legislation, environmentalists in on environmental legislation, and women and minority groups in on affirmative-action legislation helped to boost the legislation's acceptance. The process was called "third-party validation," and the Liberals exploited it blithely. But such groups are difficult allies. All special interests—from business leaders to lawyers to environmentalists to doctors to anti-smoking crusaders to right-to-smoke crusaders—generally possess an agenda of escalating requirements. The first are relatively easily met; later the demands become more expensive or difficult. Interest groups are rarely content with half a loaf; constancy of insistence is their hallmark.

And so while assorted activists had praised the Liberals during their first mandate, those same groups became increasingly critical during the second, as the government ran out of ways, or lost the will, to placate them. Despite impressive new measures extending environmental protection, Environment Minister Jim Bradley found himself and his government the object of bitter attacks from environmental groups. Despite an expanding public service, the Ontario Public Service Employees' Union attacked the

Liberals for being in the pocket of the special interests. (They meant other special interests.) Doctors were angry over their extra-billing fiasco; teachers felt they hadn't been consulted sufficiently in education reform; lawyers protested the Liberals' proposed no-fault auto insurance would leave them with nothing to do. All sides complained the government had failed to consult them, which was to say, had failed to accommodate them. Ottawa MPP Dalton McGuinty (the father of future Liberal leader Dalton McGuinty, Jr.) dubbed it Operation Alienation.[1]

To add to the dissonance, Finance officials warned that Ontario was heading into a recession. In fact, later measurements revealed that by the spring of 1990 Ontario was already in the grip of what became the worst economic downturn since the 1930s. Peterson and his advisers rightly felt that his chances would only worsen as time went on.

The premier dropped the writ July 30, 1990, and from the opening press conference, when an environmentalist disrupted his remarks, Peterson was in trouble. Protesters dogged him at every stop. His bland, stand-pat message—strong leadership and proven performance have earned us another mandate—was drowned out in the chorus of complaint. But the question remained: Could either opposition party benefit from the discontent?

The NDP entered the campaign with a popular leader and money in the bank, while the Tories had a rookie leader and were flat broke. The banks were only persuaded to lend the Tories a paltry $1.2 million for the election on the promise that the 30,000-name data base created during the leadership contest could be used for fund raising. John Laschinger, one of the few voices of experience who seemed to get along with the new crew, ran the campaign. Though a certified member of the Big Blue Machine—he had been national director of the party through much of the seventies and had served as a deputy minister in the final Davis government—Laschinger was a rebel in the Red Tory

---

[1] Georgette Gagnon and Dan Rath, *Not Without Cause* (Toronto: HarperCollins, 1991), p. 125.

camp. "Lash has a love-hate relationship with that group," says Noble, who worked for Laschinger as a management consultant after the 1987 election. Though he got his start working for Robert Stanfield, he was equally comfortable with the New Right. "Lash is always a guy who didn't have much of an ideological thrust," she explains. "He just loved the game."

There was little risk of any Big Blue tendencies surfacing; the campaign team drew heavily from the young neo-cons who had helped Harris win the leadership. Leslie Noble and Laschinger set strategy, while Alister Campbell helped out with the party platform. Clement and Big Blue Machine veteran John Tory (he had been rumoured as a candidate for the leadership, but never sought it) negotiated the media debates. Mitch Patten worked on advertising.

It was in that election, says Clement, that "you started to get that Alister-Mitch-and-Leslie core group," the group that would engineer victory five years later. Though none was thirty yet, the three had been through a surprising number of political wars together, had fought in three leadership campaigns and three elections, had developed identical political views, and had fit their complementary individual personalities into a powerful combo. Campbell was the thinker, the gleeful intellectual and motivator, as happy dissecting the ongoing neo-conservative dialectic in the United States as pumping up a roomful of party workers. (He went on to create and motivate the group-insurance division at Zurich Canada.) Noble was the hard-headed strategist, intent on transforming the neo-conservative ideology into a plan for winning power. Patten was the facilitator, the guy who figured out what it would take and who would do it. Each was impressive; as a troika they were formidable. But in 1990, their goal was simply to survive. (A couple of years later, in 1992, the group was drawn even more closely together when Leslie Noble was diagnosed with cancer. A program of surgery and chemotherapy eradicated the tumour, but it left her aware of the fragility of a life that, she says, had been lived "almost by the minute." Her friends rallied around, especially Alister Campbell, as the political bonds that linked the three became increasingly personal as well.)

The campaign team's first and greatest priority was to save the party from extinction, a genuine possibility in the minds of many observers. The very limited polling that the Tories had done indicated, as the Liberals' polls also suggested, that middle-class voters were fed up with tax hikes. During their tenure, the Liberals had raised the sales tax from 7 to 8 per cent. Personal income tax had climbed from 48 per cent of the federal tax rate to 53 per cent. This offered the team a possible strategy. Taking on taxation fit with the deepening conservatism that was becoming the hallmark of Mike Harris.

He had started his life as an MPP dutifully voting for the big-government initiatives of Bill Davis and the machine. But being instinctively to the right of the Davis government, his gut-reaction stance against government spending and intervention had manifested itself in his support for Frank Miller. Following the disastrous election defeats of 1985 and 1987, Harris was now free to follow his intuitions—a back-to-basics conservatism that emphasized lower taxes and smaller government. Conveniently, such an approach meshed neatly with the ideology of his young neo-conservative supporters, the same marriage of mindsets that had succeeded in winning Harris the leadership. Here was a logical base from which to launch the election campaign. Harris dubbed himself "The Taxfighter," promising, if elected, not to raise taxes.

But that was it. There was no other platform to speak of, not much of an advertising campaign, and no money—just a bus full of unfed reporters and the new-minted leader touring the province and promising not to take any more cash out of people's pockets. But at least one insider believes the Tories could have won that campaign, if only they'd had more money. "We were about a million dollars away from winning that election," says Leslie Noble. "We put all of our advertising into tearing Peterson down. We shoved every last vote of his loose. When the third week of the campaign rolled around our numbers started to go up and we thought, 'Oh my God.' But we had spent every last penny on tearing Peterson down and could spend absolutely no money telling people why they should vote for us." Deane Harris, however, would claim at the end of the 1990 election that his son wasn't ready to be premier yet. "I'm sure he doesn't [think so] either," Deane added. "He's as practical as I am."[2]

While many commentators predicted the Tories could be extinguished during the 1990 election, few of them cared. The Progressive Conservative Party was seen as increasingly marginal to the life of the province, a rump of rural discontents. Certainly, Harris's performance on the hustings did little to alter their views. In campaign appearances, the new leader was stiff and awkward, the pitch sounding contrived, the delivery stilted. He is little better at it today. But enough of the individual and his anti-tax message got across to shore up the party's popularity. Harris, for all his awkwardness, communicates better with voters than media observers give him credit for. On September 5, the day before the election, David Lindsay was handed polling results that suggested the Tories would do no better than they had in 1987, and might well do worse. He caught up with the leader at a Toronto campaign stop and broke the bad news. Harris dismissed it. He reviewed the campaign, riding by riding, insisting that the party was running well here, the crowds had been with him there. "I'll bet you we take twenty seats," Harris predicted, and that was exactly what they took on election day, holding onto a core 23.5 per cent of the vote. The simple message of no new taxes resonated with a surprising number of voters; perhaps the leader had as well.

The anti-tax message, however, which the other parties might profitably have read with care, was ignored in the astonishment of Rae's upset win. In what had to be considered something of an actuarial miracle, the NDP, with only 37.6 per cent of the vote, crafted a substantial majority government. Ontario was finally going to experiment with social democracy.

---

[2] "The man who led Ontario's Tories out of the wilderness," *Toronto Star*, June 9, 1995, p. B1.

Many who analyzed the 1990 results concluded that the Ontario electorate had become increasingly volatile and that voters were demanding government action to limit economic uncertainty. But the origin of the volatility was not fully understood. Despite the economic recovery of the mid-1980s, the Ontario middle class remained insecure and uncertain about its future. This much was recognized by Liberal pollster Martin Golfarb, who attributed the Liberal's loss to their neglect of the increasingly frustrated middle-income voter. "We didn't deliver for the middle class," he said after the election. "Remember, it's only 10 per cent of the population that float. They floated away from us. They used to be with us. That middle-class vote that's fickle, that's selfish, that worries about 'How am I going to make my mortgage payment because I'm overcommitted now?'—we didn't help that guy."[3]

To the vast majority on moderate incomes, increased taxation appeared to eat into whatever gains they made. The federal Conservative government, though cutting services and introducing the hated Goods and Services Tax, had proved unable to control its deficit. The provincial Liberals had briefly balanced the budget, but only by raising both income and sales taxes. In retrospect, it seems clear that the voters turned to the NDP simply because the Tories were in such sad organizational shape and their leader was completely unknown. Bob Rae had always been a popular politician. He promised he knew how to restore confidence to Ontario. Thirty-eight per cent of the voters decided to give him a chance.

The young Turks who had helped Harris win the leadership and survive the election were now in a position of extraordinary power within the party. Tony Clement, at twenty-nine, would soon assume the presidency, and his executive would boast an average age of thirty-three. The party leader shared their views on where the party and the province needed to go. And they had forged bonds among themselves that would withstand the tests of the years ahead.

[3] *Not Without Cause*, p. 125.

If Harris had succeeded in avoiding electoral oblivion in 1990, the potential for oblivion remained. Thanks to three leadership races and three elections in five years, the Tories were $5.4 million in debt. Just like the rest of the country, they were being bled dry by interest payments: $13,000 a week. But donors were reluctant to invest in a party that had gone from top of the heap to bottom of the barrel. The Liberals and the NDP had each formed a government; between them, they appeared to own all the territory available in the electorate's broad, moderate middle. Perhaps the Conservatives were irrelevant.

"There were a bunch of people saying to Harris the best thing to do now is declare bankruptcy and start over," says Clement. "They said there's no way you're going to get rid of $5 million in debt, there's nothing to raise money for. But it was a completely untenable position. We'd never get elected again." Instead, Harris shut down party headquarters, firing the nine staff left from the original sixteen. From now on, what was left of the party would be run directly out of the leader's office and Tony Clement's house. For Clement, who was now a young lawyer, it meant a lot of unpaid expenses and extra hours. It didn't matter. Not yet thirty, he was running a provincial party.

On the surface, the prospects for the Harris Conservatives appeared bleak. But there were hidden pluses. Harris's leadership was secure—who would want it?—and the party was less faction-ridden than at any time since the seventies. Moreover, the Progressive Conservative Party of Ontario was an organizational and ideological *tabula rasa*, a clean slate ready to be written on. Thanks to the new leadership-election machinery engineered by Tom Long, Harris had been chosen by the broad membership of the party and was beholden to no one in the back rooms. Thanks to the lack of preparation before the 1990 election, he now had little platform to defend.

A party that loses its constituency often vanishes, as did the United Farmers of Ontario, the government from 1919 to 1923, whose coalition of rural interests disintegrated almost as soon as it came to power. But the chance always exists that a leader can use a period of crisis to re-invent his party, to fashion a new substance as well as a new image, and to connect to a new constituency. The Tories in 1990 were poised between collapse and renaissance.

In the months following the 1990 election, Harris, as leader, did his duty. He toured the ridings, sat through endless tortured meetings with local party faithful, solicited advice, listened. He hosted fund raisers, swung his golf club at charity tournaments, shook hands with anyone who might be willing to write a cheque. The 30,000-name data base that had convinced the banks to lend the Tories their election expenses was now put to use as a mailing list. The party faithful were begged and cajoled. In return for their money, they were promised an active say in the new policies Harris was committed to creating.

The leader's meetings with the grass roots were about more, however, than raising money and improving organization and morale. Harris believed the party had to stop worrying about getting itself elected. It had to worry instead about how it would govern, what policies and principles it stood for, and the means by which it would enact them. He was convinced that the PCs needed to craft a specific mandate for governing, something not couched in electionese—"We will take concrete steps toward renewing . . . "—but a manifesto as pragmatic and specific as a budget. It was a naïve commitment. As any political strategist knows, creating a specific set of plans only offers the opposition a target of attack. But the notion fit with Harris's own pragmatism and with the ideological commitment of his advisers, who didn't want to elect a premier who would abandon the faith once ensconced on the government front bench. Both he and his young team began gravitating towards the idea of writing a policy manifesto.

The project to create that manifesto was dubbed *Mission 97*, in reference to what the Tories hoped would be the mid-point in the life of the government they would form. Throughout 1991, Harris hosted a series of town hall meetings across the province. A thousand invitations would go out; a hundred people would show up. But he listened to those who came, and they listened to him. It was clear from those meetings that the rank and file of the Progressive Conservative Party were ready for—no, insistent on—a tough platform, a platform of law and order, back to basics, and balancing the books. The leader, the ideologues, and the party faithful were largely of one mind: it was time for the party to shift emphatically to the right.

At the Tories' policy convention in August 1992, *Mission 97* became the name of the party's mission statement, a concept much in vogue in the late eighties and early nineties. *Mission 97*, as defined in 1992, was a far cry from a specific blueprint for governing. The document committed the party to "shared values based on individual rights and responsibilities" and to "implementing consistent, innovative and responsible policies."[4] Much of the statement, and its inevitable flowcharts, is in jargon—the document promises to "articulate, communicate and integrate our shared values when all strategic objectives and action plans are undertaken"—thanks, in part to David Lindsay, now ensconced as the leader's indispensable right hand, who led the consultation process and helped craft the document, and who is partial to such devices and phrases.

Lindsay had been appointed Harris's principal secretary the day after the leadership convention, having spent the previous three years serving as head of caucus services, where he proved he could run an office and hire and fire. Lindsay's Red Tory convictions had evolved, to say the least, in the years since he had first come to work for the party. His belief that government must shelter the weakest from the consequences of a harsh world had accommodated itself to his boss's insistence that the shelter must be well run and, preferably, profitable. But Lindsay's attachment to Harris was more than one of convenience. The young aide had developed a passionate loyalty to his boss, convinced that Harris was both a great leader and a potential saviour for the party. Such

---

[4] *Mission 97: Convention Participant Ideas Input Booklet* and related materials (Toronto, Progressive Conservative Party of Ontario, 1992).

devotion, coupled with his hard-headed experience as a manager of people, made Lindsay an ideal second-in-command.

Mission 97, despite its jargon, offered the first evidence of the party's commitment to a tougher line. References to individual responsibility, the work ethic, and direct democracy informed the statements and charts of the document.[5] Had anyone outside the party paid any attention to the document—and few did—they might have detected a shared commitment to retrench the party well to the right of what it had been.

The party was not shy on policy. Since 1991 it had been issuing regular reports—based on wandering policy forums and discussions with supporters—on economic development, education, public safety, and rural and northern affairs. Dubbed "New Directions," the documents contained many of the key tenets of what would become the party's election platform, including calls to reduce the size of the public service, to cut taxes and balance the budget, and to impose stricter educational standards. The doctrines put forward in 1994 in *The Common Sense Revolution* would, in many ways, repeat principles first outlined during the years in the wilderness.

But the new leader needed to do more than spout policy and court the party faithful. The small businessman from North Bay had no connections with corporate Ontario, which naturally finds its home in the Progressive Conservative Party but was feeling rather bereft of late. So Harris's next step was to court Bay Street. John Craig Eaton and George Eaton, party stalwarts through thick and thin, took it upon themselves to introduce the new leader to their well-connected and wealthy friends. Together with Bill Farlinger, they began arranging informal luncheons, get-acquainted sessions. Within a single year, starting in 1992, Harris met with more than 500 CEOs, lawyers, and other business leaders. Some of them liked what they saw. Some of them wrote cheques.

---

[5] Audaciously, the mission statement also committed the party to having a transition program and team in place six months prior to the next election.

The combination of mining the data base and building the bridge to Bay Street improved the financial situation rapidly. Stuart Eagles, a retired Marathon Realty executive, had helped reorganize the data base and get the direct pleadings underway. Thousands of $5 and $10 and $25 donations came from true believers scattered across the province. More substantial help came from the financial district. In 1991–92 the party shaved $100,000 off the debt. A year later, it had lopped off $1 million. By year-end 1993 the debt was less than $3 million, and the Tories actually had money to spend.

But if Harris was making great strides in reorganizing the party behind the scenes, the public perception of him remained discouraging. In the legislature, the leader's reputation was poor. Reporters and Liberal MPPs dubbed him Flintstone. During Question Period he came across as querulous, strident, and none too smart. Although some members of the small caucus were devoted supporters of the new leader, others were skeptical. They rightly attributed their victories in 1990 as much to their local popularity as to the leader's one-note campaign. Many were uncomfortable with the party's pronounced tilt to the right. And not all disagreed with their opponents' assessment of the leader's mental abilities. There were grumblings that Harris was so busy out talking to the constituencies that he and his party were almost invisible in the legislature. Some wondered if the leader preferred golf to politics.

In fact, the leader's absence was in part due to problems the Harrises were having at home. As Mike and Janet Harris prepared to adopt Jeffrey, their second child, they learned the infant suffered from a mild form of cerebral palsy. They were determined to continue with the adoption, but it kept Harris at home more than usual, though he refused to publicize the reason.

In May 1991, partly to counteract the impression of absenteeism, Harris led a filibuster to force public hearings on the NDP's first budget, which anticipated a $9.7-billion deficit. The highlight of the stalling campaign was a recitation by the Tory leader of all the lakes and rivers of Ontario, as a preamble to a private-member's bill on zebra mussels. The filibuster held the House to ransom for a week and forced the NDP to hold the hearings. While effective, the Tories' intransigence only deepened dislike in the House for their right-wing attitudes and seemingly blunderbuss leader.

Harris's critics misdiagnosed his wooden speaking style as symptomatic of a wooden brain, but they accurately concluded the new leader was inexperienced and prone to an over-aggressiveness that could get him into trouble, as it would do in 1994 when he waved an obscene letter in the legislature that a computer hacker had inserted into the NDP's Internet site. Harris was properly condemned for resorting to cheap tricks in order to attack the NDP government. Yet there was also a casual contempt in the dismissal of the Conservative leader as a golf pro, a good old boy from North Bay. Having had a quick look at the new leader, the Toronto-oriented media, the lawyers and professional politicians in the Liberal caucus, the elites who gathered in one another's Forest Hill, Riverdale, and Annex living rooms on Saturday evenings, concluded he didn't belong in their Ontario. Harris was as much an outsider to them as the young neo-conservatives had been outsiders in the Progressive Conservative Party a decade before.

Had they thought more carefully about Harris's résumé—his experience in business, in teaching, in local politics, in the legislature—the wiser among them might have explored further. More important, had they been able to transcend the parochialism that urban professionals mistake for sophistication, they might have realized that there is nothing inherently regrettable about coming from the hinterland and continuing to claim a connection with it.

Harris understands the feeling of middle-class suburban voters, who he rightly believes share more in common with hinterland citizens such as himself than with the downtown elites. He knows the language of those feelings. He learned during his rise to the leadership and the years of opposition how to work a room, how to keep a caucus together. And, as it turned out, he would be more committed to the power of ideas—and prepared to stake his future on them—than were the governing elites themselves. Harris was profoundly underestimated by the politicians and pundits who disparaged him. It would lead to their, not his, humiliation.

The small-town origin of Harris's opposition to ever-increasing government intervention and government debt was separate from, but complementary to, the philosophies of the young ideologues he had teamed up with in 1990. Alister Campbell, for example, with his professorial parents and Ivy League education, was from a very different background than Mike Harris. Campbell's beliefs, though sincerely held, were more abstract: that the minimalist state was the greatest preserver of democratic freedoms; that excessive taxation and regulation infringed on individual liberties; that any impediment to the free operation of the market was an impediment to economic growth.

Harris was, by nature, a more pragmatic conservative than his young advisers. He was willing to accept state intervention to address social or any other inequity, but only if it could be proved the intervention worked. While his friend Ernie Eves, for example, raged in 1995 against the new federal legislation that forced gun owners to register their weapons, claiming it was an intolerable intrusion by the state into the lives of individuals, Harris simply shrugged and said such a registry would be very expensive and there was no proof it would reduce crime.

But in the years that Harris spent leading the smallest party in the legislature, he found himself in increasing intellectual synch with his young supporters. He fumed with genuine and mounting indignation as the NDP government, under Premier Bob Rae, doubled the provincial debt, ratcheted up taxes, and imposed what looked to him like social-engineering legislation. The Liberals, under leader Lyn McLeod, decried these excesses, but that was the point. They saw them as excesses, not as wrong in and of themselves. A political field of great breadth was opening before the Tories. A fundamentalist, neo-conservative platform favouring reduced taxation, lower spending, a balanced budget, and an end to social engineering would present an emphatic alternative to the other two parties. Mike Harris and his entourage were convinced such a platform would resonate with fed-up middle-class voters. Better yet, it was what they actually believed.

However, even though the party had retired much of its debt, strengthened the riding organizations, and evolved toward a consistent and potentially popular platform, the Tories remained in deep trouble as the NDP approached the end of their fourth year in power. A series of polls and focus groups in early 1994 confirmed the problem. The Progressive Conservative Party of Ontario was disliked by most Ontarians, who saw it as simply a local extension of the despised former government of Brian Mulroney. "The PC brand was damaged goods," Tom Long recalled. "In fact, the label was virtually radioactive."[6]

Long was again becoming active within the party, involving himself both in strategy and policy sessions. Having got over the disappointment of his own failed leadership bid, he watched with increasing fascination as Harris remolded the party's ideology. And he found that he liked the new boss. Harris had come to the leadership from outside the party's traditional hierarchy, a hierarchy Long had devoted his political life to fighting. Long, who is by nature an outsider, was by no means intimate even with the other young neo-cons who were exerting such an influence on the leader. But though he remained outside the inner circle of Leslie Noble, Alister Campbell, Mitch Patten, et al., and though there was often friction between the abrasive Long and the other young Turks, they appreciated his keen analysis and fervent dedication to the cause.

As Long saw clearly, the challenge now was to transform that cause into a formula for electoral victory. Though the focus groups suggested voters were more likely to trust the Liberals to manage the economy (their federal cousins were acting very much like conservatives now that they were back in power in Ottawa), they appeared broadly sympathetic to the core values that

---

[6] Long's remarks concerning the development of the Common Sense Revolution are drawn from a speech given October 30, 1995, and from interviews with the author.

underlay the evolving Tory policy. "The voters were overwhelmingly on the same wavelength as Mike Harris on a broad range of economic and social issues," Long believes. "The only immediate difficulty for us was that they had no idea this was the case." Party polls revealed that on the issues of downsizing government, cutting taxes, and requiring welfare recipients to work, at least 60 per cent of the electorate showed strong support. But voters were also deeply cynical that any political party could or would deliver on such an agenda. The Tories' polling showed that, although Harris had been harping on the themes of tax reduction and welfare reform for nigh on four years, and though the electors believed these issues crucial, they simply weren't convinced any political party, of any stripe, would do what they promised.

The corrosive decline of public trust in political parties over the past decade is not easily measured. It finds its expression in on-the-street interviews, in conversations in people's homes. In one recent empirical measuring, more than 50 per cent of Canadians told the Angus Reid Group they were unlikely to trust the federal government.[7] This dangerous erosion of the legitimacy of political institutions has been ongoing, perhaps, since the protesting sixties. Certainly it was exacerbated in the 1970s by the oil shocks. Political leaders promised that economic crises could be managed by increasing transfers, by taking funds from better-off taxpayers and transferring them to worse-off taxpayers through programs such as unemployment insurance, job-creation, pensions, and welfare. But better-off taxpayers resist excessive taxation to support transfers. And so governments relied on annual deficits to finance the transfers, hoping economic growth would restore prosperity and make balanced budgets possible again. Federal transfer payments to the provinces increased tenfold between 1974 and 1987 and kept climbing, while deficits increased from $2.2 billion in 1974 to a high of $38.4 billion in 1984.

[7] *Angus Reid Report*, July/August 1996, p. 33.

There was no evidence such an approach would work. In 1995, two respected American economists published a survey of spending-reduction strategies used by the twenty members of the Organization for Economic Co-operation and Development—the larger economies of the developed world. They discovered that countries that had successfully reduced their deficits in the preceding years had cut spending, especially on transfer payments and in payments to public servants. The failures—such as Canada—attempted to reduce deficits through tax increases, which appeared simply to suppress the economy to the point where tax revenues actually declined despite the increased tax rates.[8]

By the mid-1980s, no one in Canada could ignore the escalating problem of debt. But the federal Conservatives' efforts were stymied by their reluctance to take on the interests that would be disadvantaged by such reforms. One indignant senior citizen on Parliament Hill could scupper the best laid plans to reform old-age pensions. Though cuts to transfers were the only and obvious solution to burgeoning deficits, the federal Tories spat out the bullet, preferring to tinker with transfers while increasing taxes. As a result, the deficit ballooned, the debt mushroomed, and the private sector was starved of much-needed investment capital. At the same time, middle-income earners became increasingly frustrated with governments that seemed to think the solution to society's woes was to make breadwinners work harder for less money.

Meanwhile, fevered growth, more speculative than real, fuelled an illusory boom economy in Ontario. Housing prices escalated in Toronto to improbable heights; it sometimes seemed as though society were being run by young men driving Ferraris who sniffed coke and played the market. But the fundamental vulnerability of the country's industrial heartland remained unchanged. Ontario's most important industries, especially

[8] Alberto Alesina and Roberto Perotti, "Fiscal expansions and adjustments in OECD countries," *Economic Policy,* October 1995.

automobile manufacturing, needed to become more productive and competitive.[9]

The Great Recession of 1990, coming on the heels of the Canada–U.S. Free Trade Agreement, exposed these weaknesses, triggering a now-or-never restructuring of the province's industrial economy. This restructuring came at a time when companies were coping with an ongoing technological revolution that did away with many existing jobs, resulting in enormous contractions of the private-sector work force—with the money saved used in part to retool key industries.

The story of Ontario's automobile industry in the early nineties is typical. The Greater Toronto Area hosts the second-largest auto-manufacturing sector in North America, surpassed only (though greatly) by Detroit.[10] The Big Five—General Motors, Ford, Chrysler, Toyota, and Honda—directly account for about 4 per cent of the province's gross domestic product, employing 150,000 workers. Several times as many people work in the industries supplying parts to the manufacturers. Ontario's steel, rubber, and industrial textile industries rely on sales to auto manufacturers. And then there is the mass of white-collar workers, from lawyers to advertising copy writers, who service the industry.

By 1995, General Motors had reduced its work force in Canada by 20 per cent. Steelmaker Dofasco in Hamilton had eliminated 5,000 workers—40 per cent of its payroll. Both had returned to profitability. The federal government had committed itself to deficit reduction, "come hell or high water," as Finance Minister Paul Martin put it. Alberta, Saskatchewan, New Brunswick, Manitoba, and British Columbia—representing Conservative, Liberal, and NDP governments—were all on track

---

[9] For a general overview of Ontario's changing economy, see *Restructuring in Ontario's Economy and Labour Market* (Toronto: Ontario Ministry of Education and Training, 1996).

[10] "Ontario's economic future is the sum of its auto parts," *Globe and Mail,* March 2, 1996, p. A1.

to balanced budgets through cuts in transfers. The exception was Ontario.

The arrival of the 1990 recession coincided with the election of Ontario's first social democratic government. Faced with a huge decline in spending, jobs, and investment, Premier Bob Rae responded, in classic 1970s fashion, by increasing transfers. He ran up repeated $10-billion deficits, spending the money on increased welfare, higher public-service salaries, and government-sponsored job creation. To keep the deficits from escalating beyond control, he also increased taxes, raising the provincial tax rate from 53 to 58 per cent[11] and sending his popularity down to Mulroney-like numbers. Although Rae attempted a partial U-turn in 1993 by clawing back the gains in public-service salaries in what he called the Social Contract and what others called Rae Days, the damage had been done. An electorate taxed to what it regarded as the breaking point viewed with implacable hostility not only the government that had brought it to this pass, but governments in general.

As a result, Ontario was beginning to show tangible signs of erosion of trust by the people in their government. Even the bureaucrats in the Finance department knew the situation was getting out of hand, worrying that an increasing percentage of the economy was going underground through untaxed bartering and other forms of tax evasion. Illegal gambling and cigarette and alcohol smuggling had skyrocketed. Of even greater concern, taxpayers appeared to have few qualms about purchasing smuggled and untaxed booze and smokes. It was this disenchanted, troubled, suspicious electorate that the Tories needed to woo and win. Harris and his young coterie were convinced voters were ready for their recipe of reduced spending, reduced deficits, and reduced taxes. The greatest challenge of all would be simply to convince the people that a political party—any political party—could be believed, particularly one that had inherited the public's abiding dislike of the Mulroney Conservatives.

[11] The provincial tax rate is a percentage of the federal tax.

In the early months of 1994, a small group of Conservative Party activists began meeting regularly at the King Edward Hotel to plot election strategy and write a party platform. When the venue shifted to the Bradgate Arms Hotel, the electoral conspirators quickly became known to Tory insiders as the Bradgate Group. By now, Tom Long had once again become a key figure in planning party strategy. So had Alister Campbell, now a young insurance executive, Leslie Noble, now a management consultant, and Mitch Patten, an executive at Municipal Gas. The pragmatic David Lindsay, as Harris's principal secretary, was the informal leader of the group.

Campbell, Noble, and Patten, who had been influencing Harris's thinking since he first considered running for leader, often gathered for dinner at Episode restaurant, in Toronto's Cabbagetown. "We're all best friends," explains Noble. "We've always socialized together, and we all sort of lived in that neighbourhood." Increasingly, Long and Lindsay joined them. Many of the key concepts that powered the Tory strategy were hatched over dinner at Episode.

Others joined as time went on. Mark Mullins, a thirty-two-year-old financial analyst at Midland Walwyn, phoned to ask if anyone needed an economist. The energetic young analyst wanted to be involved in more than the world of finance. "Most economists like to sit on the sidelines and take potshots," he explains. "I was sort of fed up and interested in seeing some changes." Before long, he was number-cruncher for the group, charged with ensuring that the financial assumptions and commitments of the Tory platform made sense. Jerry Redmond, who ran the research arm of the party in the legislature, was also on board. Pollster John Mykytyshyn sat in; so did Bill Young, chief executive officer of Consumers Distributing, as it then was, and Tom Campbell, once chair of Ontario Hydro and the elder statesman of the group. The latter two provided a business perspective that the young ideologues noticeably lacked.

The Bradgate Group's first decision was to do away with their party. The Progressive Conservative party name would cease to exist. Henceforth, the Tories would simply market themselves as the Mike Harris team, and nothing else. Polls and focus groups had shown that, while voters hated Tories, they had no antipathy for Harris; he was actually marginally more popular than Rae or McLeod. The leader of the third party may not have been a strongly marketable commodity, but at least he wasn't radioactive. The group's second, and most important, decision was to seek to take ownership of a variety of issues they believed would win public support.

The young strategists of the Conservative Party found themselves with a dilemma. The inchoate strivings of the majority of the population towards a simpler, more responsive, more responsible government fitted exactly with their own natural inclinations. Yet the abiding distrust of the electorate towards politicians had reached such a pitch that average voters were skeptical even of a party that claimed to be ready to deliver exactly what they wanted. "They wouldn't take yes for an answer," as Long later put it. The challenge was to convince the electors that the Tories not only believed what they believed, but were prepared to deliver once elected. The solution was a document they would call *The Common Sense Revolution*.

Whether you love or hate it, the CSR, as it came to be known, is unquestionably the most ideologically innovative and politically successful political manifesto in Ontario history. More than any other factor, it transformed a moribund, third-place political party into a majority government in the space of little more than a year, launching a political revolution that is still in progress. The document's duality is crucial. The CSR was both an election strategy and a statement of neo-conservative political philosophy. Its creation was an exercise both in communication and in policy. Producing a detailed policy document that would double as an election platform, and producing it well in advance of the next election, the Bradgate Group believed, would both win them the election and anchor the government. They fully realized their approach was risky. Releasing the document before an election, rather than during it—as the federal Liberals did in

1993 with their Red Book—would reveal the party's strategy to the opposition. But the group was convinced it was worth the risk. The voters would know what the party stood for, and would hear about it early enough and often enough to eventually believe that the leader meant what he said.

The strategy appealed to Harris as well. It would cap the policy documents and mission statements that the party had released under his direction through the past three years. It would both summarize and project the consensus that had emerged within the party. Harris was not directly involved in the early drafts of the document, according to those who were there, but he quickly bought into the strategy. The leader laid down only three directives, says Campbell: "He wanted a balanced budget, he wanted a tax cut, and the plan must be real." Mullins had better make sure the numbers added up.

At one session, as the various components of the plan were being debated and refined, someone—no one can remember who—suggested that the changes, if implemented, would amount to a revolution. This excited the group, until Bill King intervened. King's role had diminished over the years, as Harris increasingly relied on his new coterie of young advisers. But Harris's executive assistant had been around the leader longer than any of them and knew better than anyone how his boss thought. "Mike's not about revolution," he said. "He's about basic things, like common sense." It was a phrase, King pointed out, that Harris had used the day he was elected leader. Someone put the two together: common-sense revolution. And the document had a name. When the name was pitched to Harris, he immediately approved.

In March 1994 the wandering policy forum moved to a basement office in the Ontario legislature, and the actual writing of the CSR got underway. According to Campbell, *The Common Sense Revolution* went through thirteen drafts. "The first draft, the text was written by Tom [Long], with 'insert policy here.' It was mostly rhetorical positioning. Leslie [Noble] tore that up and did a redraft, then we started inserting the policy. I drove drafts two through seven, then it moved into the leader's office and David Lindsay quarterbacked eight through ten, along with Deb Hutton [assistant to the Tory leader] and Bill King and Peter Varley [Harris's press secretary]." The document then went through Harris's hands.

And where was the leader of the party in all of this? "The final three drafts . . . were Mike's," says Campbell. Harris, who makes no claims to eloquence, tinkered with the wording here and there, focusing the narrative on the second-person singular: how *you* will benefit from the tax cut, how *your* children will be better educated. Mostly, however, he was mastering the document himself, becoming comfortable with the numbers and assumptions, so that he could repeat its contents convincingly.

The first critical question the Bradgate Group faced was: How big should the tax cut be? They arrived at an answer quickly. Ontario had one of the highest rates of income tax in the country. Alberta had the lowest rate of any province, at 45.5 per cent. Ontario's goal would be to bring its marginal rate down below Alberta's. That would translate into a tax cut of 30 per cent off the existing marginal rate.[12] But such a tax cut would strip more than $4 billion from the $56-billion provincial budget. And it would not be progressive—that is, the richest would benefit to the same degree as the poorest. In absolute terms, in fact, the well-off would benefit much more greatly, since a cut of 30 per cent to a $30,000 tax bill is more, in straight dollars, than a cut of 30 per cent to a $3,000 tax bill.

To compensate, the Tories included a surtax, a tax on a tax. Individuals earning more than about $50,000 a year in taxable income would pay an additional amount, calculated as a percentage of the tax they already paid. This tax would compensate for a further $400 million lost to government coffers through the elimination of the business payroll tax. Despite the surtax, however, everyone's income-tax bill would go down, no matter how much they made.

---

[12] The marginal rate is the rate of tax imposed on the highest level of income.

The second challenge was to balance the budget. This would be particularly difficult, for several reasons. First, the public debt, which had doubled under the Rae government, produced an unavoidable cost in interest payments that could not be ducked, and that cost was highly volatile—it went up or down, depending on interest rates. Second, and far more important, the tax cut, even with the surtax, would take an estimated $4 billion out of government revenues, an amount that would have to be matched by equivalent cuts in spending. How could the government endure two sets of spending cuts: one to finance the tax cut and one to eliminate the deficit?

Harris and his advisers, however, were determined. The leader devoutly believed that the eleven increases to income tax imposed since 1985 were dampening consumer spending. Besides, he had crusaded as The Taxfighter in the 1990 election, and he didn't want to lose that image. For the young neo-cons, the reasoning was subtly different. They believed that, by definition, big government was iniquitous; it intruded into too many aspects of the economy and people's lives. The best permanent strategy for reducing the size of government would be to reduce the funds available to it. Tax and spending cuts would force the government to withdraw from areas of society—income redistribution, business regulation, affirmative action—that they passionately believed it had no right to be involved in in the first place. And even if their government only lasted one term, they reckoned, future governments would not easily be able to impose a 30 per cent tax increase, or run fresh deficits that created new debt, or whatever combination that would be required to get back into areas the Tories wanted to get the government out of.

And so evolved the famous "four plus two equals six" formula. The government would eliminate $4 billion in government spending through tax cuts. It would eliminate another $2 billion to assist deficit reduction. In total, the annual budget would decline by $6 billion. The plan also assumed that government revenues would increase despite the cuts to spending, partly due to the economic stimulus of the tax cut and partly because of a general post-recession economic improvement that would produce steady 3 per cent real (after inflation) growth in the province's gross domestic product.

These assumptions boiled down to a version of "supply-side" economics. Supply-side theory is, at best, deeply controversial. Also known as trickle-down theory, it argues that tax cuts generate increased consumer spending, which produces economic growth, which generates taxes that equal or exceed the size of the original tax cut. Most mainstream economists discount the theory, arguing that a version of supply-side economics practised by the American government of Ronald Reagan in the 1980s resulted in rapidly escalating deficits. Defenders of supply-side theory, like communists apologizing for the failure of socialism in the Soviet Union, respond that the Reagan government imperfectly applied the theory. Reagan cut taxes but increased overall spending to pay for his military build-up.

Mark Mullins, the Bradgate Group's economist, maintains that the economic assumptions contained in the CSR did not include supply-side-based assumptions on economic growth. In other words, his growth (and therefore tax revenue) projections were based on assumptions about economic improvement that would take place even without a tax cut. One of the CSR's inviolable elements was reducing the size of government and cutting "red tape," which would slice 13,000 positions—15 per cent of all workers—from the government payroll. Eliminating that many jobs would itself drag down the economy, which in Mullins's eyes was one of the chief arguments for a stimulative tax cut.

It was one thing, however, for the CSR to promise to cut taxes and balance the budget. It was another to say exactly where the money would come from. Taxpayers had learned the dodge about finding savings through eliminating duplication and red tape. The federal parties had been making such promises at least since 1984, and federal deficits had continued to climb. But the Tories were convinced that being specific about the cuts would not only lend credibility to their plan, it would reinforce voter convictions that their money was currently being spent badly or wrongly. In other words, the Tories were banking on voter support, not *despite* the cuts to services, but *because* of them.

Some potential areas for cuts were, however, off limits. The Ontario polity greatly values its health-care system. However much neo-conservatives might quietly espouse introducing market forces—private medicine—to increase the efficiency of health care, citizens hold a universal, high-quality, publicly funded health-care system as a sacred trust, a sadly abused phrase. And so the CSR promised no cuts to health-care funding and no new user fees. This declaration was slightly disingenuous. The document promised to freeze health-care spending at 1994 levels through the year 2000, which meant that real spending would be reduced by the amount of inflation each year. Further, as the population grew, and the budget didn't, the amount of money available per person would decline. Nor did the CSR take into account the growing strain on the existing health-care budget. Doctors were on the brink of rebellion over cuts to their incomes, and the average age of the population would increase over the next decade, leading to greater demands on health care. But for now, a promise not to cut health care, even while cutting taxes and balancing the budget, looked pretty good.

The Common Sense Revolution also promised not to cut funding to police and the courts. And it was committed to protecting "classroom funding" in education—that is, money spent on . . . on what? Here, for once, the election document retreated behind an undefined phrase.

But if a Conservative government would cut taxes and eliminate the deficit, while protecting, however nominally, health care, education, and law-enforcement spending—which, combined, account for 52 per cent of the budget—then where would the savings come from? The answer was simple: the Conservatives would take a meat cleaver to the rest of government spending. The single biggest, bleeding chunk would come from welfare. The plan promised to reduce welfare benefits to a level "10 per cent above the national average of all other provinces." Sounds good, except such a level would represent a cut of around 20 per cent from existing benefits.

How a community should succour the poorest among it has long been a matter of debate. In Ontario, since the Second World War, the response has largely taken the form of social assistance, or welfare: a grant of funds to individuals and families who are unable to find work or other means of support.

In recent years, Ontario's welfare program had gone through two financial and philosophical shifts. The first came in 1986, when the Liberal government of David Peterson launched the Social Assistance Review Committee, under Judge George Thomson. The report, released in 1988, envisioned a comprehensive overhaul of the province's welfare system. Welfare rates would be raised, and penalties for earning extra income to supplement welfare eliminated. New training programs would be introduced, and the patchwork of provincial and municipal welfare agencies amalgamated into a single system. Treasurer Robert Nixon balked at the cost of the program, which he estimated at $3 billion a year. Nonetheless, in 1990 the Liberals raised welfare rates by 16 per cent. The NDP campaigned on a promise to implement all the recommendations of the Thomson report and shortly after being elected raised rates a further 9 per cent.

But in the wake of these increases, a disquieting corollary to welfare reform began to reveal itself: the greater the benefits, the greater the numbers seeking help. The number of welfare cases had climbed steadily through the booming 1980s, from 250,000 in 1983 to 315,000 in 1990. Those numbers skyrocketed during the recession, rising to 533,000 in 1992 and 623,000 in 1993, as both provincial and municipal governments watched their budgets founder on escalating welfare costs. Worse, even after the recession ended, the welfare caseload continued to climb, rising to 623,000 in 1993 and 669,000 in 1994. When dependants were added, as many as 1.3 million people in the province depended on social assistance.

By the middle of the NDP's mandate, the government was starting to have second thoughts on welfare benefits. A planned second increase was postponed, as Treasurer Floyd Laughren watched his revenues falling and his deficit burgeoning. In early 1993, Rae began to question the wisdom of his government's welfare reforms. "Welfare isn't working," he told a group of business students. "Simply paying people to sit at home is not smart . . . . It makes little sense simply transferring money to people so they can sit at home."[13] He began to argue for reversing the trend and cutting welfare rates. He even mooted the possibility of requiring welfare recipients to take training or work. But under pressure from the left wing of the cabinet, Rae backed down. Entitlements were neither expanded nor clawed back in the last years of the government.

The Conservatives drew two lessons from the NDP experience. First, the chronic deficits of the past five years were in large measure due to open-ended welfare costs that rose irrespective of boom or bust. Second, the more benefits were raised, the more people jumped on the welfare wagon. Welfare was becoming a substitute for work.

The Tories had long complained that welfare rates were so generous they served as a disincentive to employment. In the summer of 1993, Harris had embarrassed himself when he publicized the case of one Helle Hulgaard, who said she was quitting her $41,500-a-year job with Metro Toronto's housing authority and going on welfare because, as a single mother with two children, she would make almost as much on the dole as on the job. "Helle wants to work," Harris told reporters. "But who can blame her for seizing the chance to make the same or more money while caring for her children at home?" When government officials reported that Hulgaard would, in fact, suffer a significant drop in income from going on welfare, Harris's ploy backfired. But the letters of outrage to editors suggested taxpayers were more angry at the generosity of welfare benefits than at the Tories for pulling a shoddy stunt. Welfare reform became a key to *The Common Sense Revolution*'s savings plan.

---

[13] Thomas Walkom, *Rae Days* (Toronto, Key Porter, 1994), p. 198. The passage on Rae and welfare is based on Walkom's narrative.

The document also promised to go after welfare fraud. Though public servants argued that fraud represented as little as 1 per cent of all spending on welfare, the Tories, extrapolating from estimates quoted in the Provincial Auditor's 1994 report, put the annual cost to the provincial treasury at $247 million dollars between 1990 and 1994.[14] Once in government, they would create a "snitch" line to encourage people to report suspected cases of welfare fraud.

Finally, the Tories pledged to implement workfare, a program requiring all able-bodied welfare recipients to work at government-sponsored jobs or take training. Otherwise, they would be cut off welfare altogether.

There was much more. In education, while protecting the nebulous concept of "classroom funding," the Tories promised to reduce the number of school-board trustees and possibly the number of school boards, make junior kindergarten voluntary at the board level, and raise university tuition fees, while implementing an expanded loan program for low-income university students. They also committed to scrapping the NDP's job-training program, to cutting funding to public transit, to placing a moratorium on nonprofit housing construction, to reducing funding to legal aid, to cutting workers' compensation premiums and benefits, to freezing Ontario Hydro rates, to selling off government assets, possibly including the Liquor Control Board, and, of course, to "cutting red tape."

In short, *The Common Sense Revolution* promised to revive Ontario's flagging economy by stimulating spending through tax cuts and by eliminating deficit financing. In exchange, the Tories would significantly curtail, for better or for worse, the size of the government and the role of the state in society. And when the document was ready to go to the printer, the words "Progressive Conservative Party" were nowhere to be found.

---

[14] It should be noted that the Provincial Auditor's office itself cautioned the estimates were not necessarily reliable.

In its final form, the CSR took up twenty-one pages of cheap newsprint, featured a picture of a relaxed Mike Harris in paisley tie and leather jacket on the front, and boasted a print run of a million copies. The party spent $1 million on its publication and distribution, including a 1-800 number people could call for their copy. The 1-800 number was a recent Tory innovation, and by now a trademark. Following a television statement by Bob Rae back in January 1991, Harris had been given four minutes of air time for rebuttal. Instead, he held up a policy document and invited people to call 1-800-668-MIKE for their copy. More than 13,000 calls poured in over several days. From that time on, the 1-800 number became a key part of the Tories' communication strategy.

Harris launched *The Common Sense Revolution* on May 3, 1994,[15] and immediately took to the road, flogging the party's new platform to anyone who would listen. Though he achieved little media attention, the summer-long tour help cement the link between Mike Harris and the agenda of the CSR.

But one political possibility threatened to stop the CSR cold. In the 1993 federal election, the Reform Party of Preston Manning had garnered 20 per cent support in Ontario, electing one MP and splitting the federal conservative vote in the province. If Reform competed at the provincial level, Harris didn't stand a chance. The CSR was, among its other goals, the capstone of an attempt by the Tories to keep Reform out of provincial politics, a strategy that had begun shortly after the federal election, when Tony Clement, by now the recently retired president of the party, got his hands on a mailing list of Reform supporters in Ontario (he won't say how). Conservative headquarters sent out friendly letters to them all, urging them to get involved in the Mike Harris party. Harris also met with Reform supporters—to the point where he began to complain about all the Reformers he was being asked to make nice to—and the party let it be known that its members could hold

---

[15] The document was slightly revised in the spring of 1995, to take into account the latest federal budget.

Reform and Progressive Conservative party memberships simultaneously without penalty. The Tories even welcomed federal Reformers onto some of their provincial riding executives, including future Social Services Minister Janet Ecker's riding of Durham West.

The Common Sense Revolution was intended to convince Reformers that their goals were the goals of the provincial Tories. Indeed, many observers dismissed the CSR as nothing more than a Tory ploy to keep Reform out of Ontario. *Ottawa Citizen* columnist Jim Coyle recalls a meeting with Tom Long several months after the publication of the document and shortly after Coyle had written a column congratulating the Conservatives on having beaten back the threat from Reform. Now it was time for the party plan to tack towards the centre, Coyle had argued, to recapture the soft Liberal vote. Long took Coyle to lunch to straighten him out. "We're not coming back," he told the columnist. "This *is* the new centre." In the end, the Conservatives' Reform-like platform, coupled with Reform leader Preston Manning's determination not to sidetrack the movement into provincial politics, served to keep the Right in Ontario united. Reformers and Tories would vote as one for Mike Harris in 1995.

With *The Common Sense Revolution*, Harris nailed a thesis to the door of Ontario's sacred political edifice. It was now for the other two parties to challenge it. At a fundamental level, however, the contest would be not between the Tories and the other parties, but between the Tories and the electors themselves. The CSR challenged Ontario voters to decide whether they truly had the courage to embrace a political program most of them claimed they wanted. The program itself was a relatively complex articulation of water-cooler wisdom, of locker-room punditry, of dinner-table debate. It was what the broad middle class of society had always said they desired but were afraid to demand. The CSR massaged their resentments, comforted their fears, and stoked their longings. But it was an ideology that heretofore in Ontario had dared not speak its name, that the mainstream media, the academic, social, and political elites, even much of the business community had dismissed as unjustified, petty, divisive, mean-spirited, and cruel—something to be ashamed of, something not even to be said out loud.

Now it had been said. And there was an election coming up.

CHAPTER 4

The Preplanned Miracle

One November evening in 1993, Mike and Janet Harris asked Tom Long and his wife, Leslie Pace, to join them for a glass of wine in the hot tub of the Harrises' spacious suburban North Bay home. As the four friends perched on the edge of the tub, sipping their wine, Harris offered Long the job of co-chair of the next election campaign. Long looked over at Pace, but she wasn't there. She had fallen off the edge.

Tom Long's wife wasn't the only one surprised by Mike Harris's decision. In the run-up to the provincial election, many inside the party expected him to bring in a more seasoned team of campaigners. Yes, his coterie of neo-conservative enthusiasts had helped get Harris elected leader and had stuck with him after the 1990 election, but they were frighteningly young. Long at the time was only thirty-six. If the Tories were to have any realistic hope of improving their standing, went conventional wisdom, experienced veterans such as Hugh Segal, John Tory, or John Laschinger needed to take over the job.

Tory, who was fresh from running Kim Campbell's disastrous campaign in the early fall of 1993, denies today that he expected to be brought onto the election team. "It was time for a change," he argues. Whether he wanted the job or not, he wasn't asked. Harris had decided to dance with the kids what brung him. Harris, like many politicians, values loyalty above most other traits.

Long, who quickly accepted the post, was appointed campaign chair, in charge of shaping the overall strategy; Leslie Noble would be campaign manager, responsible for successfully implementing that strategy. In splitting the leadership of the campaign in two, and asking Noble and Long to share the duties, Harris took a calculated risk. Both were smart and motivated. Both were also strong-willed and competitive. Long was still a bit of an outsider among the group. Had the two failed to get along, the campaign could have been a disaster. But Long and Noble knew the coming contest would be their supreme test and opportunity. From the first, they worked with rather than against each other. No visible rift between them ever emerged.

Long and Noble, in turn, created a campaign team of their friends. It was this team that had led the writing of *The Common Sense Revolution* and that now began to plan the campaign down to the smallest detail. Alister Campbell would be the "message guy," whose job would be to make sure that everything written, said, and done during the coming election conformed to the CSR. Paul Rhodes, a former reporter and publicist for the Ontario Medical Association, would handle media relations with the assistance of Peter Varley, Harris's press secretary. Rhodes' relationship with Long had been testy in the past, but he was friends with other members of the team and was anxious to be in on the election. Jamie Watt, a young advertising guru from London, Ontario, would work on communications and advertising. David Lindsay and Debbie Hutton—she knew Harris well from having worked as his aide during the opposition years—would be on the bus with Harris, coping with the day-to-day. As campaign secretary, Mitch Patten would be the floater, taking care of everything nobody else was doing.

Along with Bill King, a very young Guy Giorno, all of twenty-nine, would write speeches for the leader. Giorno, while a law student, had considered himself a Red Tory until one night, in a crisis of faith, he phoned right-wing commentator (and co-founder of the *Toronto Sun*) Peter Worthington on a radio talk show and was converted to the radical right. Giorno had helped out on the 1990 election campaign. This time he was going to be right at the centre of the action.

With the exception of Tom Long, the core of this team—Noble, Campbell, Patten—had worked on the 1990 campaign. Despite the new faces, the real difference this time would be the absence of seasoned veterans to catch them if they fell, no Laschinger in overall charge, no former Big Blue Machiners offering quiet, powerful advice. This election was theirs to win or lose. Their futures, as well as Harris's, would be decided by the outcome.

During the sessions that had forged the CSR and developed the strategy for the election to come, the campaign team and other members of the Bradgate Group divided themselves into Liberal and NDP sides and ran through possible election scenarios, in hopes of anticipating opposition tactics and issues. The teams attempted to put together what they figured was the most likely strategy for the other parties. This exercise led the Bradgate Group to concude that the Liberals would release a policy platform early in the campaign, as their federal counterparts had done in 1993, and that they would attempt to occupy a centre-rightist ground with modified versions of several Tory policies. The Bradgate Group further concluded that this strategy would fail, that voters would prefer a more emphatic and undiluted commitment to a right-wing agenda, but that the polls would not turn in Mike Harris's favour until the second half of the campaign, when voters would begin to display a real interest in what was happening. The analysis would turn out to be a marvel of prescience.

The team also came up with a media strategy to complement the CSR election platform. The all-important television ads would be low-cost, to concentrate on maximum saturation. They would be negative, featuring what is known as the T-bar approach of contrasting the Liberals' inconsistencies on one side of the screen, with the Tories' own clear proposals on the other. The idea was to hammer home the message that the Mike Harris team was serious about cutting taxes, cutting spending, and reforming welfare. This was no time to be subtle. The gamble was that, once voters figured out the Tories meant what they said, they would buy the package.

All that was needed now was an election. But the NDP was, understandably, in no hurry to rush into a vote. Although by fall 1994, Bob Rae had passed beyond the fourth year of his mandate, when a government would normally call an election, the NDP was wildly unpopular, scoring in the teens in some opinion polls. It seemed at times as though the government was perversely dedicated to destroying itself. If so, its strategy was three-pronged. First, it had infuriated its natural enemies, the business community, by raising the minimum wage 26 per cent, imposing employment equity, and banning replacement workers during strikes. Then it had set out to disenchant the broad middle of the electorate, by raising income taxes. Finally, it had alienated its core supporters by imposing wage cuts on the public service (the infamous Rae Days).

The NDP was activist in areas it never expected to be, and timid in areas where action was expected. Rae vetoed plans for a government takeover of the auto-insurance industry, fearing the loss of 6,000 jobs. On the other hand, a party that had damned lotteries as a tax on the poor introduced casino gambling. Once the NDP had defended the right of workers to take Sunday off. In power, it legalized Sunday shopping.

All or some of this might have been forgiven had the party of the Left managed the province's economy with some measure of competence. But if the Rae government was guilty of one mortal sin, that sin was fiscal. In the space of a scant four years, Ontario more than doubled the entire accumulated provincial debt, from $39 billion in fiscal 1989–90 to almost $90 billion in fiscal 1994–95. When Rae became premier, nine cents of every dollar spent by the government went to servicing the debt. When he left, sixteen cents went to debt servicing. The debt had doubled to 29 per cent of the province's gross domestic product.

And for what? Had the investment got people off unemployment and out of welfare and into jobs? Hardly. Even after the dreadful recession that afflicted the early years of the NDP's mandate was over, unemployment continued to stagger along at 8.7 per cent, far above the 5 per cent of pre-recession 1989. The number of people on welfare climbed every year, from 293,000 in 1989 to 678,000 in June 1995, when it finally began to decline.

Increasing spending and debt—the classic Keynesian approach to softening the impact of an economic downturn—may have actually worsened the situation. Usually, Canada's economy trails that of the United States, following the Americans into a recession, and following them out of it. But this recession was different. Ontario's economy dipped into recession in the third quarter of 1989; the rest of Canada followed suit in the first quarter of 1990. The United States didn't tilt into recession until the second quarter of 1990.

Why did Ontario sink into recession before the rest of Canada or the Americans, and why was our recession so severe? Some have blamed the Free Trade Accord, signed in 1988 between Canada and the United States. Everywhere, branch plants seemed to be closing, moving home to their American parents. Others blamed the high interest rates imposed by the Bank of Canada to suppress inflation. The high rates, they argued, also suppressed investment and encouraged people to save—rather than spend—what little they had, which would have added desperately needed economic stimulus. Some pointed to the American recession, which of course made our own recession worse. Others spoke nebulously about the restructuring of the global economy.

But a 1993 study by the University of Toronto's Institute of Policy Analysis revealed another, crucial, cause: federal tax increases by the Mulroney government. "The largest single contributing factor [to the recession] is the series of federal tax increases in 1989—in great part because many of them were increases in indirect taxes that tended to push up inflation just as the Bank of Canada was trying to reduce it," the authors concluded.[1] The tax increases not only deepened the recession,

---

[1] Peter Dungan, Steve Murphy, and Thomas Wilson, *Sources of the Recession in Canada and Ontario* (Toronto: Institute for Policy Analysis, University of Toronto, 1993), p. i.

but slowed down the recovery that finally trembled into existence in 1992. Ontario was further burdened by the accompanying rise in the provincial income tax rate and provincial sales taxes under the Peterson government. Then the NDP hastened to worsen the situation with tax increases of their own. In short, the federal income-tax increases in the late 1980s exacerbated Canada's recession, and the wave of provincial tax increases the Liberals and NDP imposed on Ontario could only deepen the pain to the nation's industrial heartland.

Unaware or unwilling to believe its economic policies were only making things worse, the NDP struggled heroically to reverse the recession, throwing $3.4 billion at its jobsOntario job-creation program. But the Ontario economy was too far gone. The jobs the NDP created were ephemeral, though the cost of creating them lingered on in public debt. In the long term, the investment probably did more harm than good by forcing the government to draw more money out of the economy to service its burgeoning debt.

Most people in the province seemed to like the premier personally; his popularity consistently scored above that of the party. The NDP genuinely appeared to be trying to do right by the province, even if things consistently went wrong. And it had arrived in power just in time for a particularly painful recession. Rae pointedly and repeatedly complained that the high-interest-rate policies of the Bank of Canada only made his job more difficult, especially since the federal government had slashed transfer payments to the province. The problem was, many people seemed to like the low inflation that came with the high interest rates. Meanwhile, 82 per cent of Ontarians approved of the federal government's budget-balancing policies.[2]

As the snows finally melted in the wet April of 1995, Bob Rae had run out of rope. A $1.2-billion splurge of new

---

[2] An Angus Reid survey after the 1995 federal budget revealed that 44 per cent of Ontarians believed the cuts were about right, while 38 per cent said the cuts didn't go far enough.

promises that winter had only deepened the public's cynicism. The legislature had sat only twenty days since it had risen in June 1994 for its summer break. It was time for a budget, but that would mean recalling the House and confronting both the opposition and the bleak fiscal numbers. Treasurer Floyd Laughren had already helpfully predicted that taxes would probably have to rise yet again in the coming year to cope with worsening debt. Rae had no intention of presenting a budget and his carcass to the opposition in the legislature. Instead, he had the treasurer release an economic statement that, in part by separating capital spending by Crown corporations from regular expenditures, appeared to show the province headed towards a balanced budget.

With this trick of fiscal legerdemain in hand, on the cold wet early afternoon of April 28, 1995, Rae called an election for June 8. "Every election is like a box of chocolates," the premier intoned, adapting freely from *Forrest Gump*. "You never know what you're going to find." The election, he promised, would be fought on the question of who best could stand up to federal spending cuts that polls showed the Ontario electorate actually supported. It was a less than promising campaign platform.

The NDP entered the campaign with around 20 per cent of the popular vote. The Conservatives were at about 25. The Liberals were above 50. All sides agreed the election was Liberal leader Lyn McLeod's to lose. A former cabinet minister in the Peterson government, McLeod had won the leadership in 1992 and was now perched comfortably with twice the popular support of either of her rivals.

In hindsight (where wisdom resides), there was every reason to discount those numbers. First, popularity going into an election has sometimes proved to be a mark of impending doom. Frank Miller enjoyed 50 per cent support going into his disastrous election of 1985. David Peterson was similarly blessed entering the 1990 campaign. Prime Minister Kim Campbell was out in front when she called the election that led to her demise in 1993. Only when voters awoke to the reality of an election campaign did their discontent with the times begin to manifest itself, not surprisingly in support for parties critical of the status quo. The question was, since the governing NDP had already been consigned by the electorate to the status of third-party-coincidentally-in-government, would they turn to the soaring Liberals or turn on them?

Most people who have met Lyn McLeod find her intelligent, sympathetic, warm, committed, and capable. The problem was, most people in Ontario hadn't met Lyn McLeod. Angus Reid pollster John Wright pointed out shortly before the election that half the people inclined to vote for the Liberals couldn't identify the leader by name.[3] Those who did know her often identified her for a less-than-auspicious reason: her apparent flip flop on the gay-rights issue. In an April 1993 Toronto by-election, McLeod had declared her support for extending benefits to same-sex couples. After the by-election, which her party won, McLeod had sent Bob Rae a letter urging him to extend equal rights for same-sex couples. But when Rae introduced the legislation in May 1994, McLeod balked, saying the bill went too far by offering same-sex couples adoption rights. When Rae, faced with rebellion within his own caucus and no Liberal support, offered to amend the legislation, McLeod said it was too late. The bill died, after a riotous session in the assembly that featured security guards donning latex gloves to remove gay protesters from the gallery. McLeod subsequently announced that Rae had so poisoned the issue her government would be unable to deal with it.

The real issue, for many voters, was not gay rights, but the credibility of the Liberal leader. Liberal strategists blamed their defeat in a by-election in Victoria-Haliburton in March 1994 on McLeod's support for gay rights. The leader, they concluded, had to back off her support, however unpleasant the optics, and it was that decision that had led McLeod to vote against the NDP bill. But Victoria-Haliburton, a quintessentially middle-Ontario rural riding, had taken a good look at the three parties and

[3] "Rivals see McLeod as soft target," *Globe and Mail,* April 27, 1995, p. A5.

chosen the Mike Harris package, a hint of swings to come. The Liberal flip flop only heightened the underlying uncertainty among electors about McLeod's dependability.

Yet few predicted, as the election got under way, that the Liberals could not count on victory. "We have this big Liberal sponge in the centre," observed political scientist Nelson Wiseman. "The NDP is discredited like the Liberals were in 1990 and the Conservative right-wing appeal isn't working." He predicted the Liberals could take as many as 100 of the legislature's 130 seats.[4]

From the start of the 1995 campaign, the political cognoscenti dismissed the Tory leader. Not only was Mike Harris the champion of a mean-spirited and impractical agenda, they felt, he was himself simplistic and—as the Helle Hulgaard case had revealed—often spiteful. Shortly after the 1990 election, he had been described thus: "A large, lumbering man with an unassuming manner, Harris was the antithesis of modern political charisma . . . . His image was hampered somewhat by his well-known previous career as a golf pro, a job not commonly recognized as preparing one for public office, and by his right-wing inclinations."[5] Five years later, little had changed. Reporters seemed incapable of writing about the new leader without referring to him as "a former golf pro." That he was, in fact, a small businessman, a veteran MPP, and a former cabinet minister generally escaped their attention.

If the pundits had dismissed Harris, the electors appeared hardly less skeptical. On his first full day of campaigning, as he walked a west-end Toronto street, Harris was confronted by what turned out to be the archetypal Ontario voter. "Your plan sounds wonderful and I want to vote for you," Peter Judd told Harris. "But I'm afraid that, when you get in there, you'll just say the same things as all the rest. You'll say there isn't enough [money]

---

[4] "Rae Calls June 8 Ontario Election," *Globe and Mail*, Toronto: April 29, 1995, p. A1.

[5] *Not Without Cause*, p. 152.

to do what you had planned."[6] In retrospect, the entire campaign was about convincing Peter Judd. An electorate disenchanted with governments that promised to right the balance even as things became more skewed was looking for a party that knew what had to be done and was willing to do it.

As campaigns generally do, the 1995 contest started slowly. But even in the first week of electioneering, there were signs of building Tory strength. Although internal party polls showed little movement, Tory signs began sprouting on lawns where they had no business being. One such place was Maple—once a village north of Toronto, today a suburban enclave within the sprawl of the artificial city of Vaughan. Maple is middle-class and commuter-based, as is much of the riding of York Centre. In the 1990 election, the Conservatives polled a lousy 9 per cent in Maple. But one week into the 1995 campaign, with the Tories running local car salesman Al Palladini and handing out at the door videos extolling the virtues of Mike Harris and his Common Sense Revolution, the lawns boasted more blue signs than dandelions.

York Centre is heavily Italian, and conventional wisdom placed the multicultural vote firmly in the Liberal and NDP camps. But many of the riding's residents, who had come to Canada after the Second World War and prospered, resented the provincial government's recent history of taxing them and giving the money to people they thought were simply too lazy to work for a living. One of these many was Nazzarene Trelle, who stood on her front lawn, a Palladini sign nearby, and protested to this writer, "I don't want to be prejudiced, but I think these people who come now, as soon as they get off the plane, they go on welfare."

Political analysts called it the Angry White Male syndrome, but there was nothing particularly male or white about it. In Markham riding, next door to York Centre, David Tsubouchi would win by a staggering 26,617 votes, topping almost every poll, including those with large numbers of East Indians, West Indians, Chinese, and Filipinos, among others. Similar ethnic groups who had not

[6] "Harris hit by hard core of distrust," *Toronto Star*, April 30, 1995, p. A6.

done as well, however, continued to support the more liberal parties. Italians in Vaughan may have loved the Common Sense Revolution, but Italians in the Toronto riding of Dovercourt stayed loyal to NDP MPP Tony Silipo. Race was not a determinant in voting patterns in the 1995 elections. Affluence was.

While Harris was out on the hustings trying to shake voter cynicism, Tom Long, Leslie Noble, and their campaign team were closeted on the ninth floor of a University Avenue office building, watching their plan unfold. Campaign headquarters—they called it the bullpen—was as dingy, cluttered, and high-spirited as a college dorm. When the election team moved in, about a month before the vote was called, they held a painting party, slathering the walls in deepest Tory blue. Peter Varley, Harris's press secretary, painted a mural of Harris in a Star Trek uniform, ordering David Lindsay to beam him up. The bullpen was equipped with an exercise bike, putting machine, a kitchen, and a mascot—Long's cocker spaniel, Dave. It was also fearsomely messy. When Dave got into some Swiss Chalet chicken and was banished from the bullpen, staff mutinied and launched a Free Dave campaign. The dog returned. The second-hand desks of the campaign team lined the walls; a large table dominated the centre. Its most important item was a telephone, a direct line to the campaign bus. When it honked, everyone scrambled to answer.

The long wait for the election call had made it possible for all parties to map out strategy to the nth degree. In the Conservatives' case, the plan was simple and direct. The campaign would focus on the key issues laid out in *The Common Sense Revolution*: cutting taxes and balancing the budget; workfare; law and order. Each week would focus on one key issue. Each day would begin with a presentation: Harris standing on top of an office building, Toronto's Bay Street skyline behind him, promising to eliminate corporate grants; Harris standing before a palatial school-board headquarters, promising to direct education funds into the classroom. This media-op would be followed by a lunchtime speech to a friendly crowd, repeating that day's mantra. The afternoon would be kept loose, to give reporters and camera crews ample time to file for the evening newscasts. If the leader was up north, plane schedules would be jigged to ensure that TV crews had plenty of time to get their tapes to the newsroom. If necessary, the Tories would offer their own runners to get the tape to the station on time.

At campaign HQ, the typical day began with a general meeting and a review of the overnight media. The team would confer with David Lindsay on the bus to ensure that the script for the day was in place. Much of the day at headquarters would consist of calling local campaigns to answer questions and to take the pulse of the ridings. In the first two and a half weeks of the campaign, when there appeared to be no momentum towards the Conservatives, Tom Long spent much of his time holding the hands of jittery candidates over the phone. Alister Campbell explained the details of the CSR to reporters, editorial writers, candidates, and anyone else who wanted to know.[7] Bill King and Guy Giorno worked over fresh drafts of speeches. Leslie Noble and Mitch Patten concentrated on logistics and whatever fires needed extinguishing.

Each night at six o'clock, the team would assemble in a room off the bullpen filled with television sets and video recorders to monitor the all-important evening news. To avoid babble, the sound was turned off; the VCRs taped the shows and assistants later transcribed the results. But for the campaigners, the words weren't important. They wanted to see the visuals. And the visuals were gratifying. There would be Lyn McLeod, standing in front of a Liberal campaign backdrop, talking about—what? There she'd be at a press conference, discussing—what? And there was Mike Harris, in a classroom. Bet it was about education. There he was in a factory. Bet it was about jobs. There he is, unveiling a city sign named Welfare, Ontario, pop. 1,300,000. Guess what that's about? For the Tories, the Liberals' indifference

---

[7] Each Tory candidate had been put through a campaign school that included detailed briefings on the CSR, followed by a test. Reportedly, one future cabinet minister failed this exam on his first attempt.

to visuals was the first and most encouraging sign that the first-place party hadn't thought through its strategy.

Spirits started out high in Tory HQ and stayed that way. The campaigners were young and filled with energy. They were noisy and irreverent and absolutely certain of themselves. Long and Noble made a point of getting along with each other, which helped relax the atmosphere. Had events gone against them, the atmosphere might quickly have soured. But, with a few early exceptions, the campaign unfolded like clockwork.

Those early exceptions came in the first week. Despite all the planning and preparation, the first few days of the campaign went rockily. The team had decided to give reporters plenty of access to Harris, to make him appear open and confident. But if the leader's openness to reporters, most of whom are by nature hostile to right-wing politicians, fostered an attitude of candour and accessibility, it also led to gaffes—two of them. On the first Tuesday of the campaign, Harris mused that universities should revoke tenure from university professors, to cut costs. It provoked protests from—not unexpectedly—university professors, who defended tenure as a necessary guarantor of academic freedom. It didn't help that Harris made the remarks in London, proud home to the University of Western Ontario. The next day, campaigning in Ottawa, he speculated that the government might close the Windsor casino, especially if competition from Detroit reduced its profits. Anyway, Harris said, governments shouldn't be relying on taxes from gambling. The casino is much loved in Windsor, especially by the businesses that profit from accommodating, feeding, and entertaining its cross-border patrons. Harris quickly recanted, promising no action without a local referendum.

The leader's handlers quickly realized that Harris's tendency to publicly chew his cud on issues could be disastrous, especially at the end of a fourteen-hour day. By week two, evening scrums were made shorter, and the leader encouraged to stick to the script. It was, said Peter Varley, "the last political lesson Mike Harris had to learn." For the duration of the campaign, at least, he learned it.

The Liberals and their even less well-known leader got off to no better a start. They entered the campaign with a muddled strategy and an inadequately prepared media plan. The party leadership, including co-chairs Richard Mahoney, John Ronson, and Deb Matthews, and campaign co-ordinator Bob Richardson, decided to introduce their unknown leader to the public through a series of scripted photo-ops. McLeod would get off the bus, greet supporters, give a rousing speech, get back on the bus. Before the first week was even over, reporters were criticizing the cocoon-like campaign, in which the leader never ventured out among the people. At one point, early in the race, McLeod called a press conference in which she promised to scrap the royal commission set up by the NDP into Workers' Compensation. She asserted that companies were avoiding setting up shop in Ontario because of the bloated Workers' Compensation system. But when reporters began badgering her for examples, which she could not provide, the press conference began to unravel. Her handlers, alarmed, cut it short, prompting shouts of outrage from the journalists. Now the cocoon myth was firmly implanted. Though McLeod later reversed the policy, hosting one scrum that lasted so long reporters' arms grew cramped from holding their tape recorders and cameras started running out of tape, the impression had been set.

The Liberals further contributed to their troubles by failing properly to counter the Tory strategy of publishing *The Common Sense Revolution* a year before the election. The Liberals waited until the first week of the campaign before bringing out their Red Book, outlining their election platform. Instead of offering a clear and cogent alternative to the radical Tory agenda, it turned out to be a watered-down—and difficult-to-read—imitation of the Tory document. The Conservatives would cut spending by $6 billion; the Liberals would cut spending by $3.5 billion. The Tories were offering a 30 per cent cut in provincial income taxes; the Liberals offered targeted tax cuts of Byzantine complexity. (Example: parents earning under $50,000 a year could deduct $1,000 from income taxes for each child under age five in day care. The deduction could also be claimed by a working parent whose spouse's income exceeded the $50,000 threshold, provided the applicant parent's income was below that threshold.) While the Tories promised to force people on welfare to work or lose benefits, the Liberals promised to reduce but not eliminate benefits for those who refused to work. They would eventually call this scheme "mandatory opportunity," the worst example of Orwellian Newspeak to emerge in Canadian politics in years. The Liberal platform was quickly branded a disaster.

Compounding the early problems of the Liberal campaign was its ill-conceived media strategy. Over at Tory headquarters, Jamie Watt had locked down the preferred advertising spots on television and radio within hours of the dropping of the writ. With the campaign already under way, the Liberals hadn't even thought their strategy out. There was no in-house advertising co-ordinator like Watt; instead, the party relied on Vickers and Benson, the party's longtime preferred advertising agency. Nor were the Liberals helped by their television ads. The five-foot-no-inch Liberal leader sat in an enormous chair and made promises about what the party would do in thirty days after an election, in ninety days, in a year. For this they spent a million dollars.

The Tory T-bar ads went for the jugular, accusing McLeod of being soft on welfare recipients and supporting employment equity. One particularly effective spot showed the Liberal leader's head perched on a weathervane, veering this way and that on everything from gay rights to workfare. Though other parties shied away from such controversial topics, Long and company believed, as they had believed when they first gathered at the Bradgate Arms in 1994, that these were the topics that tapped middle-class anger and would swing the election their way. And their ads ignored the NDP. "They're irrelevant," Long maintained.

Above all, the Liberals immolated their own campaign by misidentifying the enemy. The party was convinced it had lost the 1990 election because Liberal votes bled to the NDP. In a classic example of generals fighting the last war, the Liberals continued to fear an NDP revival, missing the greater Conservative threat.

On the campaign bus, strategists assured reporters that as long as they kept the NDP below 25 per cent, the election was theirs. "We have to come out aggressively seeking the trust of the people who say they will vote for us now. We will still run against the NDP," Richard Mahoney affirmed, ten days into the campaign.[8] But the NDP were never the threat.

Despite the contrasts in preparation and strategy, support for the Liberals held into the second week of the campaign. An Environics poll, taken during the first week, showed the Liberals had climbed to 52 per cent support, with the Tories languishing at 26 per cent and the NDP a dismal 17. The Tory overnight polls in the second week showed little change. But there was no panic, either on the bus or in the bullpen. The Bradgate Group's scenario predicted polls wouldn't begin to move until the second half of the campaign, when voters began to take an active interest in the leaders and the issues.

And there was another factor. The sensational trial of Paul Bernardo, accused of murdering teen-agers Kristen French and Leslie Mahaffy, got under way at the same time as the provincial election. The circus was taking place at a courthouse a block from Conservative headquarters. The campaign team was visibly reminded each day that the provincial election was not the only thing on people's minds.

The turning point came at the end of the third week. The week itself had been relatively quiet, as the leaders prepared for the important television debate. Lindsay and Hutton were in charge of readying Harris for the tussle. The strategy was to stay detached from the thrust and parry of the debate; instead, Harris was to look directly into the camera and repeat the Common Sense message. On the Thursday night of the debate, McLeod—who as front runner was expected to be the target of attack—went on the offensive herself, interrupting answers, castigating both Rae and Harris, and waving her Red Book incessantly.

---

[8] "Liberals expect to lose support but win election," *Globe and Mail,* May 8, 1995, p. A5.

Pundits hailed McLeod's tough, aggressive performance against Rae and Harris,[9] and Harris's own campaign team agreed. The Conservative leader appeared to have been left behind by Rae and McLeod, the principal combatants. "I felt he hadn't engaged his opponents," Peter Varley acknowledges. But Varley didn't stay worried for long. The party's overnight polls showed the first signs of increased support for the Tories. Reporters main-streeting the next day found constituents annoyed with McLeod's abrasive style. Instead, they focused on Harris's calm, emphatic message.

McLeod then became the victim of both her own rhetoric and of overwrought journalism at the worst possible time. Part way through a desultory day of campaigning, the weekend after the debate, Kelly Toughill of the *Toronto Star* asked the Liberal leader to elaborate on her policy of getting tough with men who abuse their wives. McLeod confirmed that she believed verbal abuse should be possible grounds for expelling a spouse from the home. Though the *Star* downplayed the story, the *Toronto Sun* shouted from page one: "Shout at Spouse, Lose Your House." The headline understandably infuriated McLeod, but she had been stuck with the label of politically-correct-to-a-fault, a tag usually reserved exclusively for the NDP.

Now the blows fell like hammers. The very next day the *Sun* and *Financial Post* released a Compas poll showing the Liberals and Tories almost tied at 40 and 36 per cent, respectively, with the NDP at 21. The Tories had gone up ten points since the Environics poll, while the Liberals had dropped twelve. At last, the Liberals raised their eyes from their NDP-bashing campaign strategy, to find themselves staring into the grinning faces of the Conservatives. They did their best to adjust, shifting McLeod's attack to the Tory plans for workfare and tax cuts, the first time the Liberal leader had taken careful aim at the CSR. New ads appeared, targeting the Tories and going on the attack. But it was too late. The Liberals had started out by picking the wrong

---

[9] "Grits by default," *Toronto Sun*, May 19, 1995, p. 10; "McLeod the winner—by a nose," *Toronto Star*, May 19, 1995, p. A24.

enemy and had misread the degree of voter anger over the NDP policies that the Liberals were promising to modify, not scrap. Midway through the campaign, veteran Liberal MPP Gilles Morin conceded his surprise at the hostility he faced among voters. "Some of them can be very, very harsh," the Ottawa-area MPP reported. "You just have to let that anger come out."[10]

The disastrous Liberal slide had begun, and there seemed to be nothing the party's embattled strategists could do. It was too late to revise the platform, and the very targets the Liberals now picked for their attacks on the Tory platform were the areas of the CSR that most attracted voters. As May gave way to June, McLeod began flogging the M-word in her speeches. "When [Ontarians] see the same people lining up behind Brian Mulroney, the same people that backed Brian Mulroney and Michael Wilson . . . . " But the Tories' polling had told them that the link to Mulroney had been dissolved. Their strategic decision to trash the party name had paid off. As the fourth week turned into the fifth, polls showed the Tories overtaking the Liberals, moving ahead, moving into majority-government territory. An Angus Reid poll published the Saturday before the election put the Tories at 44 per cent, more than enough for a majority government and ten comfortable points ahead of the Grits. The Liberals were in panic, their support in freefall. There were rumours of prominent Liberal candidates removing their own lawn signs, not wanting to get elected if it meant languishing in opposition. One Liberal insider confessed that, in the last two weeks of the campaign, "we figured we were losing a seat a day." The Liberals prayed for June 8 to arrive, if only to end the pain.

In the bullpen, the mood had become almost giddy. Team members began calling each other by super-hero nicknames: Wonk Man, Spin Lord. They could afford to laugh each morning, as the *Toronto Star*, appalled at the prospect of a Harris victory, worked itself into a frenzy of denunciation. The paper might hate

---

[10] Listening paid off; Morin retained his seat.

the Tories, but its readers seemed to like them fine. As the numbers climbed past 40 per cent, and a majority government became increasingly assured, the campaign team began to contemplate career choices. Most of them had jobs or hopes of jobs outside the party. Would they return to them? Or should they ride this train a little longer, right into the premier's office? Meanwhile, David Lindsay hauled out the transition briefing binders he'd prepared. It looked like they might be needed.

For Bob Rae and the NDP, the campaign had been about survival. Their strategy, such as it was, counted on popular sympathy for the premier, coupled with fears of cuts to health care and education, translating into renewed support for the government. Campaigning against the threat of the other guy is a strategy generally employed by opposition parties, not governments. But the NDP knew it was third-party-in-waiting and campaigned accordingly. The leader's tour focused on northern Ontario, southwestern Ontario, and downtown Toronto, the party's three remaining bastions of support. Rae kept up a gruelling pace; during one one-day swing he campaigned in the morning in Toronto, then flew down to Windsor, and returned by bus, stopping repeatedly to rally the troops at local campaign events. But nothing could move the numbers, which remained mired below 20 per cent.

Rae remained, by far, the most magnetic personality on the campaign trail, his oratorical skills far surpassing Lyn McLeod's and light-years beyond those of Mike Harris, who still couldn't stand before a crowd without cue cards. Rae, playing the role of Jeremiah warning the faithful against the ungodly barbarians, painted grim pictures of closed hospitals, tattered schools, needy poor. At times, carried away by his own rhetoric, he assumed the dual mantle of martyr and saviour. Once, in Timmins, late in the campaign, he looked the crowd straight in the eye and warned, "I'm the only protection you've got." Then, as though waking to reality, he turned to the local candidates behind him and added, "And he is. And he is." In the absence of a platform—for the NDP would make no promises—or a record—for the NDP's record had put them where they were—it was the most the leader could hope for. And if the crowds were small, and elderly, they were at least faithful. They were all that was left. As was he.

In the last week of the campaign, the NDP knew it would be reduced to a rump, unlikely to get far past the twelve seats needed to qualify for party status in the house. During one last swing, Rae wandered to the back of the airplane and chatted quietly with reporters. It was certain, now, the Tories would win. The premier was asked whether the people were voting against his party or for something else. "No, I think they're voting for something, this time," he mused. "Sometimes, the people just decide they want something. And cuts are what they want. But damned if I'm going to be the one who gives it to them."

The eighth of June, when it came, was anticlimactic. The networks declared a Progressive Conservative majority government less than half an hour after the polls closed. When the evening was over, the Tories had a well-padded caucus of 82 seats out of a total of 130. The Liberal caucus had actually shrunk, from thirty-four seats to thirty, while the NDP was down to seventeen from their governing high of sixty-nine.[11] And the incoming team's mandate was beyond question. The Tories had won 45 per cent of the popular vote; the Liberals 31, and the NDP 21. Since much of the Liberal platform had consisted of a weakened-strain version of the Tory platform, it could reasonably be said that 76 per cent of the voters had endorsed a program to reduce spending, balance the budget, and reform social programs.

The Tories proved strongest in the edge cities and the hinterlands. The Liberals and NDP held mostly the downtowns and the true North. The new coalition between the settler culture and the suburban middle class had been forged. The old stock in Hastings and Elgin had voted for the Tories; the new stock in Vaughan and Markham had joined them. Farmers and commuters, WASPs and *nouveaux arrivistes*, auto workers in Oshawa and computer programmers in Kanata had endorsed the Common Sense

---

[11] And Peter North, a former NDP cabinet minister who ran as an independent after a low-grade sex scandal forced him out of caucus, won re-election in Elgin.

Revolution. More, they had affirmed the values behind it, had voted to return the province to first principles of thrift, balance, and personal responsibility. These may have been simplistic precepts, and some would say they ignored those who had nothing to be thrifty with, whose lives had been knocked askew, and whose circumstances were beyond their control. But for better or worse the province had opted, firmly, for something new: the old.

Harris offered an indifferent speech on election night, despite Lindsay's attempts to inject the poetry of Robert Frost. More to the point, and more poignantly, he volunteered a rare personal remark. "My parents always wondered, I suspect, what would become of me." The restless son of Deane and Hope Harris had been elected Premier of Ontario.

2

In Power

CHAPTER 5

Season of Action

In 1985, David Peterson held his swearing-in on the expansive lawns fronting Queen's Park, and then invited everyone in for a tour of the place. In 1990, Bob Rae took power during a ceremony at the University of Toronto's Convocation Hall before 1,700 ecstatic supporters. In 1995, Mike Harris became premier amid cries of protest and alarm. Far from inviting the public in, on the morning of June 26, the new government closed the building to the public "for security reasons." Two thousand of those reasons congregated in front of the legislature at noon in the first "Embarrass Harris" rally. Unionized public servants, teachers, anti-poverty activists, natives, gays and lesbians, co-op housing and child-care advocates, and the generally enraged blew whistles, rallied each other's spirits with speeches, and vowed perpetual defiance to the incoming regime.

"We are the people of Ontario," organizer Kam Rao told the boisterous crowd. "The workers, the elderly, the disabled, men, women, young people—all of us who will be hurt by Harris's agenda of pain are the people of Ontario."

"It's going to be a long hot summer," vowed John McKinnon of the Toronto Injured Workers' Advisory Group. Indeed it would be.

Though the crowd had dwindled to a dozen or so by three p.m., when the swearing-in ceremony took place, their loudspeaker-assisted denunciations could be heard through the open windows of the legislative chamber, where tempers were beginning to rise. Incoming Solicitor General Bob Runciman, the

MPP for Leeds-Grenville, scowled at the "Mike should be embarrassed" chants that filtered into the room. But whatever the noise from outside, the place itself was filled only with friends. Families and supporters packed the visitors' galleries above the pit. The no-man's land separating the government and opposition benches was filled with beaming government supporters, first among them Bill Davis, whose seraphic grin seemed to suggest that the past ten years had been a mere unpleasant interlude. The only available seats were in the opposition benches. Many members, including about-to-be-former-premier Bob Rae, had decided to stay home. Following a rather off-key trumpet fanfare, Mike Harris and his cabinet entered to applause. The government took the reins in a brief, half-hour ceremony enlivened only by laughter from the galleries when Al "any Palladini is a palla mine" Palladini was revealed as Transportation minister. Palladini laughed too.

Afterward, the cabinet ministers milled about, surrounded by reporters who wanted instant information on what the government would do next. Many of the new ministers wore loopy grins, as though they couldn't believe they had landed here. When Palladini was asked whether the government intended to complete the construction of eastern Ontario's Highway 416 and Hamilton's Red Hill Creek expressway, it was clear he had no idea what either of them was. David Tsubouchi answered questions on welfare reform by protesting that he hadn't figured out how to be an MPP yet, let alone a cabinet minister. Harris himself was more forthright. He repeated his election pledges to move quickly in scrapping the NDP legacy, from photo radar to labour law. It was a foretaste of things to come. The protests would only get louder; the government would only get more determined.

That determination had been evident from the day the transition team, led by David Lindsay and Bill Farlinger, moved into the desks prepared for them in the premier's office on the fourth floor of Whitney Block. First, they arranged to have pink slips delivered to nine deputy ministers. These nine were mostly NDP appointments whom both sides agreed would have difficulty carrying out the agenda of the Common Sense Revolution. Their places were filled primarily from within the ranks. The most important outsider was Michael Gourley, the new deputy minister of Finance. A former career public servant teaching at the University of Western Ontario, he had been approached before the election by the Tories, who had asked him to take on the job at Finance if they won. He was at work by the Wednesday after the election.

Gourley's new boss, the cabinet secretary, was Rita Burak. During the Saturday morning meeting at the Park Plaza two days after the election, Lindsay and Harris had been impressed with her calm confidence and her willingness to work with the government in implementing its new agenda. As head of the provincial bureaucracy, the new cabinet secretary would need to co-operate with Lindsay, who as principal secretary would head the political staff in the premier's office, and so Harris gave his second-in-command much of the say in who would be picked.

One of Mike Harris's first acts as premier had been to address all the deputy ministers—the top executives in the huge provincial bureaucracy—at a closed-door session. On that occasion, he had delivered two messages. First, although the new government welcomed advice on how to implement its agenda, that agenda was not subject to debate. "I do require your absolute commitment to the final political determination of the government," Harris told them. Second, he reminded the deputy ministers that they owed their first allegiance, not to their minister, but to Harris himself. This was a timely reiteration of a political reality in parliamentary democracies. Deputy ministers are not appointed by ministers, but by the cabinet secretary, who is in turn appointed by the premier. As such, the senior bureaucracy owes its first loyalty to the chief executive—one reason that ministers are sometimes the last to know what's going on in their departments. Harris wanted to remind the mandarinate that he and his political staff intended to keep firm, central control of the government's agenda. Ministers should be under no illusion that they were sovereign within their own departments. "Rita is well known to you," he told them, "and through her you will communicate with me on a routine basis. Your reports to her will be for me only and will be dealt with in confidence." Not even Harris's most powerful ministers would know what their deputies were telling the premier.

Even more crucial than bringing the bureaucracy on side was picking a political staff. The people who staff the office of the premier are among the most important individuals in a government: they advise the leader, co-ordinate policies, create and extinguish political fires—serve, in essence, as executive headquarters. The choices were no surprise. The small group of friends who had helped Harris win the leadership, had worked with him to avoid disaster in the 1990 election, had endured the years in the wilderness, and had crafted his electoral miracle, would be the new premier's trusted advisers. They were young. Every senior political figure in the premier's office was under forty; some were under thirty. They were devoutly neo-conservative and they were very talented. They would give the government the air of cohesion and competence it enjoyed from its opening days. They would also, in their more strident moments, convey the sense of ideological fervour, of harshness, of lack of compassion or forethought, that would darken the government's record and alienate some of its core supporters.

Principal secretary David Lindsay, now thirty-six and Harris's most loyal retainer, headed the unelected arm of government. Beneath him, as deputy principal secretary, was Mitch Patten, thirty-five, who had help write *The Common Sense Revolution*, been one of the key players in the campaign, and worked on the transition. The office then split into two groups: those responsible for day-to-day issues, and those who plotted long-term strategy. On day-to-day, Debbie Hutton and Paul Rhodes were the key figures. Hutton, twenty-nine, had worked in interim leader Andy Brandt's office, after graduating from the University of Western Ontario in 1988, then joined Harris's office as an aide when he became leader. Now, as executive assistant in charge of issues management, she would alert Harris to emerging crises and contentious issues, prep him for Question Period and press conferences, and advise him on the daily agenda. Paul Rhodes, who had executed the media strategy during the campaign, became senior media adviser, counselling Harris on how the government's message was getting across on a day-to-day basis and how to sell, contain, or manipulate the story of the day.

On the long-term policy side, the key figures were to have been Guy Giorno and Jamie Watt. Giorno, thirty, who had shared speech-writing duties with Bill King during the campaign, got the job of director of policy planning. He would be responsible for mapping out and co-ordinating the government's legislative agenda and would become a key behind-the-scenes figure in the development of major policies. Jamie Watt, author of the ad showing Lyn McLeod as a weathervane that had proved so effective during the campaign, was appointed communications policy adviser. But on June 20, even before the incoming government was sworn in, it was hit with its first embarrassment. A flattering newspaper portrait of the new staff, including Watt, produced a phone call from an Oakville businessman who said Watt owed him $36,000. It turned out the young whiz kid had been convicted of fraud following the collapse of a clothing store he once owned. In the wake of this revelation, Watt sent Lindsay a letter saying he couldn't take on his new job. In the end, the role would never be properly filled, and the government would pay a public-relations price for the gap.

Finally, Harris's longtime aide and buddy Bill King rounded out the team. He was given the nebulous task of acting as liaison between the premier's office and the caucus. His most important role was to continue to sit in on meetings, offering the perspective of Mike Harris's longest serving adviser. King was becoming increasingly peripheral to the inner circle, but Harris would never abandon the one member of the team who'd been with him from the very first.

Several of the key figures of Harris's Common Sense team did not end up in the premier's office. Tony Clement might have been there, had he not chosen to run as an MPP instead. But Clement's political career had nosedived since his days as president of the party. In 1994, he had made the truly boneheaded decision to run for Metro council, a move of which Harris openly disapproved. After Clement lost, "I came back with my tail between my legs, feeling pretty horrible, figuring I'd ruined my political career," he recalls. But Bill Davis wanted Clement for his old riding of Brampton and lobbied Harris personally to grant the young politico leave to run. When Harris agreed, Clement won handily and dutifully took his place in the back benches. Though he was clearly cabinet material, Clement was kept on the sidelines, perhaps until he could convince Harris he was politically more mature.

But there were far more senior advisers to Mike Harris who chose to stay on the outside. Tom Long returned to his job as a corporate head-hunter. Leslie Noble helped launch Strategy Corp., a government-relations and lobbying firm. Alister Campbell went back into the insurance business. For these three, the thrill of politics was in the game, not in the job. But though they were never formally part of the government, their influence remained palpable. Noble and Campbell continued to talk on the phone or meet with their friends in the premier's office almost every day. Tom Long never hesitated to call or fax in his latest suggestion or advice.

And shortly after the election, David Lindsay decided to revive the Bradgate Group. The same team that had helped write the CSR and plot election strategy met in a conference room at the hotel every three or four months, when Lindsay would fill them in on the planned agenda, compare it to what had been promised in the CSR, and solicit their advice, suggestions, and occasional cries of alarm. The process was informal: the premier's staff and those outside the office exchanged ideas, plotted strategy, and shored up one another's spirits. Though Harris never attended the meetings himself, he regularly queried Lindsay on what "the campaign team," as the premier still called his young advisors, was recommending on key issues. Through these meetings and other less structured contacts, the team continued to influence the government and the premier.

If the premier's political staff was carefully chosen, the same could not be said for the political staff picked to work with and advise each minister. In some governments, especially ones in which the elected officials and their public servants are at odds, political staff can burgeon at the ministerial level, forming a parallel and competing bureaucracy. The NDP ministers employed political staffs so large they effectively acted as separate arms of government. The Tories, who were determined to keep staff levels down, kept ministerial political appointments to a minimum. A typical ministry would contain only an executive assistant to advise the minister on the political aspects of ministerial policy, a communications assistant to handle relations with the media, a legislative assistant to prep the minister for Question Period, a few policy advisers, and some support staff. The jobs involved long hours and, considering the responsibility, paid modestly. An executive assistant typically earned less than $90,000, and a communications or legislative assistant only two-thirds of that.

Nonetheless, a thousand applications arrived for the 300-odd political appointments available. Since the transition team lacked the time or interest to vet the résumés, they were photocopied, placed in binders, and sent to the new ministers. Some ministers assumed that the candidates in the binders had already been approved by the premier's office and chose their staff with little attention to background and qualifications. Others ignored the binders completely, bringing in trusted assistants to help run their departments. The results were, at best, uneven. Certain ministries, such as Finance, Management Board, Agriculture, and Municipal Affairs, would be blessed with competent political staffs: executive assistants would anticipate emerging issues, offer sound political advice, and interact well with the bureaucracies; legislative assistants would anticipate all possible assaults from the opposition in Question Period; communications assistants would feed and care for the voracious reporters. But several ministries would be plagued with incompetence in all these fields. Environment Minister Brenda Elliott's ultimate demise would be blamed, in part, on poor political advisers, while the ministries of Health, Education, and Community and Social Services would also suffer from turnover and firings, as ministers struggled to locate competent help. The Tories had only themselves to blame for the confusion. It was one area of their preparation for governing in which they failed to do their homework.

But it was the public face of the government—the cabinet—on which all attention focused in the first weeks. It is said that choosing a cabinet is the most difficult decision a new head of government ever makes. For the most part, Harris picked his cabinet well. But his own prejudices led him to make several bad choices that would force a mini cabinet shuffle a little more than a year after he took office.

Bill Farlinger, as co-head of the transition team, was in charge of vetting potential ministers. He struck a committee, consisting of former provincial treasurer Darcy McKeough, Tory insider Jim Bailey, and Rob Prichard, president of the University of Toronto. About a dozen Tory-friendly lawyers volunteered to help with the process. The team had decided to vet every MPP, both to avoid tipping Harris's hand as to who was favoured for cabinet rank, and to give the leadership a chance to discover the depth of talent in the caucus.

In 1990, the NDP had found itself hamstrung when it elected a large caucus of inexperienced and often startled blue-collar workers, union activists, social workers, and teachers. (Rae liked to joke that when the NDP discovered it had won the election of 1990, many of its members demanded a recount.) There were few professionals or people with business experience in the NDP caucus, which left Premier Rae plagued with cabinet crises and caucus revolts as he struggled with indifferent success to mine the back benches for talent. The Conservatives should have been in just as bad shape. After all, they had been the third party going into the election, with little chance of winning, according to conventional wisdom. But it turned out that Harris could draw on a surprising depth of bench strength.

The new Ontario government was formed from a caucus of shopkeepers. There were thirty-four owners of small businesses of one sort or another among the eighty-seven-member Progressive Conservative side of the house. Lawyers came second, numbering fifteen. Eight members had backgrounds in agriculture, six had worked in government or government agencies. Eight had been politicians all or most of their working lives. Surprisingly, the media were quite well-represented: five Tory MPPs had backgrounds in newspapers or television. There were three teachers in the new crowd. Only one member was a doctor—Doug Galt, a veterinarian from Northumberland.

The caucus was also a boys' club. Only twelve members, or 14 per cent of the caucus, were women. None had physical disabilities, and only one could be described as belonging to a visible minority: David Tsubouchi, the newly elected member from Markham. Though a third-generation Canadian, he was of Japanese ancestry.

The government benches boasted some obvious talent, ranging from Ernie Eves, Harris's old friend and riding neighbour, who had also been a lawyer and successful manager of his wife's family's trucking business, to Al Leach, the former commissioner of the Toronto Transit Commission, who had taken St. George–St. David, one of the Tories' few downtown Toronto ridings. Al Palladini, all gold jewellery and boisterous laugh, owned a successful Woodbridge car dealership. William Saunderson also possessed good business credentials, as a pension fund manager with forty years of experience on Bay Street. The avuncular Dave Johnson had been both an oil-company executive and mayor of East York; he had won his seat in a by-election in 1993. And there was John Snobelen, a self-made millionaire in Anthony Robbins suspenders who had made his killing in the waste-haulage business.

Cabinets are usually chosen based on considerations of geography, gender, competence, and loyalty. Harris added his own personal views on cabinet making to this mix, deliberately deciding to appoint ministers to areas in which they had little or no previous experience. At first—indeed, at second—glance, this seemed perverse. Ministers coming into a new government are always in danger of being overwhelmed. Any experience they might have in the field can only help to reduce that danger. But Harris's great fear was that his ministers would become captive to the interests that inevitably attach themselves to each portfolio. He didn't want his Transportation minister becoming a pawn of public-transit or road-safety advocates; his Education minister's job was to confront, not console, teachers and trustees; his Social Services minister was there to cut social services. And so John Snobelen, who—as everyone soon learned—dropped out of school in Grade 11 and whose area of expertise lay in waste disposal and management consulting, was sent to Education, not Environment; Al Palladini, whose knowledge of the car retail business might have suited him for Consumer and Commercial Relations, was handed Transportation; Al Leach, who had run the biggest public-transit system in the country and had been an assistant deputy minister in Transportation before that, was given Municipal Affairs and Housing.

No one was more surprised than Leach by this appointment. On June 24, the Saturday before the swearing in, Lindsay phoned the prospective members of the new cabinet, to ask if they would be available to take a call from the premier-designate between two and four o'clock Sunday afternoon. Lindsay reached everyone but Leach, who wasn't in Saturday. That evening, while Leach was with his family at Ontario Place watching a fireworks display, Lindsay bumped into him in the VP tent. He asked Leach to stay by the phone Sunday, to which Leach dutifully and happily agreed. Sunday came, with the family all gathered, including Leach's two adult daughters. Two o'clock passed, then three, then four, then five. One daughter had to leave, offering the parting shot, "I never liked Mike Harris anyway." Finally, the phone rang. It was Harris, calling to ask Leach if he would agree to serve on executive council in the portfolio of Municipal Affairs and Housing. Leach's jaw dropped. "What? I thought it was Transport!" he exclaimed. Leach would later say "that what I knew about housing you can write on the head of a pin and have room for the Lord's Prayer." Al Palladini was no less surprised to be offered Transportation. When Harris phoned and offered him the post, Palladini recalls, he answered in bewilderment, "Mike, this is Al *Palladini*." He thought Harris had mixed up his Als.

Another force—a prejudice, really—shaped the premier-designate's decision-making. Mike Harris sees himself as a self-made man, a fellow who came from modest circumstances and who rose, through his own efforts, to the top of what Benjamin Disraeli dubbed the greasy pole. Of course, the circumstances were not all that modest. Deane Harris had been a successful small businessman and the Harris children had typical middle-class upbringings. But all of us rewrite our childhoods to some extent. Harris once mused to reporters, when asked whether he could live on the baloney-and-bean diet Social Services Minister Dave Tsubouchi was recommending for welfare families, "I have in my younger days—but I wouldn't want to [again]. That's why I work so hard to try and get ahead." It prompted *Windsor Star* reporter Rick Brennan to phone both Deane Harris and Mary Coward, Harris's first wife. "He didn't eat it in my home, I can tell you that much," snorted the older Harris. Coward described eating at the Harris home as "just like going to the Royal York." The story infuriated the premier's circle.

But Mike Harris's political rise had been spectacular for someone who had dropped out of university, avoided any of the professions of the upwardly mobile, such as law, who had remained in his out-of-the-political-way home town until running for the legislature. No one could deny that Harris had worked hard. And he had looked for these qualities when selecting his cabinet. Harris was drawn to men who had come from modest beginnings and made something of themselves. "He's a self-made man," pointed out one political staffer, "and his cabinet choices reflected those prejudices."

Though Harris contacted most of his cabinet choices by phone, the most important choice was settled one-on-one. Harris met personally with Ernie Eves to tell his old friend he wanted him as both Finance minister and deputy premier. And that wasn't all. "At the end of the conversation, it was quite a lengthy one, he says, 'Oh, there's one more thing I'd like you to do,'" Eves recalls. "I said, 'Oh, really, what's that?' He said, 'I'd like you to be the House Leader.' I said, 'Are you nuts?'" But Harris insisted. He trusted his friend as he trusted no other.

The other critical economic portfolio, Management Board, would go to Dave Johnson, member for Don Mills. Johnson was raised on a farm at Greensville, near Hamilton. The affable but implacable veteran of municipal politics—one reporter observed he sounded like Kermit the Frog—would become one of the government's greatest assets: rock-solid, devoid of the edge of malice that often appeared to accompany Conservative rhetoric. He would lead the Tories through a public-service strike and major downsizing of the bureaucracy, and pinch-hit when Health Minister Jim Wilson got himself into trouble.

Wilson, who at thirty-two became the youngest cabinet minister, had so impressed Harris when he served as Health critic during the Rae years that the new premier named the MPP for Simcoe West to the biggest-spending portfolio. Wilson had worked in politics from the day he graduated from university. In age and temperament, he had more in common with Harris's youth corps of advisers than with his colleagues in cabinet. Wilson's lack of experience and discretion would lead him from one frying pan into another, but Harris would stick with his young protégé, regardless.

Pundits and opposition politicians expressed considerable puzzlement over the choice of David Tsubouchi for minister of Community and Social Services. The Markham lawyer and city councillor had no experience in social policy, though that counted as an asset, as far as Harris was concerned. Tsubouchi would be responsible for implementing the cuts to welfare and the mandatory work programs promised in *The Common Sense Revolution*. At the time of Tsubouchi's appointment, Harris would say only that the new minister "had a proven record of decision making." Cynics suspected the Tories liked the optics of giving a social affairs portfolio to the only member of caucus who belonged to a visible minority. More important, perhaps, Tsubouchi had grown up poor. His family's property had been stripped away during the quarantine of Japanese Canadians in the Second World War. Tsubouchi, like so many in cabinet, was a self-made man.

John Snobelen, who represented Mississauga North, had no inkling he'd be handed Education; he claims he wasn't expecting to be named to cabinet at all. The day Lindsay made his phone calls, the new MPP from Mississauga North had taken his phone off the hook to avoid being disturbed while he worked on some business. Lindsay reached Snobelen's wife at another number and she called a neighbour, who rapped on Snobelen's window and told him to turn on his phone. When Snobelen finally spoke to Lindsay, the perpetually enthusiastic rookie politician was both astonished and delighted at the prospect of shaking up the education system. Harris didn't want an educrat in Education; he wanted someone who could manage a corporate restructuring and saw Snobelen's experience as a management consultant as a major asset. Nor did it hurt that Snobelen too was a school drop-out who had worked for his father, taking over the family business and transforming it into a multi-million-dollar enterprise.

Waterloo North MPP Elizabeth Witmer was placed in the crucial role of Labour minister. Although thought to be among the more moderate Conservatives in caucus, the former businesswoman and teacher also had a well-deserved reputation for competence. She would face up to the political firestorms caused by the Tory's repeal of NDP labour and employment-equity legislation, in part by adhering to scripted "message tracks" that caused her never to misspeak and that drove reporters to pull at their hair in distraction.

At least Harris picked a member of the legal profession for the Attorney General's portfolio. Charles Harnick was a forty-four-year-old litigation lawyer representing Willowdale who would soon find himself battling his former colleagues over legal aid. The ministry of Environment and Energy went to Brenda Elliott, owner of an environmental products store in Guelph. It seemed a good idea at the time. Chris Hodgson, a stolid but deceptively capable Haliburton realtor—a man cut both geographically and socially from the same cloth as the premier—landed in Harris's old portfolio of Natural Resources, while veteran Scarborough councillor Marilyn Mushinski would take on Citizenship, Culture, and Recreation.

Finally, three members of the old guard, all from eastern Ontario, earned middle-level portfolios. Solicitor General Bob "Mad Dog" Runciman—notorious for his temper—had been in the legislature since 1981 and had served with Harris in the ephemeral Miller cabinet. Farmer Noble Villeneuve, a rare example of a Tory francophone, took on Agriculture, Food, and Rural Affairs, with added responsibility for Francophone Affairs. Norm Sterling, the oldest-serving member of caucus (he arrived in 1977 and had served as a minister without portfolio in the Davis years), received Consumer and Commercial Relations.

As interesting as who was in was who was out. Morley Kells and Chris Stockwell, both outspoken and visible opposition MPPs, were banished to the back benches, deprived of parliamentary assistantships and not even made chairs of any standing committees. Both did little to hide their resentment. Cam Jackson, another veteran MPP, was given the toothless job of reforming the Workmen's Compensation Board under Witmer's watchful eye. Dianne Cunningham, who had played the role of deputy leader while in opposition, in part to help unite the party after the leadership convention, may have been the most disappointed, even though she landed a portfolio. Partly because she was identified with the party's Left, partly because she had been Harris's political enemy and he does not easily forgive, the premier kept her out of the senior cabinet ranks. Though Cunningham had chaired the London Board of Education and was widely expected to take on the Education portfolio, Harris made her minister of Intergovernmental Affairs and minister responsible for Women's Issues. The latter portfolio had no priority in his government, and the former responsibility Harris largely handled out of his own office. Throughout the landmark struggles of the Tories' first two years, the capable Cunningham languished in a brackish backwater, offering high-minded speeches and little else.

Mike Harris's cabinet choices would produce a core of more or less permanently disgruntled backbench MPPs. Everyone in caucus who had weathered the days of opposition had hoped for a cabinet post as a reward, says Bill Murdoch, a farmer and member for the largely rural riding of Grey-Owen Sound. "There's ten of us didn't get a position, and I'd say all ten were disappointed. Some may have been angry." They would take out their frustrations by criticizing some government policies and even voting with the opposition on private-members' bills. Kells went so far as to write opinion articles for the *Toronto Star* lambasting his own government. But cabinet making always leaves noses out of joint, and Harris displayed considerable tolerance, at least in the early days, of his maverick backbenchers.

However, the new premier made one critical mistake in making his cabinet: he picked David Tsubouchi over Durham West MPP Janet Ecker for Social Services. On paper, in person, and in fact, the rookie member for Durham West was the preferred candidate. The mission of slashing welfare benefits and imposing workfare required a cabinet minister who could manage a large bureaucracy, work with the municipal governments that administered the programs, and handle the outrage both in the legislature and on the streets. For such a job, Ecker was unquestionably better qualified than Tsubouchi, having trained as a journalist at University of Western Ontario, worked as a communications assistant in the Davis years for several ministries—ending up as an assistant press secretary to Davis himself—and having spent much of the interregnum working as a government-relations consultant. She had also worked for the College of Physicians and Surgeons ("fishes and sturgeons," as it is universally known).

Ecker was smart and capable and knew her way around the Park. Yet she was relegated to the role of Tsubouchi's parliamentary assistant. Some said it was because Ecker was known to be less dogmatically committed to the Common Sense Revolution than many others in the caucus and had never held elected office (though neither had Snobelen). Others said Ecker had betrayed a less-than-total loyalty to Harris as a leader. Ecker herself will only say that, while she was naturally disappointed, she was grateful to know she had reached the short list. It may be that Harris felt the rookie MPP wasn't ready. It may be that as a woman from southern Ontario, the daughter of a doctor and a nurse, and a University of Western Ontario graduate in journalism, she simply struck none of the right chords. Maybe she was lucky. From her seat as Tsubouchi's parliamentary assistant, Ecker could watch and learn while he fumbled welfare reform, ultimately becoming the government's single greatest embarrassment. When the inevitable came, she was ready to fill the minister's shoes.

On the morning of the day after the swearing-in, Harris brought his new cabinet together at the Bradgate Arms. The choice of venue was deliberate. This cabinet, Harris told his ministers, would be different from those that had gone before. It would not search for policies and principles to guide the new government. Those policies and principles had been hashed out in this hotel. Each minister was given a binder, prepared by Lindsay and others in the premier's office, summarizing the promises made in *The Common Sense Revolution* that related to the minister's portfolio. Your job, Harris told them, is to make these promises reality.

The Rae and Peterson governments had each employed different cabinet structures. In its most recent incarnation, the NDP model, cabinet had been subdivided into a variety of policy committees charged with generating legislation that could be brought to full cabinet for approval. The Tories scrapped the system. They saw little need for ministers and bureaucrats to consider options, when the preferred options had already been identified. Instead, Harris and his brain trust created a streamlined, top-down cabinet structure. With only nineteen ministers, including Harris— down from twenty-six in the Rae government—the new cabinet was the smallest in thirty years. The ministry of Culture, Tourism, and Recreation disappeared, Culture being merged with the Citizenship portfolio, Tourism and Recreation being added to Economic Development. Native Affairs was shunted over to the Attorney General's office, while Women's Issues would be ghettoized along with Intergovernmental Affairs.

The Harris cabinet would require only three subcommittees: Management Board, Legislation and Regulations, and, most important, Priorities and Planning. The all-important power of co-ordinating and assigning priorities to policies resided within "P and P" and in the premier's office, which was, in turn, staffed by the young Tories who had helped write the CSR and who had run the election campaign. Nothing would be allowed to get in the way of turning the manifesto into reality.

The weaknesses of this approach were pointed out by political scientists David Cameron and Graham White, who studied the 1995 transition: "We were struck on several occasions to find both political and bureaucratic interviewees voicing what to our minds was a naïve distinction between policy and implementation," they wrote. "Policy was what was in the CSR. It had been constructed and 'road-tested' by the party before and during the election campaign. Implementation was what came after the election, once the Tories had formed the government. The election meant that the policies of the Conservatives had been approved by the electorate and now implementation could begin. There was no need for policy committees of cabinet, no need for papers presenting options or exploring the costs and benefits of alternative courses of action, apparently no significant issue for decision which had not been pre-figured and pre-determined by the CSR policy framework. Action was what was required; public servants were simply to get on with the job, and politicians were there to see the job was done. It is not difficult to see how this conception of the distinction between policy and public administration could lead a government to serious errors in judgment and vexing political problems."[1]

Those errors and problems would abound. Yet whatever embarrassments the Tories' haste and overconfidence produced, their agenda would be put in place. As one insider told Cameron and White during the transition, "The NDP assumed office, but they never took power. These guys are taking power even before they have assumed office."

[1] David Cameron and Graham White, *Cycling Into Saigon: the Tories Take Power in Ontario*, delivered at the annual meeting of the Canadian Political Science Association, June 1996, p. 21.

In their consultations with their Alberta counterparts before the election, the Tory strategists had received one overriding piece of advice: move quickly. Governments have about two years in which to implement their agendas before the necessities of the approaching election exert a fatal drag on action. Premier Ralph Klein had acted quickly to cut funding for hospitals and social services, neuter the power of school boards, and eliminate the deficit. Yet Klein's agenda paled in comparison with that of the Common Sense Revolution, which included all that plus reform of government, tax cuts, and much more. The Tories had no time to lose. Their first move was symbolic. At the conclusion of the second cabinet meeting on July 5, Harris announced that photo radar was dead, effective immediately.

The Rae government had introduced photo radar for two reasons. First, by placing unstaffed vans equipped with radar and cameras at the side of major highways to detect speeders and photograph their licence plates, the province hoped to force drivers to slow down, increasing highway safety. Second, the fines collected would be a valuable new source of revenue. In the period between August 15, 1994, and June 30, 1995, the vans nabbed 300,000 speeding motorists, bringing in about $19 million in fines. Even with administration costs (about $4.5 million), the project was a money-maker, though a far cry from the $130-million-a-year cash cow some experts had predicted.

The reasons to kill photo radar were both acknowledged and unacknowledged. Harris correctly pointed out that new technology could not catch aggressive drivers—the lane-changers and tail-gaters who are a much greater menace on highways than speeders. He argued there was no proof photo radar had reduced accidents, which was true, though only because the studies were not yet complete. For Harris, it was a tax grab masquerading as public safety. But the Tories' real objection to photo radar was that it was a statist intervention in personal liberties. Virtually all drivers in Ontario speed. Keeping to within twenty kilometres or so over the limit, provided the roads are dry and the lanes are open, is seen as reasonable by most people. While drivers were prepared to take their chances in the cat-and-mouse game with police cruisers, they saw photo radar as an unfair change in the rules.

In the 1980s, the Ontario government successfully modified the behaviour of most drivers who drank. Stiff fines, tough enforcement, and effective advertising convinced drivers, who knew in their hearts they shouldn't get behind the wheel after several drinks, to give up the practice. Only hard-core drinkers with serious problems are now, typically, caught impaired. Photo radar was intended to have the same beneficent effect. But while preliminary studies showed photo radar was forcing drivers to slow down, they didn't do so willingly. Most drivers continued to believe moderate speeding in clement weather was acceptable. They wanted police to concentrate on manic speeders and other aggressive drivers.

There might also have been another, subtler, impetus to the Tories' decision to end this form of electronic spying. The highways they monitored were primarily the domain of suburban car-owners, the sort of people who use the 400 or the 401 to get to work, the sort of people who voted for Mike Harris. Many of the supporters of photo radar lived downtown and were more likely to use public transit. In sending the hated vans back to the garage, the Tories were doing their friends a favour.

During the summer, the new government made other swift, emphatic decisions that did not require legislative approval. The same day the Tories scrapped photo radar, they abolished the NDP's Interim Waste Authority, which had been charged with finding a provincial solution to the chronic problem of where to put Toronto's garbage. Instead, each municipality would be responsible for finding solutions to its waste problems. On July 12, the new government got rid of the planned new agencies that would administer long-term health care. The NDP had intended these unionized agencies to largely supplant the work done by nonprofit organizations such as the Victorian Order of Nurses. The bad news for organizations such as the VON, however, was that, in future, long-term-care contracts would become much more competitive. The VON and other nonprofit agencies would be required to compete for contracts with for-profit agencies employing lower-paid, non-union help. On July 25, the government announced a moratorium on new construction of subsidized housing, the first step towards what would become the virtual abandonment of the province's subsidized-housing responsibilities. The province, Al Leach insisted, planned to "get out of the housing business," once and for all.

The Tories were unquestionably in control of the political agenda, but they were also jarred by the first bumps on the road to reform. Predictably, the strongest jolts were felt by the more inexperienced ministers at the cabinet table, those who were new not only to government but to politics. In early July, Al Palladini discovered the cost of musing in the presence of reporters, when he complained that he needed a limousine and driver and shouldn't be asked to give them up. He also felt there was no reason his car dealership should stop bidding on government contracts, simply because he was now a minister of the Crown. The minister quickly retracted, on orders from the premier's office. The limo and the driver disappeared.

Also in early July, Education Minister John Snobelen, who reads a great deal of new-agish management philosophy, allowed himself to be videotaped talking management babble to a collection of senior bureaucrats. Someone in his department leaked the tape to the media several weeks later. There was the rookie minister, claiming that his department needed to "invent a crisis" in education in order to prepare for major reform. A visibly annoyed Harris told reporters the next day he didn't think much of what Snobelen had said, the first instance of a technique Harris would periodically employ of dressing down erring cabinet ministers in public. The scolding often diffused the situation and actually helped to save the minister's skin. In this instance, a chastened Snobelen apologized and kept his job, though the phrase "invent a crisis" would be dragged out every time the Education minister proposed a new reform.

In late July, Social Services Minister Dave Tsubouchi fell into a trap set by a press-gallery reporter during a scrum. When the reporter asked whether the minister felt people on welfare should move to British Columbia, where it's warmer, Tsubouchi grinned and agreed that "the weather is nicer in B.C." The *Toronto Sun*, dredging up an old and mostly unused travel fund available to welfare recipients who find work in another province, published a story that implied Tsubouchi was prepared to pay the travel costs of any Ontario welfare recipients who were tempted to move. British Columbia Premier Mike Harcourt promptly told Ontario what to do with its welfare recipients. From now on, Tsubouchi ruefully concluded, he would watch what he said.

But the advantage of an activist agenda is that such embarrassments are often quickly swept into history by the next big news. The Conservatives were acting so swiftly and so radically on so many fronts that critics and everyone else had trouble keeping track of what was going on. However, there was one announcement of the summer of '95 no one would forget.

Ernie Eves had known even before he took over his job as Finance minister that the province's fiscal situation was worse than reported. The last NDP budget had predicted a deficit of $7.9 billion for fiscal 1995–96 (the year beginning April 1, 1995, and ending March 31, 1996), but that figure was predicated on robust economic growth of 4.5 per cent. In fact, the economy had contracted by 0.3 per cent in the first quarter of 1995, and the second quarter was expected to be worse. (It ended up shrinking 2.6 per cent.) Finance officials warned the incoming minister that revenues from taxes were running $1.4 billion below target for the 1995–96 fiscal year, and expenditures about $1.4 billion higher than expected, in part because of government transfers to people who were expected to get off government assistance, but didn't. As a result, the province's deficit for 1995–96 was now expected to come in at whopping $11.2 billion. Eves and Harris were determined not to let that happen. Stanching the flow would establish their credentials as a government determined to balance the budget. It would also allow the Tories to move quickly to implement one of the Common Sense Revolution's most contentious promises: to reduce welfare benefits.

Reporters gathering for a press conference on the afternoon of July 21 were handed a government financial statement that announced massive cuts in welfare spending. In one swift slash, the Harris Tories were planning to chop welfare benefits by 21.6 per cent, saving $469 million that year. More than 600,000 welfare recipients were about to have their incomes summarily slashed by more than a fifth. Eves maintained that the cuts would still leave Ontario's welfare rates 10 per cent above the national average, which was true, but only if Ontario itself (and the territories) were taken out of the calculations. If those jurisdictions were added back in, Ontario's rates would fall below the national average, according to the National Council of Welfare. Welfare rates in Ontario were now higher only than those in British Columbia and parts of Atlantic Canada.

The reaction to Eves' financial statement was swift and emphatic. The day after the announcement, the *Toronto Star*, which was rapidly evolving into a locus of opposition to everything Harris, gave its eloquent Queen's Park columnist, Thomas Walkom, a front-page podium from which to denounce the statement. Walkom linked the cuts in welfare payments to the promised tax break. "Mike Harris' Tories are keeping their word," he thundered. "They are savaging the poor today in order to reward the rich tomorrow." Metro Toronto chair Alan Tonks hinted at violence in the streets. "I'm afraid these desperate measures will make people very desperate," he warned. Social activists launched the first of what would become a steady barrage of criticism. Kerry McCuaig, executive director of the Ontario Coalition for Better Child Care, was typical: "This is an abusive budget statement," she asserted. ". . . What we have here today are men in suits making cuts to women and children."

Of all the actions taken by the Tories in a little over two years in office, the cut in welfare benefits may have been the most politically controversial. It would arm the Conservatives' many enemies with a potent accusation: the government was financing its revolution "on the backs of the poor." In fact, any program of deficit reduction had to include cuts to transfers, and welfare payments represent one of the biggest transfers. But Walkom was right. The Conservatives were not merely reducing the deficit—they were also cutting taxes. The opposition parties and the social-interest groups opposed to the Tory agenda would effectively link the two issues: the government was slashing support to the poor, not in the interest of deficit reduction, but to finance a tax cut for the middle class. It is a theme Harris's opponents have used from that day to this.

The Conservatives genuinely did not and do not see the connection. In their minds, deficit reduction was one policy, tax-rate reduction another. Taxes needed to be reduced in order to make the province more attractive to potential investors, to encourage spending and stimulate the economy, and to counteract the economic drag as subsidies were cut and workers laid off. Ontario's rate of taxation, they pointed out, was among the highest in North America. (In fact, although Ontario, like all provinces, has a higher tax rate than its American counterparts, the province's tax rate at the time the Tories took power was lower than that of many provinces.) Tax reduction, they argued, was crucial to making the province more competitive. In addition to this economic argument, the more ideological among Harris's advisers pushed the tax cut for a strategic reason. They saw it as a way to reduce the size of government and its offensive intrusion into the body politic. A government with less money, they believed, would interfere less in the individual liberties of citizens. All these goals, the Tories thought, were separate from the issue of whether welfare rates were too high.

For many Ontarians, however, the connection seemed obvious and inextricable. The government was sticking it to people without jobs or economic support, while handing the middle class a tax bonus. Ernie Eves responded to the criticism by pointing out that welfare recipients who found part-time jobs would be able to earn back the difference between the old and the new levels of benefits without penalty. For many, however, the guilt associated with the tax cut would taint their support for a government that, otherwise, they felt was on the right track.

But $469 million in cuts to welfare would make only a dent in the projected $11.6-billion deficit. Eves' financial statement also directed ministries to find a total of $500 million in additional spending cuts, pronto, and cancelled funding to one of two Metro Toronto subway lines approved by the Rae government— the first installment of what turned into a litany of bad news for un-Tory Toronto. Along with delays to various other road and transit projects across the province, the infrastructure cuts would save the government $200 million that year. Eves' axe also fell on the NDP's jobsOntario job-training program, on school boards, which were hit with a 1 per cent cut in funding (a foretaste of things to come), on funding for pay equity for low-income women, on grants and subsidies to businesses, and on municipalities, which were ordered to begin contributing to the province's subsidized child-care program. All told, about $2 billion disappeared from government spending as a result of the July 21 cuts, and the anticipated deficit dropped to $8.7 billion.

The opposition Liberals and New Democrats duly condemned all these initiatives. But the reaction to the July 21 financial statement was also indicative of where the strongest centres of opposition to the new government would be found. Complaints by Lyn McLeod that the cuts would not help put people back to work, and by Frances Lankin that the NDP estimates weren't as pie-in-the-sky as claimed (leader Bob Rae didn't even bother to show up for the event), were submerged by the criticisms of Kerry McCuaig and other activists, and by union leaders such as Sid Ryan, of the Canadian Union of Public Employees (CUPE) and Leah Casselman of the Ontario Public Service Employees' Union (OPSEU). Throughout much of the next two years, the opposition parties would struggle to capture some sense of leadership in the fight against the Harris government, only to be eclipsed by the opposition outside the legislature.

There is more to political life than cutting spending and balancing books. Sometimes issues with no immediate fiscal impact leap up and bite a government. Such a one was Ipperwash.

In 1942, the federal government seized 907 hectares of Chippewa land on Lake Huron, promising to return it after the war. The land, about thirty kilometres northeast of Sarnia, became a military base, Camp Ipperwash. Forty-two years later, Ottawa finally agreed to return the base to the natives. (The government had provided $2.4 million in financial compensation in the meantime.) But the army was slow to leave, and militant members of the band began occupying parts of the base and provoking confrontations. To avoid a serious incident, the army withdrew from the base July 30, 1995. But the situation escalated further. Members of the Mohawk Warrior Society and American Indian Movement joined the protest. On September 4, thirty-five native protesters occupied next-door Ipperwash Provincial Park, claiming it as an ancient burial ground.[2] When Ontario Provincial Police cruisers showed up that evening, police say the natives damaged and dented the cars and threw flares at the officers.

In response, the Ontario Provincial Police began a serious build-up of forces around the park. They brought in troop carriers, a helicopter, and about 225 officers, including the force's Tactical Response Unit. On the evening of September 6, on hearing reports that vehicles passing by had been damaged, they moved in force toward the entrance of the park. There police confronted a group of angry protesters, and things quickly fell apart. One native man, Bernard George, who said he approached police in an effort to defuse the situation, was instead badly beaten. (He was later acquitted of assault charges.) Police say they were hit by flying objects, including rocks. Suddenly, a school bus rumbled out of the park towards the police. The youth driving the bus would later say he was trying to come to George's aid. Although police said they were fired on, a later investigation by the province's Special Investigations Unit could provide no evidence the natives had been armed. Police, however, did open fire, claiming they felt they were under assault. Three natives were shot: one

---

[2] The federal government later confirmed this assertion.

of them, Anthony (Dudley) George, was killed. It was the first time this century a native had been killed during a land dispute in Canada. In April 1997, OPP acting sergeant Kenneth Deane would be convicted of criminal negligence in the death of Dudley George. Judge Hugh Fraser would conclude that Deane shot George knowing he was unarmed.

The day after the shooting, native leaders demanded that Mike Harris intervene. Ovide Mercredi, leader of the Assembly of First Nations, warned there was "still a real threat to [sic] the potential of violence here," and asked for a meeting with the premier. But Harris didn't want to get involved. The OPP, he said, "received no direction from politicians, nor should they." And he refused to negotiate over the status of the park until the protesters had left it. "There's an illegal occupation. They are trespassers on property that is owned by the Crown."

On September 12, Mercredi showed up at Queen's Park, even though Harris had not agreed to meet with him. Mercredi's influence within the native movement was on the wane. Though he continued to advocate using legal means to resolve land disputes, his words were being flouted across the country. Protesters had barricaded themselves both at Ipperwash and at Gustavson Lake, in British Columbia. In Ottawa, Mercredi's office had been trashed by militants who claimed he had not given enough support to protesters. Upon his arrival at Queen's Park, a small, motley band of natives who had been camping out on the lawn for weeks tried to rush the doors, which were once again barred. When Mercredi finally got into the building, he waited an hour and a half before Harris and Attorney General Charles Harnick finally agreed to meet with him. The meeting was brief and tense, and nothing was accomplished. Uncharacteristically, the premier refused to answer questions from reporters, repeating through a press release his refusal to get involved in the stand-off.

But Ipperwash just wouldn't go away. The opposition parties smelled more to the story than the government was revealing, maintaining that the crisis would never have occurred had the Tories taken seriously native claims that the park was on sacred ground. And there was evidence that not only government officials, but the premier's office itself, knew what was happening before the police moved in at Ipperwash. The most damaging question was: had anyone in the government influenced the tragically wrong strategy of the OPP?

Over the succeeding months, in dribs and drabs, based on leaked documents and requests under the Freedom of Information Act, a partial picture emerged. On September 6, mere hours before the police moved in, Debbie Hutton attended a meeting of provincial bureaucrats and political advisers who were monitoring the situation. As one of the premier's trusted confidants, her role was to advise the group of the concerns being passed to the premier's office from people in the community, including Lambton MPP Marcel Beaubien, and to relay back to the premier any responses from the police. Minutes of the meeting record Hutton as saying the premier's first priority was to get the protesters "Out of Park only—nothing else." Native leaders, quoting a source at the meeting they will not reveal, claim someone—they will not say who—ordered an OPP representative in attendance to "get the fucking Indians out of the park." The implication is that the statement came from Hutton or had been passed on by her from Harris himself. Native leaders and opposition politicians suspect this direct interference by the government caused the OPP to abandon its usual policy of waiting out such occupations and to become more confrontational.

Since this revelation, there have been widespread calls for a public inquiry into the Ipperwash affair. Harris has refused, maintaining that an inquiry would be wrong while court cases are underway. As this book went to press, Deane's appeal of his verdict had not been heard, and one other court case and a lawsuit brought by the George family against the government and police remained unresolved.

Privately, government insiders acknowledge that sending Hutton to that meeting was a mistake. "She should never have been there," one said. Hutton's presence tied the government to police actions that the Tories should have wanted no part of. Several advisers to the premier vehemently deny that Hutton or anyone else offered any advice to the police, at that meeting or afterward; rather, they say, the OPP insisted on handling the situation as it saw fit. However, they acknowledge Hutton did pass on to police the concerns that had been expressed by people living around and driving by the park. "Deb expressed concern that we were getting phone calls," one senior adviser confirmed. "Remember, the local MPP and people were down there with phone calls and concerns. You've got natives with guns occupying the park—what's the government doing? Deb conveyed that concern."

Does conveying concern equal influencing tactics? The premier's advisers think not. Had Hutton "reflected the concerns of the local MPP and reflected the concerns of the community? That's logical," one adviser commented. "[Was it] a directive from the premier? No." It is reasonable to believe that Hutton did not order or advise the police to take a strong stand against the Indians occupying the park. She would know the political dangers of such a tactic. But it is also reasonable to assume that a senior adviser to the premier, in passing on the concerns of both the premier and of local residents, was seen to endorse those concerns and therefore telegraphed to police where the government's sympathies lay.

The public has shown little inclination to blame the Tories for the debacle at Ipperwash. That may change, if and when a public inquiry is able to clarify the government's role. But if nothing else, Ipperwash was an embarrassing reminder that the Harris government would not always get to decide what would be on the agenda.

By the late summer of 1995, certain traits of the new Tory government were starting to emerge. One of most important became apparent in the battle over legal aid. The government, which had subsidized 60 per cent of the $317 million spent on legal aid the previous year, suspected the plan was being poorly administered by the Law Society of Upper Canada and might be better run by the government itself. For the first but not last time, the Harris government was willing to jettison its getting-the-government-off-your-back principles, if it believed others were doing a poor job of carrying the load. The fund in 1994 had run a $70-million deficit, and although the society had placed caps on compensation, meaning some lawyers would not be fully paid for the work they had done, another large deficit was predicted for 1995. In early August, the government announced plans to make it tougher for applicants to qualify for legal aid. On September 11 Harnick warned that lawyers who were owed legal-aid money might not get it.

The profession reacted with predictable anger, accusing Harnick of ignorance and incompetence, and threatening to refuse legal-aid cases. About 6,900 of the province's 17,000 lawyers do some legal-aid work, meaning a boycott had the potential to bring the court system to a standstill, which could lead to waves of dismissals of criminal cases by judges.

Faced with this legal storm, Harnick backed down, assuring his fellow lawyers they would be paid whatever they were owed. The government also offered to abide by the funding arrangement agreed to between the law society and the NDP, which was a mixed blessing for the society, since it was precisely that four-year agreement that was leading to the annual deficits. The society should have been pushing for a new agreement, on the grounds that everyone had underestimated how heavily the fund would be used. But it would have appeared unconscionable to demand a new agreement at this stage, and so the government offer was accepted. Henceforth, legal-aid underfunding would be the society's problem to deal with, not the government's.[3]

Harnick had threatened the lawyers with a truly Draconian solution, imposed without consultation. When the lawyers

---

[3] But if the political dust-up was finally settled, the fundamental problems remained. To keep the plan solvent, the society has strictly limited the number of lawyers allowed to accept legal-aid cases. In 1993, the legal-aid plan issued 220,000 certificates; the projected number for 1997 is 80,000. Alarmed at the number of people who qualify for legal aid but do not receive it, law professors Frederick Zemans and Patrick Monahan recently recommended that management of the plan be taken away from the society and given to an independent government body. See *From Crisis to Reform: A New Legal Aid Plan for Ontario* (North York: York University Centre for Public Law and Public Policy, 1997).

threatened the equivalent of a strike, the government compromised, accepting a solution that appeared to be a backdown but was, in fact, more than might have been expected. Had the Tories simply asked the law society to abide by the NDP agreement, the society could have agitated for a better deal. Instead, to avoid losing control over legal aid altogether, it agreed to abide by the old terms.

Staff in the premier's office drew a vital lesson from the first confrontation with a powerful group: an entrenched interest will accept substantial change as a means to avoid cataclysmic change. Therefore, to obtain substantial change, threaten cataclysm. This approach of starting from an extreme position would become one of the government's favourite tactics.

The afternoon of September 27, 1995, was wonderfully autumnal, the sky, purged of humidity and smog, a crisp blue, the temperature mild, the leaves showing their first hints of colour. It was a perfect day for the Speech from the Throne, and a perfect day for a demonstration. Outside the legislature, 5,000 protesters—more than twice the number that had greeted the swearing-in of the government three short months before—jeered, chanted, waved signs, and banged drums. They filled the driveway in front of the main entrance and the grounds beyond. Union leaders, anti-poverty activists, students, the geriatric songsters The Raging Grannies— all had come to protest the convening of the thirty-sixth legislature of Ontario and the reading of the new government's first Speech from the Throne. And things were getting out of hand.

Police had erected flimsy metal barricades in front of the steps leading to the main doors. A vanguard of protesters, surging past the platform where the speakers had harangued the crowd, pushed over the barricades and rushed up the shallow flight of steps, intent on forcing their way into the building. The doors were barred with wooden beams, and a line of police formed in front to protect them. Inside, more police waited, shields and batons at the ready, a German shepherd barking in excitement. The demonstrators pushed as close to the police as they dared.

Every now and then, pressure from those behind thrust someone at the front forward. The police lashed out with their batons, striking at least two women and drawing blood. The pungent odour of pepper spray filled the air.

You could smell it in the chamber, where, above the dull roar of the protesters outside, Lieutenant Governor Hal Jackman read the half-hour text prepared for him. Normally, the throne speech is an event marked with some pomp, the lieutenant governor arriving in an open carriage to fanfares and salutes. All that had been abandoned in anticipation of the protest outside. The throne speech also generally offers a much-anticipated outline of a government's priorities. But after the summer Ontario had just been through, no one was in any doubt about this government's priorities. The only surprise came when Jackman, upon arrival at the Speaker's chair, found no copy of the speech present. A clerk was sent scurrying to locate one. "I thought I might have to ad-lib this," the lieutenant governor joked.

In the hour before Jackman's arrival, as the mob roared and the confrontation escalated, the legislature's security service had closed all entrances to the building. In doing so they barred minister without portfolio Cam Jackson and Liberal deputy leader Sean Conway from getting inside. When, shortly after the throne speech concluded, Conway, who has a high appreciation of both parliamentary prerogative and political theatre, finally made it to his seat, he immediately rose on a point of personal privilege to demand an investigation. "Today, for the first time in twenty years, I faced staff of this place who know that I am a member here and who would not let me or some other people they know to be members into this building for His Honour's address," he fumed. "I can't imagine a more fundamental point of privilege." NDP House Leader Dave Cooke chimed in, "I'd like to know who's setting policy for security around this place." It would turn out to be a prophetic question.

The occasion ended in farce. At first, nervous police refused to let guests, including Bill Davis, leave the building after the speech was over, fearing mayhem. Then a bomb threat was phoned in, and everyone was ordered to vacate through an underground tunnel. With the object of their wrath no longer around to hear them, the crowds gradually dispersed.

In the melee on the legislature steps, opponents of the government thought they had scored a victory. Pictures of baton-wielding police confronting enraged and bloodied women on the steps of the Ontario legislature made it onto the evening news and the next day's front pages across the country. The Queen's Park demonstration became a staple of opposition strategy over the next year, leading repeatedly to violence, though none of it serious. But if the intent of the strategy was to alarm moderate citizens and make them rethink their support for Mike Harris, there is little evidence it succeeded. The government's level of support remained firm, the protests serving only to further polarize a province already divided.

September 27, 1995, represented not simply a throne speech and a protest, but the second in an escalating series of clashes between two opposing coalitions. Inside the legislature, a government of the middle class, a government of suburban tracts and small towns, was carrying out its promise to wrench the province from a debilitating dependence on the state. Outside, a growing coalition of urban intellectuals and artists, single mothers, students, and advocates for the poor strove to stop them, in what would turn out to be a rehearsal of spectacles to come.

With the Speech from the Throne read and the legislature officially in session, the Mike Harris team was ready to launch the legislative portion of its revolution. The government's opponents expected the session to focus on the repeal of much of the NDP's legislative accomplishments. But behind the arras, more important deliberations were underway. For the Tories had come to two key conclusions. First, a public-servants strike was inevitable, and they had better prepare for it. And second, they needed a bill, a big bill, an omnibus bill, to give them new powers to restructure the province. The set was being built for the first winter of confrontation.

CHAPTER 6

The Battle of the Bully Bill

In the early autumn of 1995, Mike Harris and his inner circle were faced with a growing and potentially fatal political problem: the Common Sense Revolution seemed in danger of collapsing in the face of the province's deteriorating financial state. The first two quarters of 1995 had shown negative growth. Revenues were $1.4 billion below expectation. Some members of caucus were quietly urging the government to reconsider the tax cut. "We're not barbarians," one parliamentary assistant confided in the autumn of 1995; if a retreat on the tax cut was necessary, the MPP said, many in the government were prepared to do it. But as far as Harris and his principal advisers were concerned, the tax cut was inviolate. "Many Ontarians still don't like us, as they don't like all politicians," Harris had warned his cabinet at the Bradgate Arms back in late June. ". . . They want to believe we will keep our promises, but are waiting for the first sign we will break them. If we do, the survey data is clear: retribution will be swift."[1] Harris had campaigned as the Taxfighter in 1990. He had demanded that tax cuts be the cornerstone of the Common Sense Revolution. He had no intention of backing down now.

In this he had the full support of Tom Long, who continued to follow the political play-by-play from his position at the executive-search firm Egon Zehnder International, and who continued to send in plays from the sidelines. When the Bradgate

---

[1] Taken from ministerial briefing notes, cabinet meeting of June 27, 1995.

Group met that fall to wrestle with the problem of making the numbers add up. Long's advice was emphatic: "If we get to the point where we have to do more to get to our deficit targets, I'll tell you exactly where we should come down," he said in a later interview. "We should cut more government spending." The staff in the premier's office agreed. Harris agreed. Eves, though uncomfortable with the size of the cuts he was being asked to contemplate, also agreed. By October 1995, Finance and the premier's office had both decided the cuts to government spending would have to go from $6 billion to $8 billion.

With the July 21 financial statement, the Tories had already gouged as much from welfare as they dared. And under the prodding of Management Board Chair Dave Johnson, they had sliced and diced $770 million from no fewer than 375 different programs, including everything from the farm-tax rebate, to criminal prosecutions, to grants to TVOntario, the Art Gallery of Ontario, the Royal Ontario Museum, and other cultural institutions, to family counselling programs for abusive husbands, to worker-retraining programs, to blue-box subsidies, to transit subsidies, to the home oxygen program—"Breathe slower," reporters joked— to television commercials about violence against women. And 1,000 public servants had received pink slips.

So the next round of cuts couldn't come from social services or through trimming the fat from existing programs. That left the MUSH sector: municipalities, universities, schools, and hospitals. Grants in those four areas equalled $16 billion annually, 30 per cent of the provincial budget. But if those institutions were going to have their provincial subsidies slashed, they would need tools to raise the money on their own. Those tools could only come in the form of legislation.

Eves had rejected calls by Liberal Finance critic Gerry Phillips to bring in a proper budget, even though the province hadn't seen one since the spring of 1994. The government wanted to hold off on its good-news tax cut until the bad-news spending cuts were largely out of the way. Instead, Eves committed to a major economic statement in November, in which the government would outline the next and largest round of spending reductions. Logically, that would be a good time to introduce the legislation giving the health-care, education, and municipal sectors new means to raise revenues.

The municipalities were an obvious candidate. Each year, the government handed over $1.5 billion in transfer payments to help towns and cities pay for things like water, sewage, road, and public-transportation costs. Much of that money would have to disappear. But the problem for the government was that municipalities and school boards had only one way to make up lost revenues from the province: they would have to raise property taxes. And the Tories emphatically did not want to see property taxes going up. They knew the taxpayer would rightly blame them as well as the municipalities. User fees might be the solution. The municipalities could dissipate the cuts by charging fees for ambulance services, garbage pickup, and the like. But the municipalities were restricted in the user fees they could charge, so legislation would be needed to give them new powers.

The province transferred almost $8 billion annually in direct grants to universities and school boards. Some of that would have to go. The universities could compensate for lost grants by being allowed to increase tuition. It might be necessary to grant school boards the powers to impose user fees on things like busing and school supplies to help them make up the loss. And they should be permitted to abandon some mandated programs, such as junior kindergarten and adult education. That would require legislation, too.

The government couldn't look to the health ministry for savings. *The Common Sense Revolution* had promised no cuts to funding. But within that ministry's $17-billion budget, there was considerable room for increased efficiency. The medical community generally agreed that hospital closures were necessary; since 1987, almost 10,000 hospital beds had been vacated across the province, the result of budget cuts and new procedures that made hospital stays shorter. Meanwhile, home care, nursing-home care, and other forms of community health care were chronically underfunded. The logical solution was to close some hospitals and divert the savings to community care. But no government had ever found the courage to close hospitals. The politics of it were too painful to contemplate.

When Frank Miller, as Health minister, tried to close a few rural hospitals in the 1970s, the protests forced him to abandon the scheme and probably contributed to a heart attack he suffered. The NDP, under Rae, had asked district health councils to come up with plans for restructuring, but they had been given a leisurely timetable, so as not to interfere with Rae's hoped-for re-election. The Tories wanted to speed up the process, but Health Minister Jim Wilson wasn't eager to repeat the immolation of Frank Miller. Instead, the Tories decided to hand the problem over to an independent commission, which would have absolute power to choose which hospitals closed, and which would work to a strict timetable. The commission was there to save more than just the Health minister's skin. The premier's advisers also wanted to distance Harris as much as possible from the closure decisions, especially since he had suggested during one campaign appearance that the Tories had no plans for closing hospitals. Creating the commission would be one goal of the legislation.

Hospitals weren't the only problem in health care. Newly graduated doctors were stacked like cordwood in the urban centres of the province, while the rural and northern regions were badly underserviced. Many of those underserviced areas, including Jim Wilson's home town of Alliston, were in Conservative ridings. Wilson wanted powers to force doctors into underserviced areas. The Tories were also convinced a lot of money was being wasted on doctors who prescribed unnecessary treatments and drugs. But, again, they lacked the legislative power to police payments.

Finally, the Ontario Drug Benefit Plan, which subsidized the prescription costs of low-income citizens, was vacuuming more than $1 billion a year out of the treasury. Wilson, Harris, and the premier's office all agreed that drug costs were not health costs. It was time to slap user fees on free prescription drugs, requiring yet another legislative change. The cuts to hospitals alone would save the Tories $1.3 billion, which could be reinvested in long-term care and home-care programs.

In September, not long before the throne speech, David Lindsay and Rita Burak, the cabinet secretary, had hosted a one-day brainstorming session. "We pulled all the ministers and all of their executive assistants and all of their deputy ministers together," Lindsay recalls. Everybody hashed through the numbers: how much needed to be cut, how much each ministry should be expected to contribute, where the cuts might come from in each ministry. After the meeting, ministry staff contacted such "stakeholders" as the Ontario Hospital Association, the major universities, and the Association of Municipalities of Ontario. If you found yourself losing this much money from us, they were asked, what new powers would you need from us to make up the difference? The ministers then fed the information they received back to the premier's office.

It was clear by now that so many changes from so many ministries would pose a formidable logistical challenge. Pushing through the various pieces of enabling legislation could tie up the legislative calendar for months. But what if it were passed all at once? What if the hospital-restructuring commission, the curbs on doctors' privileges, the tuition hikes, the municipal user fees, and all the rest were bundled into a single all-encompassing bill? Not only would it speed up the timetable, the entire herd of opposition oxen could be gored at once, reducing the political fallout. Thus the omnibus bill was born.

Lindsay and Rita Burak supervised. "Cabinet office would put all the logistics together, and we would work out strategically what we wanted to achieve," said Lindsay. The actual package was assembled by Guy Giorno, the long-term policy adviser. He co-ordinated the material funnelled to him from the ministry bureaucracies through the cabinet office. As pieces of the package were assembled, Giorno then shipped them over to the Finance ministry. Since the bill would accompany the economic statement, it would have to be presented to the legislature by Ernie Eves. And here the process broke down.

Perhaps the largest bill ever put before the legislature of any province was being assembled in incredible haste. Ministers had little time or opportunity to vet the recommendations coming from their bureaucracies. Instead, the recommendations were often simply shovelled up by the deputy ministers straight to cabinet office and Giorno. But Giorno, though widely respected for his intelligence, had little experience in government and none with the bureaucracy. He didn't perceive that many of the recommendations were simply wish lists of new powers that senior bureaucrats had longed for but never been given. Worse, once the legislative provisions were sent over to Finance, they disappeared into a black hole of secrecy. The omnibus bill would accompany a financial statement, and Finance officials are justifiably paranoid about leaks. They can cost a minister his job. Eves' officials drafted the bill without letting anyone outside the ministry see its actual wording. Lindsay, Giorno, cabinet ministers all appealed in vain to see what the legislation would look like.

And then, at the critical period of preparation, just six weeks before the economic statement and the new omnibus bill were due, Ernie Eves confronted a personal crisis that forced the government's most powerful minister to temporarily abandon his post.

Justin Eves spent Thanksgiving Saturday night of 1995 with some friends at a local Parry Sound hotel. The son of Ernie Eves had faced more than the usual challenges of having a politician for a father. He had also struggled with a learning disability, which he'd overcome, earning a degree at Curry College in Boston, which specializes in teaching students with learning disorders. Now the twenty-three-year-old was back in the Sound, working for the family trucking firm, and having his share of fun. After the bar closed, Justin and two of his friends headed west on a two-lane highway to visit some buddies at a hunt camp. The October evening was wet and cool, the roads slick with rain and fallen leaves. Justin was driving. He was also speeding and not wearing a seat belt. Somehow he lost control, and the car veered off the road and slammed into a rock face. His two friends were slightly injured. Justin was killed.

Friends remarked that Ernie Eves was calm in the days following his son's death. He spoke, dry-eyed, at Justin's funeral, talked of the many times they had gone fishing together, in the Sound, in the Florida Keys. "We fished all over," he told the thousand mourners at the Parry Sound Pentecostal Tabernacle. "It was the one thing Justin knew he could do better than me, fishing." But if he remained composed in public, in private Ernie Eves was devastated. For two weeks, he disappeared from his job, remaining in Parry Sound with his wife and daughter. "The greatest crisis this government has faced was the death of Ernie's son," says one adviser. The loss of Justin "took Ernie out of the picture," another related. "In a way, for a little while, it took Mike out of the picture, too." The premier was distracted, unfocused. The political chain of command had temporarily dissolved.

There may never have been a Canadian head of government more intimately allied to a finance minister than Mike Harris is to Ernie Eves. They are more than political allies. They are close and trusted friends. They had known each other since Harris's days on the Nipissing school board. They golfed together; they and their wives vacationed together. Eves still calls the premier Mikey. It was Eves who, more than any other, had convinced Harris to run for the leadership of the party. Harris, on becoming premier, made his friend not only Finance minister, but House Leader—Harris's old job—and deputy premier as well. As one confidant put it, "When word got out that Mike and Ernie were having dinner together, all policy work stopped. Because whatever they decided over dinner was going to become policy."

It had been a difficult year, personally, for Ernie Eves. His father, Harry, had died of a heart attack only eleven months before. Ernie gave the eulogy at the funeral. "Doing a eulogy to your own father—I couldn't do it," his close friend Bob Drummond confessed. "But he did it, and his voice didn't even waver, and it was just as though he was addressing the legislature.

But he was hurting. I knew he was really, really hurting. But he didn't show it."[2]

Harry Eves' son had spent, as had Deane Harris's son, an active youth. Ernie was famous for fast driving—setting, one friend said, a land speed record for getting from Windsor, where he grew up, to a party in Point Pelee. But he was a good kid, had served as an altar boy, played the accordion, run the mile in 4:34, sneaked onto the Roseland golf course at twilight to putt for nickels, once caddied for Sammy Davis Jr. "I think I'm somewhat introverted by nature, as I believe Mike is," Eves has said. But it didn't stop either of them from cavorting.

Harry Eves, who'd started as a labourer and worked his way up, moved his family to Parry Sound, a small central-northern Ontario town on the shores of Georgian Bay, when he became a plant supervisor. Though Ernie was seventeen when the family arrived in Parry Sound, and would spend much of his adult life as a politician in Toronto, he would sell himself as a Parry Sound boy, a product of a small town and an up-by-the-bootstraps father. Ernie took care of his own bootstraps, by becoming a lawyer, by marrying his high-school sweetheart Vicki—whose family owned a prosperous trucking firm—by eking out a razor-thin win in Parry Sound during the 1981 election (it earned him the nickname "Landslide Ernie"), and by forming a personal and political bond with the rookie in the next-door riding of Nipissing, Mike Harris.

"We think alike," says Eves. "We do the same things . . . . I think it's because we both have small-town, small-c conservative upbringings, both, one way or another, have been exposed to small business, both understand what it means to make a payroll, regardless of how big or how small, and we both had parents that had to work very hard to be successful . . . [and who] instilled in us the need to work hard and never to forget where you came

---

[2] Biographical material on Ernie Eves is derived from interviews and from a previous profile of the minister by the author. See "Mike's Right-Hand Man," *Ottawa Citizen*, July 4, 1995, p. A1.

from." The only difference, perhaps, was that Eves was softer on some social issues than his friend Mike, breaking ranks with him and the party to support women's health centres (which performed abortions) in the days of the minority Peterson government. Although when it came to gun control, he was once quoted saying it would be a cold day when the federal government got him to register his rifle.

Eves was very close to his father, especially as a child. And it was painful, knowing Harry hadn't lived to see his son sworn in as Finance minister. "But I have a tremendous faith," Eves says. "I believe he was there one way or another." Now, less than a year after losing his father, Eves had lost his son. Not surprisingly, for the two weeks following his son's death, Eves stopped being Finance minister and adviser to the premier.

The political culture is ill equipped to handle a personal crisis. Political offices are competitive, powerful places. There is little room for the kind of selfless compassion and support that people in crisis need. As one adviser put it, "Emotions are not things that are dealt with in a political office very well." And the death of Justin Eves hit Harris hard as well. It was a grim and silent Mike Harris who emerged from the Eves house the day after Justin's death. For several days afterward, he was not himself — "he just sort of tuned out," one adviser said. Harris was intensely jealous of his family's privacy; the publicity surrounding Justin's death only worsened the pain he felt for his friend.

Michael Gourley, the deputy minister of Finance, helped bridge the crisis. Gourley was the first deputy minister appointed by the new government, and for good reason. He had served as a senior manager in half a dozen government departments, including Finance; he had private-sector experience as a systems analyst for Canadian National Railways; at the time of his appointment, he was vice-president, administration, at the University of Western Ontario. Gourley and his staff were able to keep the process moving in Eves' absence.

Eves says he was glad to return to the job at the end of October. "Actually, I welcomed the opportunity to come back to work. It provided an outlet for me to not think about other things, to work a little bit harder, I think, than I had before." But Eves' absence and the secrecy surrounding the new bill left the Tories ill-prepared to introduce their massive legislation. Only on the eve of its presentation were staff in the premier's office shown the first copies of the text. Until then, neither they nor the cabinet knew what the bill actually said. Only Eves knew. And part of the time he had been away.

At such a critical time, the government desperately needed a coherent communications strategy. The bill's "message track"— the rationale to be offered by ministers and advisers—should have been carefully worked out and drilled into the appropriate ministers and advisers. But since the resignation of Jamie Watt, the premier's office had lacked a communications adviser. In the absence of any more thoughtful preparation, senior media adviser Paul Rhodes chose to downplay the bill, shrugging it off as a compendium of housekeeping measures, mostly dealing with such things as how to close exhausted mines and issue building permits. The hope was that the bill's size and scope would make it so difficult to absorb, reporters and opposition politicians would give up and move onto something else.

The government called for a lockup on November 29, the day the statement was released. Lockups are usually confined to budgets. Reporters are shown the documents, but kept from telephones or any other kind of outside communication until the markets have closed and the budget is presented in the House. Strictly speaking, this lockup wasn't necessary. An economic statement is not a budget; it contains none of the tax measures that should require reporters to be kept isolated until markets have closed. But in another sense, the lockup was appropriate. The November 1995 economic statement was the most important financial document tabled by the Harris government, eclipsing any of its budgets to come. For now, it showed, clearly, starkly, the dimension of the coming rents to Ontario's social fabric.

In his statement to the legislature, Eves proclaimed cuts of $6 billion to government spending over three years. Coupled with the $2 billion taken out of the budget in July, this represented a loss of $8 billion in government spending: 14.2 per cent of the 1994–95 Ontario budget. Six billion dollars of the cuts were now identified. Four hundred million dollars was excised from grants to universities. In exchange, administrations would be allowed to increase tuition 20 per cent. Since the overwhelming majority of university students are the children of the middle and upper-middle class, the cut represented a rare attack on the pocketbooks of the Harris government's core constituency. Another $400 million was sliced from transfers to school boards; in exchange, NDP plans to make junior kindergarten mandatory were dropped. Municipalities were told block grants would decline by $657 million over two years; in exchange, they would be granted new powers to charge user fees and issue licences. All seniors not on welfare were expected to pay the first $100 of their annual prescription drug costs, along with a dispensing fee of up to $6; poorer seniors and those on welfare would be expected to pay a $2 dispensing fee.

As reporters struggled to master the ninety-one pages of announcements, graphs, and charts, the government quietly introduced a foot-thick piece of legislation known as Bill 26, the Savings and Restructuring Act, into the legislature. Most reporters filed their first day's stories unaware the bill had passed first reading.

For the first few days, the Tories' strategy of downplaying the bill appeared to work. The press gallery at first attempted to ignore the new legislation and concentrate on the seismic cuts contained in the economic statement instead. To most journalists, including this writer, Bill 26 looked like a "process bill": legislation that changes the way decisions are made, without actually coming to any decisions. Such bills are difficult to understand and difficult to sell to editors and readers. But the opposition parties, stymied for months by the Harris juggernaut, realized they finally had an issue on which they could take a stand. The new bill contained regulations imposing user fees on seniors and low-income earners who purchase prescription drugs, but *The*

Common Sense Revolution had promised in bold type, "Under this plan there will be NO new user fees." The Tories insisted that the drug "co-payments," as they called them, didn't violate that promise, because prescription drugs weren't covered under the Canada Health Act. It was the kind of shoddy, technical excuse for a broken promise that Mike Harris had vowed to avoid, and the Liberals, in particular, decided to nail him to the wall of the legislature on it. And if voters had trouble grasping the hundreds of legislative changes contained in the bill, they could certainly understand that a government that wanted to pass so many changes all at once was probably up to no good. One columnist dubbed it "the bully bill," and for the opposition, that became its name.

The day after the bill was introduced, an exasperated Speaker Al McLean expelled six MPPs. "Why did you lie to the people of this province?" the indignant Liberal leader Lyn McLeod raged, knowing full well the accusation of lying will get you kicked out the House. Deputy leader Sean Conway does such things much better. "With bald-faced amorality, you lied!" he roared. "You lied through your teeth! You're a liar! That's what you are!" Health critic Elinor Caplan managed to work up tears as she hurled her epithets.

Slowly, it penetrated the media's skulls that the new omnibus bill was about more than mine closings. It was even about more than user fees for prescriptions. The bill amended no fewer than forty-seven existing laws. It contained the mandate for a new hospital restructuring commission, which would have the authority to close hospitals across the province at will, without requiring cabinet approval. It included provisions to force newly licensed doctors to set up practice in "underserviced" areas of the province. It allowed inspectors to examine doctors' medical records in search of fraud, disqualify medical procedures they considered frivolous from payment under OHIP, and deny doctors the right to practise medicine without appeal. It deregulated drug prices, granted the municipalities broad powers to impose new licences and user fees, granting them also the power to privatize utilities without having to hold a referendum. It directed

142

arbitration boards to take the financial state of municipalities into greater account during wage settlements, reduced the obligation of the government to comply with freedom-of-information requests, and made it easier for conservation authorities to sell off land, the government having already cut their funding. Most significantly, perhaps, it gave the provincial government unlimited power to merge and abolish municipalities without their consent. Under the Constitution, municipalities are considered creatures of the provinces. They exist by provincial sufferance. Bill 26 would turn them into abject creatures indeed.

The government was intent on getting the omnibus bill passed before Christmas. The opposition was intent on stopping it. There was no legal way, however, to prevent the bill's passage, thanks to legislation the NDP had passed that reduced the power of opposition parties to obstruct the business of the House. House Leader Ernie Eves was proposing two weeks of public hearings on the bill in December. The Liberals knew they had to keep the issue alive until after Christmas. They wanted province-wide hearings in the new year. Eves refused.

Wednesday December 6, after another raucous Question Period, thirty-three opposition members refused to vote on a routine motion concerning the bill. Under parliamentary rules, they were required to leave the chamber. When Speaker Al McLean cited Liberal MPP Bernard Grandmaître, he dutifully left. But when Alvin Curling's name was called, the former Housing minister refused to get out of his seat. McLean ordered sergeant-at-arms Tom Stelling to eject him by force. But Curling's seatmates linked arms with him, defying the sergeant-at-arms and the Speaker. Other opposition MPPs rushed to surround the rebel. "Where is your force?" Curling asked Stelling. "This is it," Stelling confessed. "Well, we have a long wait here, Tom," Curling replied. It was an outrageous violation of the rules of the legislature. And it worked. Flustered and confused, McLean ordered a recess. He left the legislature, but Curling stayed, all night as it turned out. Surrounded by a praetorian guard of opposition MPPs, sustained by pizza, propped up with pillows, and warmed by a blanket that covered a bottle discreetly brought in for calls of nature, Curling sat out the night.

The next morning, shortly after 10 a.m., Curling left the chamber, with a new appreciation of the hardness of the legislature's seats. Under the regulations of the House, by delaying his departure until after ten, he had made it impossible for the House to sit that day. Since the House did not sit on Fridays, Curling had effectively shut down further debate on the bill until the following week, the last week the legislature was scheduled to sit before the Christmas break. It would be virtually impossible, now, to pass the bill before Christmas.

Shortly after Curling made his grand exit, surrounded by cheering opposition MPPs and swarmed by reporters and television cameras, Ernie Eves placed a call to NDP House Leader Dave Cooke and Liberal House Leader Jim Bradley, who was in Cooke's office. Staff outside the door could hear Cooke delightedly advising Eves, "That kind of language won't get us anywhere, Ernie." The three house leaders agreed to meet immediately. Bradley, a wily veteran of legislature wars, knew the opposition had used up just about every trick in its bag. It was time to deal. "I'm going to help you out of this," he told Eves. "I'm going to solve your problem for you." The opposition parties dropped an earlier demand that the bill be broken into several pieces of legislation. They would settle for a single month of province-wide hearings. The bill would then be passed in a one-day sitting of the legislature at the end of January. Eves, who knew the alternative was to force the House to sit through Christmas, agreed.

The Liberals had hogged the spotlight during Curling's Stand, but now NDP leader Bob Rae had his day. During Question Period the following week, he and other opposition members peppered Municipal Affairs Minister Al Leach with questions about the bill. Rae, who's read a few pieces of legislation in his day, pointed out that the wording of Bill 26 appeared to allow municipalities to impose gasoline taxes, income taxes, and sales taxes. It even possibly permitted a poll tax. A poll tax, such as the one Margaret Thatcher attempted to impose in Britain—the furor helped bring her down as Conservative Party leader—taxes each person in a household a certain amount, as opposed to taxing the property itself. Poll taxes are unpopular because a poor couple with six children could pay vastly more than a wealthy widower living alone.

Leach believed the new legislation did not allow for poll taxes. But as Rae read the fuzzily worded passage to him, the Municipal Affairs minister became increasingly befuddled. "To the leader of the coalition, I had that right there to read back to you. Completely lost. Mr. Speaker, give me two minutes. Let me take that on notice and I'll get back to you," he babbled. "Mr. Speaker, I'm completely lost" became a standard punch line in the premier's office. "It is not clear what Mr. Leach meant by referring to Mr. Rae as coalition leader," the *Globe and Mail* dryly reported.

Leach's befuddlement grew out of the process that created the omnibus bill. By having ministry staff shovel forward recommendations straight to Burak and Giorno, and then having Finance ministry staff draft the legislation, individual ministers were left in the dark on the portions of the bill affecting their ministries. They were stuck with publicly defending a piece of legislation they had had little to do with and didn't understand. As the committee hearings in Toronto got underway, it became obvious there were all sorts of things in Bill 26 that shouldn't have been there. Hearings had barely begun before Health Minister Jim Wilson promised to modify the health-care portion of the bill. Municipal Affairs Minister Al Leach promised to resign before letting the municipalities impose gasoline or poll taxes.

Tony Clement, now a parliamentary assistant to Citizenship, Culture, and Recreation minister Marilyn Mushinksi, was on one of the committees examining the bill. It quickly became clear to him and others on the committee that the government had been shafted by the bureaucrats. "The bureaucracy tended to put in every item that had been on the shelf for the past five years," he believes. "It was almost like a wish list." And that wish list had been shovelled from deputy ministers to Giorno with little supervision by the ministers who would have to carry the political ball.

"The ministers . . . did not do as good a job as had to be done to make sure the stuff was on the agenda. Some of it was totally off our agenda." The committee members, along with Finance ministry staff, went to work at drafting amendments to excise the more obnoxious clauses from the bill.

Bill 26 set a precedent that would become a pattern with the Harris government. Time after time, staff from the premier's office would seize control of an issue and try to manage it, only to be slapped in the face by public reaction. Then other elements within the government, or allies outside it, would come to the rescue. Undaunted, the premier's staff would launch the next big crisis. In part, Lindsay and his staff adopted this tactic because it worked. The government generally had its legislative way in the end. In part, it was a product of their messianic zeal to reshape the province in their political image.

The young whiz kids in the premier's office were strong on strategy and ideology, but they lacked the tactical experience that comes with long political service. They should have been tempered by the premier himself—Harris had fourteen years of experience in the legislature to draw on—yet Harris would repeatedly allow his government to be hijacked by the grand schemes of his political staff, each time at political cost, each time having to be rescued. This was the price Harris paid for delegating much of his own power to his advisers. But it was a price he was willing to pay to achieve the fulfillment of his Common Sense Revolution.

By the time January 29 rolled around, the government had tabled more than 160 amendments to the omnibus bill. The wording was clarified to make sure municipalities couldn't actually tax gas, income, and heads. Jim Wilson put on hold plans to force doctors out of urban centres, and the more Draconian powers given to the province to search files and suspend physicians were taken away. The worst excesses of the bill, the excesses that had so unnecessarily embarrassed the government, were gone. But its core remained intact. The health-care field was set for a major restructuring. And the province now had the power to remould municipalities when and as it saw fit.

The Conservatives might have learned a few lessons from Bill 26: that shoving massive pieces of legislation through the House can be more trouble than they're worth; that the more time you spend in consultation and preparation, the less you spend in damage control; that the premier's office is not infallible. Instead, they took away another lesson: if you push forward a revolutionary bill, you should expect to take a few hits, but the bill will get passed, and all the furor will soon be forgotten. A few months after the bully bill became law, it had disappeared from public memory.

Though Clement and his committee colleagues had to sit through 367 deputations complaining about the bill, and suffered the embarrassment of pushing through all the amendments, he nonetheless defends the process. "The way we've decided to run the government is revolutionary," he maintains. It involves "change first, then consolidation. We can't put things off, because we'll get too close to an election and we'll lose our nerve."

Bill 26 didn't serve as a warning to the government. It served as encouragement.

CHAPTER 7

Season of Discontent

In late February 1996, the Ontario public service went on strike
for the first time in its history. The work stoppage did not take
the Mike Harris government by surprise. The premier and his
advisers had expected a strike from the day they took office—not
only expected it, encouraged it.

And they won it.

Once the legislature was in session life in the premier's office on
the fourth floor of Whitney Block had settled into a predictable,
if taxing, routine. Each morning at 8:30, in a notoriously
cramped meeting room, the key members of the Harris inner circle gathered to plan the day. David Lindsay chaired the sessions,
with Mitch Patten taking over when Lindsay was absent. Paul
Rhodes would brief the group on what the boys were saying in
the newspapers and on the radio and TV. Debbie Hutton would
lay out what to expect from the opposition that day. Guy Giorno
would report on how long-term plans were proceeding. Bill King,
as caucus liaison, had little formal role, but always an opinion.
Rounding out the group was Scott Munnoch, who organized the
premier's schedule.

The meetings were lively, rudely humorous and animated,
founded in many ways on the esprit that had been forged in the
election bullpen. The most important task each morning was to
identify any issues the premier needed to know about. It was also

the one regularly scheduled opportunity for the inner circle to discuss where the new government was going and how it planned to get there. The whole thing lasted about an hour. After the morning meeting, Lindsay and Hutton would brief the premier. This was Harris's best opportunity to ponder the various recommendations coming to him from his advisers and to make his own.

Those who have watched Mike Harris over the years describe his decision-making process as complex, intuitive, and intensely focused. That focus is both an asset and a liability. Harris tends not to think in a linear, step-by-step fashion. Rather, he takes in information from all available sources, from ministerial memoranda to taxi drivers. (A conversation with a cabbie in New Jersey some years back led Harris to briefly pursue the idea of asking people to exchange their illegal weapons for cash or rewards.) The information he receives from these disparate sources is then filtered through Harris's own matrix of values: the lessons he learned from his father, the moral and cultural precepts of North Bay, his own experiences. Once the information has been assessed by these core values, Harris makes a decision. During that decision-making period, woe betide anyone who wanders in, hoping to talk about something else. "He'll look at you like, 'I'm over here. What are you doing talking about something that's over there?'" one former staffer revealed. Harris will angrily reject attempts to get him off whatever topic he is focusing on. It can lead to powerfully concentrated analysis. It can also lead to a narrow, blinkered obsession with whatever is at hand. "It's both his greatest strength and his greatest weakness," one associate has remarked.

In the afternoon, Harris's attention shifted to the legislature, the premier arriving for Question Period at about two p.m., followed possibly by a scrum with reporters after it ended an hour later. But even in the early days of the Mike Harris government, such scrums were relatively rare. From the time the Tories took power, the strategists in the premier's office had concentrated on shifting the focus away from the premier and onto the cabinet members. Until June 8, 1995, Mike Harris had been the

Mike Harris—summer of 1967—Table Island, French River.

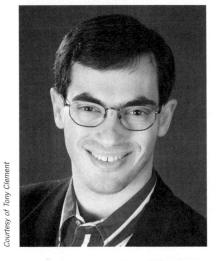

Some of the faces behind the Common
Sense Revolution and the 1995 campaign
victory. Clockwise from top left: Tom
Long, Alister Campbell, Leslie Noble,
Tony Clement.

During Harris's first two years as premier, his youthful political staff wielded a remarkable degree of power and influence. Left to right: Guy Giorno, Paul Rhodes, Mitch Patten, David Lindsay, Bill King, Debbie Hutton.

Bill King, Executive Assistant to the Premier; businessman Bill Farlinger, a key fundraiser and co-chair of the transition team, who was rewarded with the chairmanship of Ontario Hydro; and Mike Harris—May 1996.

Mark O'Neil—Toronto Sun Syndicate

The first serious Queen's Park demonstration of the Harris years accompanied his government's first throne speech on September 26, 1995.

A grim Mike Harris leaves the home of Ernie Eves, soon after Justin Eves' tragic death at Thanksgiving 1996.

Ian MacDonald—Toronto Sun Syndicate

Canapress Photo Service

Treasurer Ernie Eves receives
a congratulatory pat on the back
from Premier Harris after
presenting his first budget on
May 7, 1996.

UPSEU head Leah Casselman
pickets the Ministry of
Community and Social Services
during the public servants' strike
in late winter 1996.

Craig Robertson—Toronto Sun Syndicate

The first Harris cabinet:
Front row: Norm Sterling (Consumer and Commercial Relations), Noble Villeneuve (Agriculture and Rural Affairs, Francophone Affairs), Ernie Eves (Deputy Premier, House Leader, Finance), Mike Harris (Premier).
Second row: Jim Wilson (Health), Charles Harnick (Attorney General), Dave Johnson (Management Board), Bob Runciman (Solicitor General and Correctional Services).
Third row: William Saunderson (Economic Development, Trade and Tourism), Dianne Cunningham (Intergovernmental Affairs, Women's Issues), Elizabeth Witmer (Labour), Chris Hodgson (Natural Resources).
Fourth row: Al Leach (Municipal Affairs and Housing), Al Palladini (Transportation), John Snobelen (Education), David Tsubouchi (Community and Social Services).
Back row: Cam Jackson (Minister Without Portfolio, Workers' Compensation), Marilyn Mushinski (Citizenship, Culture and Recreation), Brenda Elliott (Environment and Energy).

Remarkably, of the original eighteen ministers, only Brenda Elliott would be dropped during the first two years.

Three of the government's most important ministers, left to right: Dave Johnson, Jim Wilson, John Snobelen.

Stan Behal—Toronto Sun Syndicate

The two faces of the megacity
debate: Al Leach, minister of
Municipal Affairs and Housing
(above), and John Sewell, former
Toronto mayor and leader of the
Campaign for Local Democracy
(below).

T. Bock—The Toronto Star

The largest protest against the Harris government came during the Toronto Days of Action in October 1996. But it certainly won't be the last.

Progressive Conservative Party of Ontario. Now that the promised revolution was underway, it made sense to distance the premier from the day-to-day actions of the government, so that he could dodge the inevitable political flak. Individual ministers would carry the various policy balls: Elizabeth Witmer on labour legislation; Jim Wilson and Al Leach on the omnibus bill; Dave Johnson on negotiations with the public service. Nor did the media seek the premier out; his answers were typically so vague and rambling they were seldom worth quoting. Real information came from the cabinet ministers and the political staff. This led to the impression that the individual ministers exercised considerable control over their departments' agenda.

In reality, policy continued to be determined and co-ordinated out of the premier's office. Lindsay, Patten, Giorno, Hutton, and Rhodes were, collectively, more powerful than any member of cabinet, with the possible exception of the economic ministers: Finance Minister Ernie Eves and Management Board Chair Dave Johnson. This was nothing new in Ontario politics. As Harris had reminded his deputy ministers in June, the senior ranks of the bureaucracy answered directly to cabinet secretary Rita Burak, who answered directly to the premier. Such a system provides a direct line of communication between the premier's office and the senior bureaucracy, bypassing the ministers. In many cases, as Bill 26 revealed, policy initiatives developed by deputy ministers strongly influenced the views in the premier's office, which shaped the policy or legislation, and then communicated the decisions back to the ministers, who served as front men and women, selling the legislation to the public. (In the case of Bill 26, the Finance ministry was the final author of the legislation.) The flow was not uniform; some ministers were more powerful than others, some more in tune with the flow and able to control it. Some ministers were sometimes in the loop, sometimes out of it.

As premier, Mike Harris saw himself as an arbiter. He was happy to approve the initiatives of others, as long as the ideas were workable and there was time and energy available to implement them. It would be an overstatement to say Harris is a passive premier, but he is far less interested in micro-managing the government than his two predecessors. As a chief executive, he could best be described as a combination traffic cop and judge. Nonetheless when Harris decided, for personal and sometimes unpredictable reasons, that one initiative should take priority, or another be shelved, that decision was law. And when Harris's passions were aroused, as they still could be, he was capable of hijacking his own agenda. The personal obsessions of the premier would become increasingly an engine of government in the second year of its mandate.

The real crucible of decision making was the Priorities and Planning Committee. This small committee of cabinet contained the most powerful ministers of the Harris government: Finance Minister Ernie Eves; Labour Minister Elizabeth Witmer; Management Board Chair Dave Johnson; Health Minister Jim Wilson; Environment Minister Norm Sterling; and Economic Development Minister Bill Saunderson. Harris himself chaired the weekly meeting, which set the government's legislative agenda. Discussion in P and P, as it was called, was less structured than at cabinet; deputy ministers sat at the cabinet table with the ministers and debate was informal. Ministers not on the committee would attend to pitch their legislation or take instruction. Here, the priorities of the government were hashed out and conflicts resolved. An initiative passed by P and P was an initiative passed. The full weekly cabinet meetings were largely pro forma affairs. Only a reckless minister would raise fundamental objections at cabinet to a proposal already approved by P and P.

The November 29, 1995, economic statement and the introduction of the omnibus bill would have been enough to keep any normal legislature occupied from Labour Day to Victoria Day. But the thirty-sixth parliament was no ordinary legislative session. It was possibly the busiest sitting in the history of the province. Their Alberta cousins had advised the Ontario Tories to move quickly.[1] Jamming the early months of the mandate with the most difficult pieces of legislation required to launch the Common

Sense Revolution would also keep the opposition off-balance. Harris and his advisers followed that advice with a vengeance. Besides the omnibus bill, during the fall session the government introduced an avalanche of new legislation and regulations, affecting everything from prisons to the minimum wage.

The minimum wage was indefinitely frozen at $6.85 an hour. With inflation, it would fall in real terms 1 to 2 per cent each year of the government's mandate. This would make it easier for employers to hire entry-level workers, but would condemn those workers to a lower standard of living. Solicitor General Bob Runciman followed with news that halfway houses for young offenders were being closed immediately. These homes helped people serving time in provincial jails[2] to prepare for their release. Instead, Runciman said, an electronic-bracelet monitoring program would allow the province to keep tabs on convicts who had been released from jail but were not yet entitled to full parole. Until the program was in place, inmates would simply have to make do with the overcrowding. Critics rightly warned that closing halfway houses makes it more difficult for inmates to prepare themselves for a return to the community. There were about 300 people in halfway houses at any given time. Today, due to budget

---

[1] Alberta Conservatives are happy to take credit for much of the electoral and legislative success of their friends in Toronto. According to the former treasurer Jim Dinning, senior bureaucrats and political advisers burned up the phone lines and shuttled regularly between Toronto and Edmonton in the months before and after the 1995 election. "The airlines could have dedicated a special flight for them," he joked. The Ontario Tories vehemently deny the claim, saying they limited their consultation to half a dozen trips and some phone calls. The Alberta Tories themselves were acolytes at the feet of the New Zealand politicians who launched their major restructuring in the 1980s. Herman Schwartz, of the University of Virginia, recently prepared a compelling comparison of the Alberta and New Zealand experiences, and the links between the two governments, entitled *Kiwi or Not Kiwi: Exporting the New Zealand "Model" to Alberta, Canada*. It can most readily be obtained on the Internet, at http://darwin.clas.virginia.edu/~hms2f.

[2] Those whose sentence is less than two years serve that sentence in a provincial jail; sentences of more than two years earn a stay in a federal prison.

and eligibility restrictions, about 100 people are on the bracelet program; the rest languish in jail. But it saved $11 million.

However, no sooner did one cry of protest arise than it was drowned by even more anguished wails. On October 4, the Tories moved to repeal the NDP's Bill 40, which had altered the province's labour legislation. Gone were NDP changes that outlawed the use of replacement workers during a strike. Gone were provisions making it easier to organize unions. Gone also were regulations that allowed agricultural workers to organize. In their place were new rules requiring a secret ballot during strike votes or union ratification. Most important, there were changes to successor rights.

Successor rights protect the pay and privileges of employees whose companies are sold to another concern. In the non-unionized portion of the private sector, these rights are generally minimal. During a merger or buy-out, workers must cross their fingers and hope there's a place for them in the new order. Their only real protection is the Employment Standards Act, which guarantees them a minimum number of weeks of severance pay. Workers who belong to a union, of course, have a collective agreement that the new owner must respect. As part of their labour-law reform, the Conservatives exempted provincial public servants from the protection of successor rights. Now the Tories would be able to sell off, contract out, or otherwise privatize government operations without the disincentive to potential buyers of having to retain the wages, benefits, and job-security provisions of the former public servants' contracts.

Private-sector corporations would have hesitated taking over road maintenance, safety inspections, and the host of other government services on the block if they had to pay their workers government rates and offer them government-level job security. The leaders of the Ontario Public Service Employees Union, usually called OPSEU, were enraged by the loss of successor rights, which would have been the union's principal tool in fighting the expected wave of Tory privatizations. The Conservatives had campaigned on a promise to eliminate at least 13,000 jobs from the 80,000-member Ontario public service, mostly by privatizing and contracting out government services. There were rumours as many as 27,000 jobs could disappear before the Tories were done. The union's leaders quickly decided that, if their workers were to have any protection, they would have to force the Tories to embed in their next contract the successor rights they had lost through legislation. They knew, of course, the Tories would never willingly agree. What they didn't know was that the new government had already accepted the inevitability of a strike, one it was determined to win.

Mac Penny had worked for the Conservatives since joining their caucus services division as a researcher in 1982. When the new government was sworn in, he landed a job as executive assistant to Management Board Chair Dave Johnson, who would be in charge of downsizing the public service by at least 13,000 jobs, and who would also head the negotiations for a new contract with the 67,000 members of OPSEU. According to Penny, Johnson and others in the government expected a strike from the first day they took office. "We knew that the mood simply wasn't there" for a settlement, he remembers. The government had no intention of giving back to the public servants through collective bargaining the successor rights it had just legislated away. Rather, government intended to claw back even more. "Bumping rights" allow someone whose job has been declared surplus to take over the job of someone with less seniority, who in turn can bump someone else. Under the existing collective agreement, the province had to give six months' notice to lay off a worker. If it was laying off more than twenty workers, notice extended to eleven months. But the threatened worker could then bump another worker with lesser seniority, and a layoff notice had to be given to that worker. Before the process was finished, it could take two years to actually lay someone off. The Tories didn't have two years. They wanted bumping and other job-protection clauses stripped out of the new OPSEU contract.

The Tories knew that the union would never willingly surrender such protections, when it was clear the government planned to lay off many of its members and sell others into private-sector slavery, especially since the NDP government had give OPSEU the right to strike in 1994. This was not an act of altruism on the NDP's part, although Bob Rae had certainly hoped the move would salve some of the hurt from the imposition of the Social Contract. As Rae neared the end of his mandate, he too had concluded that the public service was too large and too well protected. Under existing conditions, the government could do little to claw back benefits. Without the right to strike, disputes between the government and its employees invariably ended up in arbitration, and arbitrators almost never eliminated existing rights and benefits in a contract; on the contrary, they usually gave the union at least some of what it wanted, which is how the contracts had become so well padded in the first place. By giving the union the right to strike, the NDP was also giving itself the power to confront the union without having to worry about an arbitrator emasculating its demands. Ironically, however, the move served only to hand a potent weapon to Rae's Conservative successors.

The incoming Tories had been blessed by a second stroke of good luck. Ontario public servants had been without a contract since January 1, 1994. In the spring of 1995, with the Social Contract negotiations finally out of the way, when government and union negotiators finally got down to the business of negotiating a new contract, OPSEU brought to the table demands for wage increases to compensate for the losses of the Social Contract. But Rae had instructed the bargaining teams to seek concessions. The job-security provisions of the existing contract were too rich even for his blood.

There was one ploy the union could have attempted that might have saved its job-security protection. It could simply have offered to renew the existing contract. "That would have been very tempting," believes Angelo Pesce. Pesce was the chief negotiator for the Rae government throughout the contract negotiations. A simple offer to renew, he says, "would have been very tempting for the government, and very tempting for the bureaucracy." It would have purchased several years of labour peace and allowed the NDP to bridge the divide separating it from its fractious public-sector unions, who were supposed to be its allies but had become enemies. And a contract would have given the government something to boast about in the upcoming elections.

But in the spring of 1995, OPSEU was engaged in an internal power struggle. After a bitter fight with the union's old guard, Leah Casselman, a forty-one-year-old former prison guard, became the new president of the union the day Bob Rae called the election. Casselman said she phoned Rae immediately after her victory and urged him to conclude a contract. Rae refused, insisting he couldn't tie the hands of whoever formed the next government. In retrospect, Casselman later maintained, not having a contract was a blessing in disguise. "They would have simply rewritten the law, stripped away our [successor] rights, and then said, 'So what are you going to do now?'" she said. "It would have been an illegal strike, and that would have made it doubly harder to get our members out." True, but at least the contract's bumping rights would have remained entrenched.

OPSEU sent union protesters to heckle Rae during the campaign. He phoned Casselman and asked her to desist. Negotiate an agreement, she replied, and they'll desist. Not during an election, the premier declared.

"Then you'll have to live with the consequences," she told him.

"No, actually, Leah, you will."[3]

When Pesce met with his new boss, Management Board Chair Dave Johnson shortly after the election, he quickly learned that the minister, a veteran of both municipal politics and corporate boardrooms, hated lengthy briefings. If you wanted to get a point across, Pesce discovered, you had to do it quickly. The chief negotiator took the lesson to heart. At an early meeting between Johnson and his staff and the Management Board negotiators, Pesce presented a diagram of a set of scales on an overhead projector. One half was labelled "wants"; the other, "gives."

---

[3] *From Protest to Power*, p. 64.

"If you want a settlement," he told Johnson, "you have to have this balance between things you want and things you're willing to give. The more you load up the wants side, and the less you put in the give side, the more things go out of balance."

But Johnson only had wants. He wanted to eliminate successor rights; he wanted to make layoffs quicker and easier; he wanted to reduce the government's obligations under the pension plan. And he was prepared to give virtually nothing that cost money.

"If you do that, you get a strike," Pesce told Johnson.

"Fine," Johnson replied.

From that moment on, says Pesce, "a strike was inevitable."

There was one strategy the union could have employed to retain its privileges. It could have dragged out negotiations indefinitely. As long as the provisions of the old contract remained in effect, the Tories were limited in their ability to conduct mass layoffs. Since a strike would be a high-risk strategy for a union that had never struck before—how many of its members would go along?—the Tories worried that the union would instead mire them in endless negotiations in which the government couldn't afford to get mired. It was committed to immediately cutting up to $8 billion in spending, and unless it could downsize and privatize the work force, it would never make those targets. "We knew it was going to be a tight thing," says Penny, "because we had to get the contract in place for this fiscal year. We had to have it, *had* to have it. There's no way we could do what we're doing now without it."[4] Though the government could nudge the matter along by applying the labour law—imposing deadlines, threatening a lockout, and requesting a mediator—to a certain extent, it was the union's call. The Tories were gambling that, sooner rather than later, OPSEU would lose patience and call a strike vote. "To some degree we were counting on the militancy of the union," Penny says. "We felt we could simply outwait them."

Talks lumbered along through the fall, while attention focused on the news of the latest slashes. Suddenly, in late

---

[4] The fiscal year beginning April 1, 1996, and ending March 31, 1997.

November, while the two sides were still outlining their positions on the main agreement, the government negotiators announced they were applying for conciliation, the last formal step of negotiations before a strike vote can be called. The news stunned the union's chief negotiator, André Bekerman. "Normally that's done when you're at some sort of crossroads," he says. "We were still presenting our packages." Now it was clear to the union that the government wanted to hasten the strike.

By early February 1996, with Bill 26 out of the way, public attention began to shift to the state of the public-sector contract talks. Conciliation had been underway since January 8. After five months of talks, even the most minor of the more than 100 issues on the table had not been settled. The negotiations, as expected, had boiled down to several key points of contention, all related to job security. Though public servants hadn't seen a pay raise since 1991, and had actually seen their average pay of $40,000 temporarily cut during the Social Contract, the union was not pressing for increased wages. Instead, it was fighting to preserve job security. It wanted successor rights entrenched in a new contract, it wanted extensive retraining guarantees for laid-off workers, and it wanted bumping rights protected. The union also hoped to gain access to pension benefits for laid-off workers, an access that had been limited by yet another provision of the omnibus bill. The Tories refused even to consider the matter.

On the first weekend of February, the union walked away from the conciliation talks, finally giving the Tories exactly what they had hoped for. A new contract had to be in place on or about April 1, if the government was to be able to accurately forecast for the 1996 budget how many jobs would disappear and when. By walking away from the talks, OPSEU set the strike clock ticking. Under the province's labour law, a strike can begin fourteen days after the conciliator tables a report saying no agreement has been reached. But first, the union needed to conduct a province-wide vote of its members, asking for a strike mandate. Assuming they got that mandate, a strike could begin in late February. Just about perfect timing, as far as the government was concerned.

The OPSEU leaders understood the risk they were taking by calling a strike vote, but they felt they had no choice. In months of negotiations, the government hadn't budged a millimetre. Only the threat of a strike, they concluded, could force the Tories to offer at least some of the concessions the leadership needed if it was to have any credibility in the eyes of its members. The final decision was Leah Casselman's. "Government work doesn't necessarily have as huge an impact as you'd like it to have," she later explained. "We had to determine what would have the most impact on the government and on the public to get this thing settled as soon as possible. So we had to make sure there was snow on the ground." If Ontario's motorists couldn't navigate its highways because the plows were behind picket lines, they would soon be pressuring the government to settle, or so the new head of OPSEU believed.

Casselman had been in the president's chair only ten months, but she fully knew that OPSEU was a fractured, fractious place, known within the labour movement as "Lebanon." The union embraced workers ranging from stridently militant jail guards, who had already flexed their muscles with illegal walkouts, to timid clerical workers in the office towers beside Queen's Park. The union had already suffered the ignominy of Rae's Social Contract; many wondered if it would have the discipline even to secure a strong strike vote from its membership, let alone take those members out on their first-ever strike.

Casselman's decision to break off talks was probably a tactical misjudgment. Had she forced the government to walk away from the table—which it would have, eventually—she would have had a powerful public-relations weapon. Even the Tories' supporters were sometimes uncomfortable with the government's bullying tactics. Instead, it was the union that appeared determined to force a confrontation. Yet if Casselman was guilty of tactical misjudgments, she was also an effective leader of her volatile troops. When the results of the strike vote were released in mid-February, 66 per cent had voted in favour—hardly an overwhelming mandate, but impressive from a membership that had no history of labour militancy, that had never even taken a strike vote before.

In some ways, the contest was a battle of wills between two effective and determined leaders. Fifty-one-year-old Dave Johnson had kept a relatively low profile in the first months of the mandate. In scrums and at press conferences, he displayed a remarkable effectiveness as a government spokesman. Avuncular yet uncompromising, he conveyed exactly the impression Harris and his advisers wanted for the government: reasonable, anxious to be fair, but determined to protect the interests of taxpayers as it set about reforming its public service.

It was a role Johnson was well suited to play. Raised on a farm in Greensville, near Hamilton, the son of a mechanic and part-time farmer, he had earned his science degree at McMaster University and a master's from the University of Waterloo before going to work for Imperial Oil, where he eventually reached the executive offices. In 1972, he entered municipal politics, running for alderman in the Toronto borough of East York. He later served as East York's mayor for ten years and enjoyed his share of contract negotiations with public-service unions. Both government negotiators and Queen's Park reporters would be impressed with Johnson's clear-sightedness and the relative absence of Tory cant from his public utterances. But it was also clear he was sternly determined to win the fight with OPSEU, to settle only on his terms.

Casselman was also raised on a farm, in Morewood, near Ottawa, in a family of Loyalist stock. She also went to McMaster University, but her degree was in sociology, and her profession was jail guard. In 1984, she joined the executive of OPSEU and in 1995, on her second try, captured the presidency, taking over a union that had been strained by its failure to get the Rae government to back down on the Social Contract. Other labour heads were skeptical of Casselman's ability to confront the Tories or to successfully wage a strike.

During the negotiations and the strike that followed, Casselman repeatedly found herself tactically outmaneuvered by

Johnson. Before the strike vote was even held, the government publicly released its "final offer" to the union, which restored the 2 per cent pay cut imposed by the Social Contract, and also restored merit pay, adding a total of 5 per cent to the pay of about one-third of the employees. The government also offered some limited "bridging" assistance to employees laid off before they could fully access their pensions, and it promised to make "reasonable efforts" to protect the benefits of provincial servants whose jobs were privatized. Finally, the government offered to double the severance package of laid-off workers to a maximum of fifty-two weeks of pay. But the key demands—strict limitations of bumping rights, no entrenchment of pension and successor-right benefits, and a six-month maximum layoff notice—remained unaddressed, and the union swiftly dismissed the offer as regressive and cruel. To many ordinary citizens watching the dispute, however, who envied the public servants their $40,000 average annual salary and who rarely enjoyed the job-security benefits that even the stripped-down contract would contain, the government's offer seemed more than fair. The union knew it couldn't count on public sympathy.

Following the strike vote, the two sides went back to the table for a final week of desultory talks, but by now it was clear to everyone a walkout was a virtual certainty. "It may be inevitable," Johnson conceded on February 21. Indeed, the government had already put together an operations manual, detailing ministry by ministry how it would continue to maintain services during a strike. The union and the NDP had negotiated essential services agreements as part of the new strike weapon. Jail guards, snow-plow operators, staff at public-health labs, were all to continue to work in the event of a walkout, albeit at reduced levels. Fully 12,000 of the 67,000 OPSEU government workers would stay on the job during the strike. Ironically, so many government workers had claimed they should be deemed essential—partly to keep their pay cheque, and partly because everyone likes to believe they are indispensable—that the government negotiators had been forced to demand limits. Otherwise there could have been a strike with no one off the job. The Tories were convinced that, by forcing the union to observe the emergency-services agreements and by working their managers to the brink of collapse, they could keep the government functioning through a strike indefinitely.

The union had set a strike deadline of February 26. To minimize fallout, workers who had no direct contact with the public would walk out first. If the government failed to blink, the strike would gradually escalate. The goal was to maximize inconvenience to the government while minimizing public irritation. But the union management lacked that level of control over their members. On Monday, February 26, about half the public servants in the province walked off the job. By the end of the week, the rest were out. The union's strategy of gradual escalation had failed. Now the question was, how would the union fare in total war?

Until now, things had gone pretty much as the government had hoped. It had been OPSEU that had broken off the talks, had publicly spurned the government's final offer, and had called the strike. From the start, public sympathy appeared to be with the Tories (polls taken during the strike would show the majority of people thought the public servants were in the wrong), and it was clear the union leadership wasn't firmly in control of its own members. If the leadership couldn't keep members from walking off the job, perhaps it wouldn't be able to keep them from crossing the picket lines, either. But the best-laid plans of even Tories go awry.

On Sunday February 25, the day before the strike began, the *Toronto Star* carried a front-page story, "Tory Strike Plan Revealed." In it, "senior government sources" stated that the government planned to bring in 5,000 replacement workers to break the strike. "Replacements will not be brought in en masse by bus, but will be strategically placed where needed, and introduced to the workplace in small numbers at first so as not to attract too much attention," William Walker reported. When the news broke, the senior strategists over at the Management Board "went ballistic," as one insider put it. As far as they knew, the government had no plans to bring in replacement workers. They were confident that, between the essential-service agreements and the managers at their disposal, they could keep the government functioning indefinitely during a strike. Replacement workers were unnecessary and dangerous; they would only inflame the union members and increase both their militancy and solidarity.

More to the point, the Management Board was supposed to be running the strike. Johnson's staff was livid at staff in the premier's office for trying to put their own spin on the situation. Their anger only deepened the next day, when Harris proceeded to make things worse. Scrummed by reporters before the cabinet meeting, the premier spoke with unnecessary candour. A confrontation, he suggested, had become inevitable the day the NDP gave the public servants the right to strike in 1994. "They were given this candy, this new tool, by Rae and they are determined to go and use it and try it, and I'm not sure there was anything we could have done to stop them," he mused. Reporters jumped on the line; it revealed an attitude of callous paternalism by the government towards its workers. In two days, just as the strike was getting underway, two separate incidents had damaged the government's credibility, forcing it to switch to damage control. And the premier had only himself to blame.

Unfortunate off-the-cuff remarks remain one of Mike Harris's chronic weaknesses; although he tempers his opinions most of the time, in periods of high drama or acute stress, he tends to reveal the sort of ill-humoured defiance he displayed in the letter he had written to the editor of the *North Bay Nugget* twenty years before. The trait emerged during the early days of the election campaign, when he talked about closing casinos and revoking tenure; now it had surfaced with a vengeance with the "candy" line during the strike. Eight months later, he would display it again when deriding the protesters at the Toronto Days of Action, and it would haunt him during the Megacity debate, when he would compare hospital workers trying to keep their jobs to workers at a hula hoop factory. As a leader, Harris struggles to control his resentment towards those whom he believes take more than they give. His inability to manage these feelings has repeatedly landed him in trouble.

But the fault during the OPSEU imbroglio had to be shared with the staff in the premier's office. Someone close to the premier deliberately sought to inflame the situation by threatening the use of replacement workers. Just as in the Bill 26 crisis, the group around the premier had pushed too hard on an issue, enraging the opposition and causing even supporters of the government to wonder at its tactics, not to mention its humanity. And once again, the premier's staff had to be rescued. Behind the scenes, Johnson let the premier's office know in no uncertain terms that he was in charge of negotiations, and he would manage this strike. Harris agreed. From that moment on, Johnson became the public face of the government as far as the strike was concerned. There would be no more false leaks, no more embarrassing quotes.

As the lion of March arrived, and the strike quickly spread and deepened, Ontarians discovered the extent—or lack—of their dependence on the provincial public service. For a while, meat shortages were feared, as provincial meat inspectors walked off the job. But other plants, which used federal inspectors, were able to keep the shelves filled. Transferring property, getting a driver's licence or birth certificate, checking for liens against a vehicle and other regulatory chores all became difficult or impossible. But these aren't activities people pursue every day, and a general suspension of the regulatory rules by the Tories got most people through the period. Poorly plowed highways offered the most visible evidence of the strike, and several spring-blizzard pile-ups were blamed, by the government and the union, on each other's perfidy. Welfare recipients lost access to their case workers, but they got their cheques nonetheless.

A strike is a contest in which a union attempts to make it so costly for the employer to function that it accedes to the union's demands, while the employer seeks to carry on despite the picket lines until the workers are forced to return to their jobs. During the public-service strike, the services most needed were provided, thanks to the essential services agreements; the services not provided turned out not to be needed by most citizens. But the Tories didn't have things their own way entirely. For one thing, the picket lines were firmer than the government had believed possible. Only about 5,000 workers, or 10 per cent of the union, crossed the lines during the strike. This was a considerable achievement, considering the traditional lack of militancy by most OPSEU members, and considering the 10,000 picket lines it had to maintain across the province. The union didn't succeed everywhere; at one location in midtown Toronto, all the workers in a government office simply decided to stay on their jobs, and did. (The union didn't seem to notice.) But for the most part, the picket lines held.

In the early days of the strike, there was a notorious lack of picket-line discipline. After a week, however, things toughened up, and getting into government buildings became considerably more of an ordeal, involving, at the minimum, a fifteen-minute wait before picketers would let a pedestrian or car through. That toughening coincided with the arrival on the picket lines of teachers, auto workers, and steelworkers. These more experienced unions decided they couldn't afford to let OPSEU crumble in the first major confrontation between labour and the Harris government.

The government also came to regret its emergency services agreement with the jail guards. At provincial prisons the picket lines were brutal things to cross. Guards who showed up for work often caused more harm than good, vandalizing their own work places, and inciting the inmates to violence. Mini-riots became a chronic problem. Lack of proper supervision probably led to a riot among young offenders at the province's Bluewater facility. When the youths were transferred to another facility, they were beaten by guards, causing a public outcry. Six months later, sixteen-year-old James Lonnee, who co-operated with police in the investigation of the Bluewater incident and later complained he was being beaten by fellow inmates for talking, was killed in jail. The public-service strike may have been one, albeit indirect, cause of his death.

The disturbance that caught everyone's attention, however, didn't occur in any jail, but right in front of the legislature, on the morning of March 18. "The riot at Queen's Park," as it became known, was the most spectacular clash before the legislature ever seen. And the most unnecessary.

March 18 was neither the first nor the most destructive confrontation between demonstrators and the Mike Harris government. Police had drawn blood during the protest over the throne speech back in September. And on February 7, only a few weeks earlier, student demonstrators had smashed through the front doors of the legislative building, wreaking tens of thousands of dollars of damage. The vandals were a militant minority of the 800 protesters who were demonstrating against the hikes in tuition fees. In a matter of minutes, they ripped from their anchors the metal barricades protecting the front entrance. When police retreated into the building, the students used a concrete ashtray pedestal to smash through two sets of barred doors, then poured into the ornate, red-carpeted lobby of the legislature, where some twenty police, now the last visible line of defence, barred their way.

After twenty tense minutes of stalemate, with the protesters shouting defiance and defacing walls and furniture while the police held their ground, the protesters retreated with the constabulary in pursuit. Four students—two of them from high school—were charged with break and enter and mischief and with intimidating the legislature. (This last, obscure, charge was later dropped.) It cost the province $20,000 to restore the lobby and repair the doors. Yet these acts of violence and vandalism by protesters who appeared bent on storming the seat of provincial government provoked remarkably little public outcry. Things would be different when the striking public servants blocked the entrances to the legislature.

With the exception of the one-day sitting January 29 to pass the omnibus bill, Ontario's legislative assembly had been in recess since before Christmas. But everyone knew—indeed, there were numerous press reports warning of it—that OPSEU and its allies would stage some kind of major demonstration when the legislature resumed sitting at 1:30 p.m. on Monday March 18. The question was, would the strikers try to keep the MPPs from entering the building?

The answer to this question became evident early Monday morning when staff arriving at Queen's Park found the only entrance to the legislature completely blocked by demonstrators. For security reasons, both the centre and west gates had been closed throughout the strike, making the east gate the only way to enter the building directly. By dawn Monday, that entrance was surrounded by hundreds of demonstrators, most of them teachers and steelworkers. Steelworkers also guarded the subway entrance to Queen's Park—called "scab alley," it had been a convenient way for strikebreakers to get to work, until the steelworkers shut it down—as well as the entrances to the adjacent office complex, where much of the provincial bureaucracy worked.[5]

Anyone who wanted to enter the legislature or the office blocks that morning had to join a long line at the east gate waiting to be allowed through the picketers. Every fifteen minutes or so, a few people in the line would be permitted to go inside. While they waited, they were subjected to taunts, jeers, screams, ear-piercing whistles, and general intimidation. The rules weren't firm; at times the entrance to the legislature was blocked completely, at times reporters were spirited through the lines, the better to observe and report on the demo.

Fearing just such an obstruction, some MPPs and senior staff had spent the night in their offices. Others, who had arrived at five or six a.m., found the lines were already up, but were able to get in through various entrances. Soon, however, the entrances to all the office buildings of the precinct were blocked, and employees had no option but to run the gauntlet at the east gate, where

---

[5] Queen's Park officially consists of the legislative building, the grounds that surround it, and several large office blocks to the east of the legislature, one of which is the Whitney Block. All the blocks are linked to one another, and linked as well, through underground tunnels, both to the Queen's Park subway station and the legislature.

more and more people gathered and the congestion and confusion grew. Although the crowd was noisy and the atmosphere intimidating, the situation wasn't violent. However, unknown to strikers, staff, and politicians, a critical breakdown in communication had occurred among the several police forces on the scene.

Policing at Queen's Park had always been a knotty affair. Three different kinds of police were responsible for the security of the building. Fifty special constables of the Ontario Government Protective Service, or OGPS, handled routine security. They were under the direction of six OPP officers, seconded to the legislature to supervise its security. But the OPP officers answered, confusingly, both to their regular superiors and to the Speaker and his staff. This meant that the police officers at Queen's Park took orders, in part, from superiors who had no training in policing. To make matters even more muddled, the OPP's responsibility extended only to the building itself. The grounds outside the building, where demonstrations and protests took place, were the responsibility of the Metro Toronto Police. Yet there was no formal co-ordination between the two forces—quite the opposite. Metro Police and the OPP tended to resent the other's presence.

Both forces had a policy of not helping strikebreakers proceed through picket lines, a stance that angered the Tories, who felt that Metro Police, especially, were on the side of the strikers. "Their leadership was disreputable," one adviser to Harris later complained bitterly. "To serve and protect the public was a joke. To serve and protect the Ontario Public Service Employees Union was the joke in our office." In refusing to help workers cross picket lines, however, both Metro Police and the OPP were following a long-established policy of neutrality during strikes. They monitored picket lines in case of violence and would create a passage through a line in an emergency. To do more, police claimed, would be to favour the employer in a labour dispute.

The OPP, however, viewed the legislature as a special case, which it was, in two senses. First, blocking access to the legislature for its elected representatives by any means borders on treason. The legislature of the province is sovereign; its representatives and the representatives of the Crown are the embodiment of the people and their government and must not be intimidated by anyone. Furthermore, the OPP at the legislature answered to the Speaker. And Speaker Al McLean saw it as his job to ensure that Ontario's parliament functioned, strike or no strike. So when he ordered the OPP to produce action plans to ensure all MPPs made it into the legislature on March 18, the OPP complied. Those plans included the use, if necessary, of force.

Management Board, in its strike preparations, had never envisioned the use of police to force a breach in a picket line. Its preferred tactic was to seek a court injunction ordering OPSEU to let workers through. OPSEU generally respected court orders. In the days leading up to March 18, as it became clear the legislature would become a focus of protest, staff at the Management Board contacted McLean's office to see whether the Speaker wanted advice or help on planning for the day. The offer was rebuffed; McLean felt that taking Management Board advice would violate his neutrality.

Thus, as the fateful day approached, several separate entities formed conflicting plans: the government, OPSEU, Metro Police, and the OPP. The government, the union, and the Metro Police assumed that the same rules of engagement would be followed that had obtained throughout the strike—pickets and temporary blockages, with the government ready to seek a court injunction if things became too frustrating. OPSEU looked on the legislature as just another office building and planned to block access as much as possible. In this, the union was simply extrapolating from the status quo, since McLean had been tolerating pickets at the legislature for weeks, even though they had at times become quite obstreperous.

The union had no way of knowing that McLean and the OPP had decided that with the return of the legislature on March 18, the rules would change. If necessary the OPP's riot squad, offically known as the Crowd Management Unit, would create a cordon that would guarantee the MPPs could get through the strikers. Not only was such a use of force unprecedented, it's doubtful, in retrospect, whether McLean had the legal authority, as a building manager, to order the police to use force during a labour dispute. But even more mind-boggling, having made these preparations, McLean and the OPP *didn't tell anyone*. They didn't warn OPSEU or the government that the rules of engagement had changed, that crowd-control police would be brought in. They didn't even bother to advise the Metro Toronto Police. It was positively Strangelovian: a weapon of deterrence had been created without the other side being informed that the weapon existed.

On Monday morning, Metro Toronto Police were appalled to find the OPP riot squad, complete with Darth Vader helmets, shields, truncheons, and pepper spray, present at the Park. At one point, with several dozen MPPs congregated and waiting for access, Metro officers pleaded with their OPP counterparts to attempt a parley with the OPSEU picketers. Perhaps they could be persuaded to let the MPPs through. The OPP agreed, Metro Police made their pitch, and the MPPs were led in peacefully. But that hopeful precedent failed to set a pattern. Increasingly, the OPSEU strike marshals lost control of the pickets, many of them from the Steelworkers union.

Around 11:30 a.m., after Metro Police were unable to convince picketers to let a group of MPPs enter through the south entrance of the Whitney Block, the OPP riot squad prepared to move in. Witnesses said they heard the police beating their shields and vowing to "whack 'em and stack 'em" as they got ready to engage the strikers. When the vans containing the MPPs returned, this time at the north entrance of Whitney, the riot squad deployed, using their shields and batons to shove the picketers aside. Those who resisted received a smart whack to their knees. One picketer was struck on the head by a truncheon on its backswing—accidentally, it appears— and fell senseless to the ground. Members of the legislature were forced to step over his recumbent body on their way into the building. And television cameras caught it all.

OPSEU marshals, as horrified as the Metro Police at the OPP's tactics, offered to help arrange safe passage for MPPs. But before their offer could be taken up, the riot squad deployed again, this time at the Frost Building, forcing a passage through hundreds of screaming protesters so that several vanloads of MPPs could get through. In this instance, Metro Police officers assisted, though they kept their batons sheathed.

By two p.m., with the bulk of the MPPs safely inside, the forces of OPSEU and it allies began to disperse, and the situation outside the legislature gradually returned to normal. But things were anything but normal inside. During the throne-speech fracas back in September, MPPs had voiced their outrage at not being allowed into the legislature. Now the opposition was incensed at the steps taken to get them in. Opposition leaders demanded a public inquiry. "Nothing that happened on that picket line warranted the excessive force that we saw used," protested Liberal leader Lyn McLeod. "We're speaking in the legislature about crimes by the police," charged renegade NDP MPP Peter Kormos, seldom a stranger to inflammatory rhetoric. At first, Harris wasn't inclined to grant the opposition wish, saying he wanted to wait for a report from the office of the Speaker. But on March 20, when it became clear the other parties were going to hammer at the issue indefinitely—while trying somehow to link the government to the actions of police—Harris made a quick, smart decision.

As late as noon that day, the premier's staff were advising him against a public inquiry; it would simply drag out the unpleasant event for weeks or months, they feared. But in the House that afternoon, the opposition was once again feasting on the issue. They cried "Shame!" and "Whitewash!" as a shaken Al McLean recommended that a parliamentary committee study the affair. Eves, whose desk is beside Harris's, huddled with the premier for a few moments, then rose to announce the government agreed a public inquiry was necessary. Mikey and Ernie had gone and made policy on their own again. The announcement stunned MPPs on both sides of the House. "We are not looking for a public inquiry in order to have the government be able to sweep all of the questions under the rug," a nonplussed McLeod asserted, desperately searching for something to complain about. The premier's staff were no less bemused.

The inquiry, a one-person affair conducted by former Supreme Court justice Willard Estey, began hearings in May, but didn't deliver its report until the following year in the middle of the megacity mess, where it got lost in the fuss of the moment. In his conclusions, Estey meted out blame to all sides, but aimed his most probing criticism at McLean and the OPP. He questioned McLean's judgment in ordering police to prepare extreme measures, noting that he probably lacked the authority and certainly lacked the experience to supervise such a police action. He also criticized the OPP for planning and carrying out the action without warning or consulting anyone in advance. He recommended that in future the OPP be removed entirely from the responsibility of policing Queen's Park, and its operations handed over to Metro Police. In response, Speaker Chris Stockwell has indicated that Queen's Park will create its own, independently managed, security service.

The good news for all sides was that the violence at Queen's Park had no real effect on the negotiations between OPSEU and Management Board; talks had continued, on and off, throughout the strike and were, by the time of the March 8 riot, starting to show some progress. Those close to the talks could see an eventual end, if not around the corner, at least down the road.

As the strike entered its fifth week, both the government and the union found themselves surprised at how long it was lasting. The Tories had been convinced OPSEU would bow to the inevitable and accept the final offer—with a couple of small face-saving sops added—after a few days on the crumbling picket line. OPSEU's determination to stay the course, and its ability to keep those picket lines going, rattled the government strategists who monitored the progress of the dispute. Management Board representatives had repeatedly gone to the Ontario Labour Relations Board in hopes of forcing meat inspectors back to their jobs and prison guards to curb their subversive actions, but the board had sided with the union—a lesson the government would bear in mind when amalgamating school boards and municipalities a year later. And the police, as far as the Tories were concerned, were behaving like de facto allies of the union.

Moreover, although it was hidden from the public, the situation at the province's ten psychiatric hospitals was seriously deteriorating. Patients were receiving food, shelter, medication, and little else, but they had far greater needs. "The patients were really starting to suffer," one senior government source conceded. "The situation in the hospitals had become a real problem." Meanwhile, co-ordinators at the government's strike headquarters reported that, after five weeks, the managers who were trying to keep the public service running were exhausted and frustrated.

Nonetheless, Management Board staff and government negotiators believed they still had the necessary reserves to carry on the strike for several more weeks. Their ultimate weapon, back-to-work legislation, was not even close to being used. Such legislation usually includes arbitration, but the Tories theoretically could have ordered the workers back and simply imposed a contract on them. Such a heavy-handed tactic would have revealed the government to be both desperate and dictatorial. It would have repudiated the Tories' stated commitment to collective bargaining and would have poisoned the labour environment in government offices for years to come. Still, the government was ready to resort to legislation rather than admit defeat; its strike strategy always envisioned such legislation as a last resort. But even as the fifth week of the strike began, government negotiators had been given no inkling that cabinet might wield the legislative club. It seemed that the Tories were prepared to tough it out a while longer. The same, however, could not be said of the union.

Several factors had conspired to make it necessary for OPSEU to settle the strike. First and foremost, its strategy had failed. The leadership had hoped the government would find itself unable to function without its unionized workers, that ministries would seize up without public servants to process the paper work, that the wrong people would get welfare cheques, that provincial jails would become so many Atticas, that supermarkets would start to run low on meat and eggs, that highways would become impassable. But the union had negotiated too much away with its essential services agreements. The provincial public sector, though tattered and frayed, continued to function with relatively minor inconvenience to the general public.

The second factor undermining OPSEU's resolve was the government's failure to bring in back-to-work legislation. All along, union leaders had hoped that the Tories would become so frustrated they would use the legislative hammer, then send the contract dispute to arbitration. The union knew the government could simply legislate its preferred contract, but the leadership was banking on the Tories' unwillingness to endure the radioactive work places such an action would create.

As the strike dragged on, however, it became increasingly clear that the government was coping without most of its workers, and that a legislated end was not yet in the cards. Governments usually introduce back-to-work legislation because the public becomes so annoyed by service disruptions that constituents complain to their MPPs, who pressure cabinet to end the strike. But more than a month into the strike, the Tory caucus was, if anything, more militant than the Management Board. At one meeting, when the government's chief negotiator, Peace, appeared before the caucus, he was denounced by the MPPs for giving too much away and had to be rescued by Johnson.

Worst of all, OPSEU found itself once again outmaneuvered by the Management Board, whose negotiators were simultaneously bargaining with a smaller public-service union, the 5,000-member Association of Management, Administrative and Professional Crown Employees of Ontario (AMAPCEO), the unionized middle managers of the public service. On March 12, four days after the Queen's Park riots, reporters learned of a recently inked tentative deal between AMAPCEO and the government that essentially mirrored the last offer of the government to OPSEU, with a few added sweeteners. Once the AMAPCEO deal was made public, it was obvious to most observers that the tentative agreement foretold the shape of the final settlement with OPSEU. Striking workers increasingly and publicly asked their union leaders why it was taking so long to reach a similar deal. "It hurt us," Casselman acknowledges. "The bargaining teams did a lot of soul-searching at that point." The embittered president still hasn't forgiven the AMAPCEO leadership. "They've got a lot to learn about trade unionism," she maintains. "The employer used them masterfully. If they'd come to us and talked, we could have got a good deal for both of us."

Finally, the union was hurting financially. The strikers had received their last government pay cheque by the third week of the walkout and were now living on about $100 a week strike pay. The union had drained its $3 million in reserves and was financing the pay with $30 million in loan guarantees from other unions. At a weekly cost of about $5 million, the longer the workers stayed out, the more they would have to contribute to pay back the loans. Since there would be at least 13,000 fewer of them, the burden would be even more severe.

On Friday March 30, five weeks after the strike began, both sides announced a tentative deal. It had almost been scuppered at the last moment. Though the outline of an agreement had been in place two days before, angry senior bureaucrats in the Ministry of the Solicitor General and some hotheads in the premier's office insisted on the right to lay criminal charges against any jail guards who might have incited violence and intimidated workers. The union, in response, demanded immunity from all strike-related crimes. Throughout Friday morning and early afternoon both sides refused to budge, as despairing negotiators watched their tentative agreement slipping away. At the last minute, however, Dave Johnson contacted Solicitor General Bob Runciman. Both agreed the jail guards weren't worth prolonging the strike for. They in turn telephoned David Lindsay, and convinced him it was time to declare victory and move on. Lindsay agreed, Harris gave the nod, and the deal was done.

At a Friday afternoon press conference, Casselman put the best possible face on the situation. "It's an agreement that many said was impossible," she told cheering supporters. "Public-sector workers have made major gains." In fact, they had won a slightly more generous severance package than the "final offer" of February and minimally increased protection for privatized workers. They had not restored the successor rights they lost in legislation, and they had been forced to give up most of their bumping rights. The government was free to begin laying off workers and contracting out services. One year later, it had already eliminated 11,500 jobs.

There is an imperative to some strikes that defies logic and can only be understood by the heart. The OPSEU strike was driven by such an imperative. The union could have won virtually all of the concessions it eventually won without a strike, something Casselman and her advisers knew. But a union cannot agree to the loss of 13,000 of its members and a raft of job-security concessions without a protest. The strike was as much a gesture of defiance as a negotiating tactic. Pesce likened it to the Second World War. "There was no way to stop that war. Nothing Neville Chamberlain could have done would have prevented it. It just had to happen." The public servants' strike of 1996 had to happen.

And, just as inevitably, the government had to win.

CHAPTER 8

Rolling Heads

On May 8, 1996, after two years of waiting, and eleven months after the election of the Harris government, Ontario finally got a new budget. But Finance Minister Ernie Eves' first formal financial accounting was an anticlimactic document. The good news, a 30 per cent reduction in the marginal tax rate (the first tax cut in Ontario in twenty-five years), with the first phase to kick in July 1, had long been anticipated. The bad news, the cuts to spending needed to finance the reduction in taxes, had already been announced in various economic statements and business plans. Even the loosening of gambling restrictions was expected, confirming that modern Ontario governments are addicted to gambling regardless of political stripe. When Bob Rae was in opposition, he had criticized lotteries as a tax on the poor, who were most likely to play them. Once in office, he opened the province's first casino in Windsor and approved another for the Rama reservation, near Orillia, moves Mike Harris in opposition denounced as a government tax grab disguised as entertainment. But in office, Harris approved a third casino, for Niagara Falls, and Eves' first budget legalized electronic slot machines in bars and up to fifty permanent fixed-site charity casinos. The Tories' weak excuse for surrendering to the sin of wagering was that illegal gambling had become so rampant that legalization represented the only means of controlling the trade.

As also expected, the budget revealed a rapidly shrinking deficit. The deficit for fiscal 1995–96, just ended, had come in at

$9.1 billion, a good $2.1 billion below what it might have been without cuts. Eves now projected a 1996–97 deficit of $8.2 billion and reiterated the government's pledge to reach a balanced budget by the year 2000.

One year into his mandate, Mike Harris could survey the political landscape from a pinnacle of political success. He had carried out all the earth-shaking commitments required for the opening stage of his revolution. He had shifted the bias in labour law away from the union and towards the employer, weathered and won the province's first public-service strike, pushed through his enormous omnibus enabling legislation, and set his government solidly on the road to health-care reform. And through it all, he had retained his popularity. An Angus Reid poll released in early June put the Tories at 53 per cent support, eight points above the vote they received in the 1995 election. Most of the province appeared ready to accept, and possibly even welcome, the Tory medicine.

Mike Harris, however, had no intention of slowing down. "We've only just begun," he vowed on June 27, as the legislature finally recessed for the summer, a year and a day after the Tories took office. As if to prove the point, Municipal Affairs Minister Al Leach had introduced only two days before a policy paper promising a graduated end to rent controls.

For two decades, the province had struggled to manipulate supply and demand in the rental market through price controls, a policy that had been introduced by Bill Davis on the fly during the 1975 election. NDP leader Stephen Lewis had so nurtured public sympathy during that campaign with horror stories of the poor and elderly forced out of their apartments because of steep rent increases that Davis was forced to announce the abrupt policy shift to win back eroding urban support. For the next two decades, all three parties struggled in vain to develop a rental policy that worked. No one was willing to suggest abolishing rent controls entirely, but without the discipline of the market to regulate supply and demand, construction of new rental housing dried up, existing supplies deteriorated, and vacancy rates plummetted. The worse the distortions became, the more painful the adjustment promised to be.

Leach proposed that rent controls remain on all units with existing tenants. Once a tenant vacated a unit, however, the landlord could set whatever rent the market would bear. Housing experts predicted that within five years, most apartments in the province would be renting at market value.

The elimination of rent controls, however gradual, should have been greeted with a storm of protests by tenants. Fear of such protests had kept previous governments from making the move. And tenant activists promised to fight "tooth and nail" against the new scheme. But the protests never materialized. It may have been that the same protesters who would have manned the barricades over rent control were already at the barricades fighting other Harris government policies. It may have been that most renters, after suffering two decades of lousy maintenance and near-zero vacancy rates, were ready to try their luck on the open market. Whatever the reason, the new tenancy legislation, finally introduced in November 1996, reached second reading in June 1997 with, comparatively speaking, nary a whimper.

With the MPPs back in their constituencies—a sure sign of the arrival of summer—Mike Harris asked his principal secretary David Lindsay to undertake a month-long review of cabinet, mostly from a cottage on Lake Simcoe. The centrepiece of the review was an interview with each cabinet minister, a sort of job-performance evaluation, which Lindsay conducted by telephone from a doughnut shop in Jackson's Point, there being no phone available at the cottage. By mid-August, Harris was ready to shuffle.

On August 16, the premier announced two major changes to his cabinet and one minor adjustment. Community and Social Services Minister Dave Tsubouchi was transferred to the less onerous ministry of Consumer and Commercial Relations. Janet Ecker, until now Tsubouchi's parliamentary secretary, took his place. Brenda Elliott, former minister of Environment and Energy, was dropped from cabinet altogether. She was replaced by veteran Norm Sterling, who moved from Consumer and Commercial Relations. As well, Dave Johnson lightened Ernie Eves' load by assuming the role of House Leader; Cam Jackson ended his job as minister without portfolio responsible for workers' compensation and started work as minister without portfolio responsible for seniors, and Rob Sampson, member for Mississauga West, joined the cabinet as minister without portfolio in charge of privatization.

Of these changes, the least surprising was the demotion of Tsubouchi, whose landing was far gentler than many had predicted for him. In the Tories' first year in power, the Social Services minister had caused the government more embarrassment than any other member of executive council. Tsubouchi was kept in cabinet, in part, because he was the only member of a visible minority in the Tory benches, and because Harris accepted that the rookie minister had faced an impossible task.

As minister supposedly responsible for delivering succour to the poorest in society, Tsubouchi's mandate had been, in fact, to increase their hardship. It was he who was charged with slicing the income of welfare recipients by 21.6 per cent; he who was charged with forcing them to work for the money that was left. The situation would have been difficult enough for the most adept and experienced of politicians. But even though Tsubouchi was, in fact, more experienced than most in his caucus, having served on Markham council for six years, he seemed to have learned nothing while there, at least in regard to debate. On the floor of the House, the performance of the bearded, mild-mannered amateur poet and actor was fumbling, repetitive, sometimes almost incoherent. "Well, Mr. Speaker . . ." he would begin, like an actor who had forgotten his lines, desperately improvising while he waited for a prompt. None came.

The opposition would have targeted Social Services as a key area of attack regardless of who held the portfolio. But when it became apparent that Tsubouchi was the weakest actor in the Tory cast, they tore into him with the gusto of undergraduate film critics. On the Liberal benches, the charge was often led by

Dominic Agostino, the newly elected member for Hamilton East. Agostino's body-builder physique, combined with a Steeltown pugnacity and almost infinite capacity for self-promotion, served him well in the early days of the legislature. His breathless depictions of single mothers driven to despair by Conservative heartlessness left Tsubouchi constantly on the defensive.

But Tsubouchi's great bane during those first months of the legislative session in the fall of 1995 was Bob Rae. The former premier had returned from his post-defeat summer vacation rested and not in the least chastened by having been reduced by the voters from majority government to third party. It was universally understood that Rae would soon step down as leader, probably in 1996. (He eventually resigned his seat on January 29, the day the legislature passed Bill 26.) But until then, the caucus was in no hurry to see him go. The former Rhodes scholar remained a formidable debater, the best orator in the House, and knowledgeable as only someone who has been premier can be. Rae made Tsubouchi's life hell.

On October 3, 1995, Rae rose in the legislature for his first question of the day. The Liberals had already been hammering away at a recent Tsubouchi gaffe; the minister had advised shoppers on welfare that they could absorb his government's cuts by buying dented tins of food or waiting for tuna to go on sale for sixty-nine cents. Now Rae rose, right hand in jacket pocket, as was his custom, and solicitously asked Tsubouchi if he knew just where one might find tuna at such a low, low price. (Across the province, editors had already sent reporters scurrying to supermarkets in search of sixty-nine-cent tuna. Some store managers put the stuff on sale in response to the publicity. This may have been the first time a Social Services minister was able to influence the price of a commodity.)

Any first-year spin doctor knew Rae's question was a trap. A competent politician would simply sidestep it: "Mr. Speaker, the question is not really how much this costs or how much that costs, but how this province can escape the deficit monster the honourable member opposite unleashed on the people . . ." and so on. Instead, Tsubouchi assured the leader of the third party that tuna was commonly available at that price. "In fact," he added helpfully, "even if it's not priced at sixty-nine cents, quite often you can make a deal to get it for sixty-nine cents."

After a moment's stunned silence, the House erupted. The sounds might have resembled outrage to those listening in on television, but in fact most members were roaring with laughter, including government backbenchers, several of whom looked up at the incredulous reporters in the gallery and shook their heads in woe. The only people not laughing were Tsubouchi and Harris. The premier hunched forward in his chair, staring grimly at his desk. When Speaker Al McLean finally got the House to quiet down, Rae affected an air of bemusement. "I can honestly say I was not anticipating" the response, he told the House, "but I'd like to ask him, when was the last time he bartered for food?"

In the wake of such debacles, the Tories tried to improve the rookie minister's verbal fencing skills, bringing in a communications expert on a $25,000 contract. But her efforts produced little visible effect, and within a few weeks of the tuna incident, Tsubouchi was at it again, this time apologizing to the House after *Toronto Star* reporter Kelly Toughill pointed out to him that new regulations would cut welfare payments for 115,000 people with disabilities, something the Tories had promised not to do. In his apology Tsubouchi lamely claimed that the cuts were inadvertent. A patently angry Harris berated his own minister in front of reporters. "That's no way to run a government and it better not happen again," he warned.

By the end of the fall session, the Social Services minister was a marked man. He had made too many gaffes, parried questions from politicians and reporters with too little skill. He exuded an air of confusion and fear, the very opposite of the take-charge attitude the government wanted to convey. As one observer of the Queen's Park culture has noted about the key to success for rookie MPPs, "It is not necessary to be right all the time, but to be right about important things most of the time, and to know that the important things are often the small things. It is also important not to make the same mistake twice, and to stop making mistakes altogether after an initial grace period."[1] By Christmas, the grace period for Tsubouchi had expired. He bided his time and waited for the shuffle.

In the end, Tsubouchi simply lacked the necessary ruthlessness for his portfolio. A right-wing government imposing right-wing policies brands itself a hypocrite if it uses the terminology of the Left. When Solicitor General Bob Runciman closed halfway houses for inmates, he was unapologetic. It wasn't his job, he said, "to provide Holiday Inn-type accommodation for people who have broken the law." Had Tsubouchi been equally frank, had he shot back at Rae and Agostino that taxpayers were tired of seeing their hard-earned money handed over to people who sit at home and do nothing, he would at least have displayed the courage of his party's convictions. Instead he mumbled, offered inane advice, and sank his future in the ministry. After the August 1996 shuffle he was rarely heard from again.

Brenda Elliott's demotion was also no surprise. Government insiders had been prepping the press gallery for it for weeks, quietly hinting to reporters that Elliott was "lacklustre," that she made no impact at the cabinet table, that her ministry was moving too slowly on environmental deregulation. The gallery swallowed these pronouncements and duly regurgitated them. When government advisers, who are there to offer a positive spin to the most dismal disasters, disparage one of their own cabinet ministers, journalists assume the truth must be at least as bad as the allegation. Yet the quiet character assassination of Elliott was, in some respects, surprising. Just how had she failed to perform?

Granted, Environment carried a much lower profile under the Tories than it had in previous governments. Under Ruth Grier for the NDP and Jim Bradley for David Peterson, it was a

---

[1] An anonymous source, quoted by Carolyn Thomson in her essay "'This Place': The Culture of Queen's Park," *Inside the Pink Palace: Ontario Legislature Internship Essays* (Toronto: Ontario Legislature Internship Programme/The Canadian Political Science Association, 1993), p. 5.

powerhouse ministry, with a hefty budget, a sheaf of regulations and legislation regularly before the public and the House. Since taking power, the Tories have slashed the Environment ministry's budget by 37 per cent and staff by 31 per cent. But all ministries had suffered serious cutbacks. Over at the related Ministry of Natural Resources, Chris Hodgson lost 30 per cent of his personnel and a quarter of his budget, while being praised—at least inside government—as a tough, competent minister.

The environment was bound to have a smaller role in a Harris government, regardless of who was in charge. Harris is a conservationist rather than an environmentalist. As a hunter, fisher, and tourist-resort operator, he sees the natural environment as a resource to be husbanded, to be carefully managed and preserved for future use, not simply protected for its own sake. While some environmentalists believe that humankind has invaded and despoiled what should be the sovereign preserve of nature, threatening both its survival and ours, Harris sees many environmental regulations as simply unnecessary disincentives to business. The environment, under a Harris government, is something to be monitored and regulated, but the regulations are relatively few, and monitoring largely up to those being monitored. The important thing is to keep the lakes clean and well stocked with game fish, the air as pure as you can get it without shutting down the factories, and the woods healthy enough to sustain forestry, hunting, and tourism.

Elliott did her best to fulfill these goals, loosening restrictions on garbage incineration, closing branch offices (the regional office for Muskoka is now in Thunder Bay, which is closer to Manitoba than to central Ontario), cutting regulatory red tape and staff. Yet in the premier's office, there was dissatisfaction that the minister was not moving fast enough and a feeling that she lacked political judgment.

This lack of judgment manifested itself most obviously in her choice of staff, where Elliott showed neither good political radar nor an eye for talent. Some of her political staff advised her poorly and failed to connect with their counterparts in the premier's office.

There were accusations of cronyism and incompetence. And when Elliott began replacing individuals and reducing their number in an attempt to improve her standing, her choice of a former campaign worker as executive assistant only deepened the suspicions.

Elliott also had a cross to bear in Ontario Hydro. As minister of Energy, she was responsible for the utility, even though it operates at arm's length as a Crown corporation. But the biggest challenge facing the energy utility, under the Harris government, is whether all or part of it should be sold off, in hopes of improving competitiveness and lowering rates. To get answers, Harris appointed his friend and former fund raiser, Bill Farlinger, as chair of the utility. Farlinger had direct access to the premier, bypassing the Energy minister and weakening her authority.

Another, subtle, factor that may have influenced Harris's decision to fire Elliott must be mentioned. She is a girl in what is still very much a boy's club. Being a woman does not disqualify you from Mike Harris's confidence: Elizabeth Witmer was already a powerful minister, and Janet Ecker, after her penance, was about to become one. But male cabinet ministers who got themselves into at least as much trouble as Elliott had during the Tories' first year got off much more lightly. John Snobelen had embarrassed himself with the "invent a crisis" video, and failed to come up with a "toolkit" of education reforms, yet he survived with his portfolio intact. Tsubouchi was demoted in the shuffle, but not fired. Only Elliott got the axe. Her fall may have been the result of personality and gender as well as competence. At times of crisis, collegiality can be a vital asset to a worker. The ability to fit in and get along can serve as powerful protection against mediocre performance. Elliott lacked not only the necessary savvy of a political operator, she was not one of the self-made men Harris likes around him. Nor did she possess the social warmth that might have helped her form a bond with her boss. Brenda Elliott lost her job, not simply because her performance in her portfolio was weak and because she displayed bad political judgment but, perhaps, because she could never be Mike's friend. The combination proved fatal.

August of 1996 witnessed one other change in the positions of power in the Ontario government. Speaker Al McLean was pushed from his chair by allegations of sexual harassment and by Harris's own lack of support.

A Simcoe County farmer by profession, McLean had won the Speaker's chair, with the support of the rural members of the Tory caucus, over Margaret Marland, the member for Mississauga South. But he had proved an indifferent Speaker at best, displaying a delightful talent for malapropisms—he repeatedly referred to the omnibus bill as the "ominous bill"—and a penchant for referring to the honourable members as "youze" that did nothing to enhance his tenuous control of the legislature. The thirty-sixth parliament of Ontario was bound to be a fractious place, no matter who was in the chair, but McLean was clearly out of his depth. Under his rule, Question Period regularly descended into a shouting match, during which opposition members openly derided the Speaker for his timidity. Back in December 1995, McLean's indecisiveness over the opposition's refusal to vote on Bill 26 had led to the stand-off that weakened his own credibility as much as the government's. Worst of all, his mishandling of security arrangements before the March 18 confrontation at the legislature helped contribute to the debacle. Testimony at the Estey inquiry had already criticized McLean's decision to change the security rules as one of the chief causes of the fiasco.

But the Speaker serves at the pleasure of the House, which means in a majority government he serves at the pleasure of the administration, and Harris had shown no signs he wanted McLean to leave, despite his troubles—until Sandi Thompson, a former staffer in McLean's office, filed a complaint of sexual harassment against him. She would later charge that she had engaged in a brief sexual relationship with McLean and that when she tried to end it, he threatened to fire her. After Thompson went public with her complaint, newspapers circulated stories of other complaints about the Speaker.

"Oh God. They're sure trying to crucify me," McLean moaned to a reporter who contacted him about the allegations. It was not a dignified response, but then McLean had hardly cut a dignified figure during his time in the chair. Finally Harris had had enough.

Unlike many American neo-conservatives, Mike Harris and his advisers have steered away from espousing what are called "family values"—conservative Christian attitudes to sex and marriage—and with good reason. Conservative moral values do not necessarily equate with neo-conservative attitudes towards government. To be logically consistent, neo-conservatives must believe that government should play the smallest possible role in all aspects of society, the moral as well as the economic. Harris and his advisers believe, philosophically, in keeping the state out of both the boardroom and the bedroom. Furthermore, family-values conservatives oppose premarital, adulterous, and homo-sexual relationships, yet Harris and his advisers knew full well that all three could be found in the government. Harris himself is on his second marriage. Should the premier ever mount a holier-than-thou platform, his advisers feared he might be hanged on it. And their refusal to be caught sermonizing has served them well. When Transportation Minister Al Palladini's involvement in a palimony suit became public in November 1995, the opposition didn't even try to paint the unseemly affair as typical Tory sleaze. Harris stood by Palladini, allegedly saying that if everyone in cab-inet who had committed adultery were forced to resign, he might have trouble making quorum.

Harris's refusal to brand himself a social conservative has produced grumblings of discontent from suburban and rural Tory backbenchers. Many of them identify with American and some Canadian conservatives who espouse a minimalist state econom-ically, while trying to force prayer back into the classroom and homosexuals back into the closet. They resented it when Health Minister Jim Wilson and other Tories joined to defeat a private-member's bill, introduced by York Mackenzie MPP Frank Klees, that would have required doctors to consult with parents before providing treatment to anyone under sixteen. Then Attorney General Charles Harnick opposed a private-member's bill from

Scarborough West MPP Jim Brown that would have, among other things, imposed curfews on teen-agers. Led by Brown, about thirty MPPs have formed a semi-secret family-values caucus, whose members lobby cabinet for more action on their agenda and occasionally express their discontent to the media. As yet, they have exerted no visible influence on the government's agenda.

But Harris does believe in acting swiftly to contain crises related to character issues. He bounced Bill Vankoughnet from caucus, after the Frontenac-Addington MPP was picked up during a john sweep on Queen Street West. (Vankoughnet apparently offered the undercover cop posing as a prostitute his business card identifying himself as a member of provincial parliament.) Vankoughnet was readmitted after confessing his guilt and attending john school. When the sexual-harassment allegations against McLean surfaced, both House Leader Dave Johnson and Harris urged McLean to step aside until the matter was investigated. At first the Speaker fought back, launching allegations of his own against Thompson, hiring a private investigator, and making public the results of a lie-detector test that appeared to clear him.

However, without the support of the government, McLean's position was hopeless. On September 18, he announced he was temporarily leaving his post for reasons of health. When the legislature resumed on September 24, backbench Tories—the same ones who had got McLean elected and who stood by him to the end—won a delay on a vote to remove him as Speaker. But McLean, knowing the inevitable, submitted his resignation the next day.[2] A record eight candidates vied to replace him and it took seven ballots to elect, remarkably, Etobicoke MPP Chris Stockwell.

---

[2] Thompson has sued both McLean and the Legislative Assembly for wrongful dismissal, and filed a complaint with the Ontario Human Rights Commission. McLean denies all accusations of wrongdoing. Attempts at a negotiated settlement collapsed in June 1997. As this book went to press, the case remained before both the courts and the board, with legal costs to the taxpayer headed for the mid six figures.

Stockwell is a character. Hot-headed, opinionated, passion-ate, abrasive, he had a reputation in opposition as the most pugnacious heckler in the House and had displayed a visible lack of respect for Harris. The member for Etobicoke had publicly contemplated running for the leadership in 1990, because he felt the Nipissing MPP's agenda was too right-wing. Before the 1995 election, he opposed, in caucus, the Bradgate Group's plan to cut taxes while balancing the budget. And he made no secret of his suspicion that Harris wasn't too bright. "These days, anyone can become premier," he once joked.[3] Nonetheless, because he had been such an effective opposition critic, Stockwell had expected a cabinet post in 1995 and didn't hide his resentment when he was frozen out. For Harris, Stockwell presented a problem similar to the one that had confronted Bob Rae in 1990: what to do about a maverick caucus member. In Rae's case, the problem was Welland-Thorold MPP Peter Kormos, whose cowboy boots, Corvette, and radical left-wing views made him a charming but unpredictable rogue. Rae's solution was to put Kormos in cabi-net, following Lyndon Johnson's maxim that it's better to have a potential enemy inside the tent pissing out than outside the tent pissing in. To his dismay, Rae discovered that Kormos "ended up inside the tent pissing in."[4] Rae quickly fired him.

Harris had no intention of letting Stockwell get that close to power. When the first cabinet was named, Stockwell received nothing. Several weeks after the swearing-in, the frustrated MPP fumed about his exile over lunch in his favourite Italian restau-rant. "All right, so I'm not in cabinet," he complained. "But did they make me a parliamentary assistant? No. Did they even give me a committee to chair? No. And what committee did they put me on? The ombudsman committee!" (Many expletives have been deleted.)

But despite the freeze-out, Stockwell mostly held his tongue in public, hoping to make it into cabinet in round two. As rumours

[3] "Stockwell lands a job—and a jab," *Toronto Star* Oct. 4, 1996, p. C5.

[4] *From Protest to Power*, p. 134.

circulated in the summer of 1996 about an impending cabinet shuffle, he let it be known that he was ready and very, very willing to heed the call. When he was disappointed yet again, Stockwell figured he had nothing to lose when the speakership became vacant. On the surface, he looked like a very long shot, since Harris was known not to support him. But many backbench MPPs, angered by the leadership's abandonment of their friend McLean, resentful at having their family-values issues ignored, restless as backbench MPPs always are in a majority government, decided to remind their leader that they were not dead yet. When the vote result was announced, Harris, ashen-faced, quickly left the chamber.

Stockwell proved to be a good choice, quickly bringing the legislature under control. No one knows a heckler like a heckler, and Stockwell let the members know that, while fun was fun, the business of the House took precedence over theatrics. With firmness and humour, he kept both opposition and government members in line. He reined in Question Period, the most raucous part of the legislative day, by not hesitating to cut off opposition members whose questions went on too long, or ministers whose answers meandered. Under his guidance, the House became a more ordered place.

The most potentially damaging resignation to hit the Harris government came in December 1996, when wunderkind Health minister Jim Wilson was forced to step down. Not only did Harris lose a valuable minister and hand the opposition fresh ammunition, the resignation came in the midst of a fractious dispute with the province's doctors, a dispute the doctors eventually won.

Jim Wilson had been practising to be Health minister since he left university. The Wilsons were a solid, established family in Alliston, once a small town in Simcoe County that catered to potato farmers, now the home of the Honda auto-assembly plant and a bedroom community for Toronto. The Wilsons had roots in the Conservative Party stretching back 150 years. Wilson's great-great grandfather was a leader of the Conservative Party in the 1850s, and the Wilsons always helped deliver the area's

Catholic vote for the Conservatives. Young Jim, after flirting with the priesthood at university, joined his father working in the office of MPP George McCague, who became a cabinet minister in Bill Davis's later years. Soon after, he landed a job working for Perrin Beatty, then federal minister of Health. In 1990, he ran in McCague's old seat and joined the thin ranks of Mike Harris's Tory opposition, where he distinguished himself as health critic both for his intimate knowledge of the portfolio and for his apoplectic fits during Question Period. He face was known to literally go purple with indignation. Though he was only thirty-one when the Tories came to power, Wilson knew the Health portfolio like no one else, and Harris appointed him to the post.

Wilson combines a passion for work—his first boss forged his birth certificate so he could get a job while underage at the local IGA—with a keen intelligence and an amazing lack of discretion. All these qualities had been brought to bear during his tenure as Health minister, enabling him to push for reform in areas where previous governments had retreated in fear, but also leading him to consistently undermine his own best efforts.

Health is perhaps the most contentious portfolio in the Ontario government. It spends by far the most money: the $17.7-billion budget represented fully one-third of provincial spending in 1996–97. And the money goes to something that affects every citizen and becomes more vital the older one gets. Not surprisingly, the rhetoric surrounding the issue is often of the "lives are at risk" variety. Yet for all the passion that surrounds the health-care debate, there is, strangely, a surprising degree of consensus. Almost everyone in Ontario agrees that the province's public health-care system is a good thing and should be retained. Arguments for privatizing the system are relegated to the lunatic fringe of public debate. Universal public health care is a cornerstone of Canadian society, as it is of every major industrial society outside the United States.

There is also general agreement that the system, whatever its strengths, is not working at peak efficiency. Health-care costs in Ontario rose 227 per cent between 1984 and 1992, when spending was capped. The increases were partly the result of a society growing older, partly the result of poor cost control. Yet service has deteriorated. Waiting lists for heart surgery and cancer treatment have grown alarmingly. Between 1993 and 1997, according to the Cardiac Care Network of Ontario, the number of patients waiting for heart surgery doubled,[5] and by March 1997 the average wait for non-emergency cardiac surgery had reached two months. And as service has declined, so has remuneration. Doctors' incomes have been capped and clawed back, while the number of nurses has decreased. Although some markets—Toronto and Ottawa, especially—are saturated with physicians, others—including Jim Wilson's Alliston—can't keep their doctors for love, and have no money.

The most remarkable aspect of the health-care debate is that, despite the rhetoric that accompanies it, something close to consensus also exists on how to deal with the problems. The major political parties, much of the policy establishment, and most doctors and nurses agree that money needs to be diverted away from hospitals and towards other health-care sectors. As far back as the 1970s, Bill Davis recognized that the province had been over-building hospitals for decades when he assigned Frank Miller the thankless and ultimately futile task of trying to close a number of smaller facilities. Bob Rae realized it when his government ordered district health councils to prepare plans for reductions in hospital spending. Fully 25 per cent of the 32,000 acute-care beds that existed in Ontario in 1991 had been closed by 1996, mostly due to declining need: new procedures make prolonged hospitals stays unnecessary.[6] Yet the political costs of closing hospitals meant that, while entire floors sat empty, the hospitals themselves stayed open. By the time Mike Harris became premier, everyone in politics and in health care agreed that some hospitals needed to

[5] From 800 to 1,600.

[6] Day surgery as a percentage of total operations went up to 69 per cent in 1995–96, from 63 per cent in 1990–91.

be closed, with the savings diverted to home care, long-term care, and other community-based health services.

Equally vexing was how to reform the role of doctors, who in Ontario are paid on what is called the fee-for-service basis. Under this system, a doctor sees a patient, then sends in a bill to OHIP for that service. In an attempt to keep the $3.8 billion spent on doctors' salaries from escalating, the Peterson government limited and the Rae government capped the amount it would reimburse doctors for each patient visit. Doctors responded by increasing the number of patients they saw. The government countered by clawing back a portion of a doctors' income, once it exceeded certain limits. This left doctors increasingly angry and frustrated.

One of the cardinal flaws of a socialized health-care system is that the market functions despite the system's best effort to suppress it. In an open market, doctors could expect a certain income from their skills. In a closed market such as the Canadian health-care system, doctors will increasingly seek redress if the amount they are paid falls too far below what they would receive in a competitive market. In Ontario's case, that redress has taken the form of flight. Doctors have increasingly emigrated to the open-market United States. In 1995, according to a University of Toronto survey, thirty of ninety-five doctors who graduated from the university's family medicine program moved to the United States. And those doctors who remained agitated for increased wages.

Despite the growing salary conflict between the doctors and government, a consensus existed on how to deal with this problem, as well. Both sides accepted that newly graduated doctors needed to be encouraged to set up shop outside of saturated markets and that the fee-for-service model needed to be modified. One model often cited as an alternative is known as capitation. Under this system, patients sign up with a doctor, who is remunerated based on the size of his or her client list rather than how many patients are seen per day. As part of such a model, doctors would be encouraged to give up their high-overhead independent practices and pool their resources in larger clinics. Such an approach, advocates maintain, would eliminate the expensive and often wasteful practice of pushing unnecessary treatments on patients to boost fee-for-service incomes, would reduce waste by reducing overhead, and would provide patients with stable long-term community-based medical care.

Unfortunately, in health care there is a wide political distance between idea and action. Too many interests, from the patient to the doctor to the government health expert, view any change as coming at their expense. All this Jim Wilson knew when he took on the Health ministry portfolio in June 1995. But unlike previous ministers, he was prepared to move swiftly to restructure health care. Wilson brought to the debate one great asset and one great liability. His asset was his determination to see through major reforms in health care. His liability was a youthful, pigheaded inability to recognize that even Health ministers can't simply govern by executive fiat.

Wilson's first assault was three-pronged. He took on the problem of hospital closures, underserviced areas, and doctors' pay. The vehicle for his assault was the omnibus bill. First, the bill provided for the creation of the Health Care Restructuring Commission. The commission would be charged with examining and acting on the proposals of district health councils across the province, who had been ordered to create plans for local hospital restructuring by the Rae government. The commission would have to work swiftly. As part of his November 1995 economic statement, Finance Minister Ernie Eves had already announced plans to swipe $1.3 billion from grants to hospitals. To give the commission the clout it needed and to distance himself from the political fallout, Wilson endowed it with absolute power to decide which institutions stayed open and which closed, although later events would reveal that the government could influence its decisions when it really wanted to.[7]

On the second front, the problem of out-of-control doctors' salaries, the original version of the omnibus bill gave Wilson's ministry broad powers to examine doctors' records, in search of fraud or unnecessary treatments, since no one knew how much some doctors were padding their incomes through unnecessary procedures. But during the hearings that led to the bill's amendments, outraged doctors warned that such unfettered powers of search and seizure were intrusive and probably unlawful. And their younger representatives threatened a mass migration to the United States if Wilson went ahead with the third component of the assault: refusing billing numbers to newly graduated doctors who wanted to practise in overserviced areas. In the end, faced with the doctors' revolt and warnings from the information and privacy commissioner Tom Wright that the proposed legislation violated a patient's right to privacy, Wilson was forced to water down the search-and-seizure provisions of the omnibus bill, and to promise he would hold off implementing the billing-number restrictions while the matter was studied further.

As a final goad to the leadership of the doctors' lobby, Bill 26 took away the power of the Ontario Medical Association to set fees on behalf of doctors and to represent them in binding arbitration. The OMA, though riven by its own internal dissent, was recognized as the bargaining agent of all the province's physicians. In a classic divide-and-conquer strategy, Wilson sought to weaken the body and negotiate directly with each of the societies representing family physicians and the various specialties.

If the doctors were alarmed by the audacity of Wilson's first assault, they were aghast at the second, launched in early 1996, when the Health minister attempted to impose further cuts to doctors' pay. The reasoning, as Wilson saw it, was simple. Since the government had committed to retaining existing spending levels on health care, then that meant freezing total payments to doctors at $3.8 billion. But the number of doctors in the province

---

[7] Senior officials in Wilson's department have repeatedly sent letters to the commission, asking it to reconsider initial judgments. Deputy Minister Margaret Mottershead, for example, wrote the commission urging it to reverse its decision to close Ottawa's French-language Montfort hospital, after Prime Minister Jean Chrétien and Quebec Premier Lucien Bouchard protested the closure. And Wilson summarily torpedoed the commission's plans to close and amalgamate rural hospitals, by announcing in June 1997 new guidelines that could see all 66 of them remain open.

continued to increase, as did the number of patients. The only solution was to reduce the incomes of the doctors. The cutback took two forms. In January, Wilson eliminated the $36 million the government spent each year subsidizing doctors' malpractice insurance. Then in the summer, he increased the clawback on physicians' billings from 6 to 10 per cent. And he lowered the total income cap already imposed on doctors.

This was a remarkable decision for a Harris Conservative. Wilson and Harris should both have known and accepted that market forces influence wages in every field, socialized as well as open-market. Even if you felt, as many do, that doctors were overpaid and ungrateful for the security that a state-sponsored health-care system provided; even if you believed that—since other sectors of society have had to accept reduced job security, wage rollbacks, or both, as part of the province's economic restructuring—doctors should have to accept their share of the burden; even if you believed doctors needed to be taught a lesson, the fact remained that doctors were worth what they were worth, and alternatives existed if they were paid significantly less than what the American market would pay. One alternative was to strike. And that's what the doctors threatened to do.

Jim Wilson could have learned a lesson or two from Dave Johnson. When Johnson had faced down the province's public-service union, he matched words to deeds. The Management Board chair never staked out a position beyond the one he was willing and had the power to defend. He never allowed rhetoric to unnecessarily inflame the rank and file. He spoke calmly, and carried the appropriate stick. Wilson took the opposite approach. He acted swiftly, rashly, and unilaterally. It is an approach the premier's advisers have a fondness for, but it leads to complications. In the case of the doctors, the complication was that, unlike other elements of the public service, the services of physicians are essential and their withdrawal deeply discomfiting for the employer, as Wilson was about to learn.

In response to the loss of malpractice insurance, obstetricians and gynecologists announced in March 1996 that they would stop taking on difficult births. Wilson accused doctors of holding mothers for ransom. When the doctors didn't bend, Wilson blinked, restoring the malpractice subsidies. When the salary cap and clawbacks were announced in July, the protest repeated itself on a larger scale. Groups of both specialists and general practitioners announced they would stop taking on new patients. By the fall of 1996, as many as half the province's baby doctors were refusing new cases. They were joined by a coalition of 8,000 other specialists and by many of the province's family physicians.

The government found itself in an impossible position. It had sought the publicly laudable goals of controlling spending on doctors' salaries, reducing fraud, and distributing their services more evenly across the province. All it got in return was the threat of the greatest medical disruption since the extra-billing fight of 1986. Doctors, who traditionally were core supporters of Conservative governments, now counted on the side of the Harris regime's many enemies. The government had no choice but to negotiate a deal with the doctors, throwing its plans for health-care reform in the trash heap, while opening itself up to accusations of pandering to the privileged medical elites even as it laid off nurses and closed hospitals.

Throughout the summer of 1996, Wilson and his team negotiated with representatives of the OMA. The government had learned that, whatever its weaknesses, the doctors' union was the only effective voice on behalf of the entire membership. Finally, on October 19 they reached a tentative deal. The government would eliminate a 6.5 per cent clawback on billings. It would reduce a second clawback from 3.5 per cent to 2.9 per cent. And most of the malpractice insurance cuts would be at least temporarily restored. In exchange, the OMA agreed to the policy of forcing newly graduated doctors to serve in underserviced areas.

But the OMA then proceeded to prove what the Tories had claimed, that it was not a reliable bargaining agent for doctors. When the societies representing the various specialties and family physicians sent the matter out for ratification, it was soundly rejected by 76 per cent of the OMA's 23,000 members. They were not prepared to condemn medical students to exile in communities they themselves had no desire to live in. And the compromise did not go far enough to address the chronic complaint of many specialists and family physicians that they were grievously underpaid. Once again, the doctors threatened province-wide action. Once again the OMA and the government searched for a solution.

At the root of the dispute was the future of the single-tier health-care system. The doctors understood that the government couldn't increase spending on salaries indefinitely. Their response? Delist an increasing number of medical services, permitting physicians to charge whatever they could get. But delisting increases the range of medical services that are available to the better-off but unavailable to the poor. Such a system would not only violate the Canada Health Act and risk the cutoff of federal funding, but would undermine the foundations of universal health care.

In November 1996, with no deal and no sign of a deal in sight, the doctors across the province began a sort of work-to-rule, refusing to take new patients and refusing to work after-hours and evenings. In smaller communities, patients of older doctors scrambled frantically to get on somebody else's roster before the freeze kicked in, often to discover that the rosters were full. On the same day a new GP opened her office in Peterborough, she was besieged by hundreds of phone calls and dozens of patients who lined up outside. The province began contemplating flying in doctors from other jurisdictions to cope with the spreading withdrawal of services. Wilson, true to form, threatened to punish doctors who withheld services, a threat he had no power to carry out. And then came the unpleasantness of the weekend of December 7.

On the morning of December 5, the Specialists Coalition of Ontario held a press conference calling on all doctors to launch a one-day complete shutdown of all but emergency services, scheduled for Friday December 13. The coalition, which represents specialists as opposed to family physicians, had as its vice-chair

Dr. William Hughes, who participated in the conference. The specialists' move was a clear escalation of pressure on the government, and Brett James, Jim Wilson's communications assistant, decided to put his own spin on the press coverage. In the course of a telephone conversation with Jane Coutts, health reporter for the *Globe and Mail,* James, who is a gregarious twenty-something—a thesis remains to be written on the impact of excessive youth on the fortunes of the Harris government—mentioned Hughes' name.[8] "You know, Jane, if you wanted to have fun some time, you should ask Bill Hughes how much he bills in a year," James recollects saying.

"Why, is he the top biller?" James says Coutts asked.

"I don't know, but he's up there," James replied.

The next day Coutts called back. "You know, Brett, what you said yesterday, I feel obligated to write about it."

"What do you mean? . . . What are you talking about?" James replied, shocked.

"You know, the fact that a member of the minister's staff wanted to tell me that Dr. Hughes was the province's top biller."

"No," James insisted. "I never said he was the top biller, those were your words."

Coutts remembers a different version of the story. "What he [James] said was, 'Ask him about his billings sometime' and I said, 'Why, is he a big biller?' and he said, 'Number one.'"

James says at that point he was "at a loss for words," as well he might have been. Whether he had told Coutts that Hughes was the top biller or near the top was irrelevant. He had disclosed financial information about a doctor, a matter protected under provincial privacy legislation.

---

[8] Information relating to the conversations is taken from: Tom Wright, *A Special Report to the Legislative Assembly of Ontario on the Disclosure of Personal Information at the Ministry of Health* (Toronto: Information and Privacy Commission, 1997). The conversation is based on James's recollection of events, as told to the commission. Coutts and the *Globe and Mail* refused to co-operate with the inquiry, on the grounds that the media should not participate in government investigations. Jane Coutts, however, agreed to share her recollections for this book.

Realizing what he had done, James contacted Wilson's executive assistant, Catherine Steele, and the deputy minister of Health, Margaret Mottershead, and confessed his sins. Before long, he was also trying to explain the affair to the director of legal services and to Wilson's policy adviser. At three p.m., Steele phoned Wilson, who was in his constituency. Shortly after four p.m., Steele asked James for his resignation. He handed the letter in at 4:30. Shortly thereafter, Wilson phoned Hughes to apologize.

But Wilson also knew the matter wouldn't end there. Why had James said what he'd said? Did he have access to the billing records of doctors who were leading the fight against the government? If he had them, people would ask, did Wilson have them as well? Either act would be a gross violation of privacy legislation and cause for the minister's resignation. When the *Globe* story hit the streets Saturday—"Minister's aide out of job after using OHIP billing data"—doctors and opposition leaders began asking exactly those questions.

David Lindsay was thinking the same thing Wilson was thinking. Wilson phoned Lindsay at home. "I'm thinking maybe I should resign," Wilson acknowledged. "Well, come in and let's talk about it," Lindsay replied. When they met Monday December 9, Lindsay and Wilson had already talked to Harris. Harris had decided to accept Wilson's temporary resignation, while privacy commissioner Tom Wright was asked to investigate. "It will only be for a few weeks," Lindsay assured the once and future minister of Health. "As soon as everything's cleared up, you'll be back." Lindsay had already phoned Dave Johnson, asking him to come over. It wasn't the best time—the busy Management Board chair had been hoping to do some Christmas shopping. When Johnson arrived to find Lindsay sitting with a dejected Wilson, he stopped in his tracks.

"Oh no," he moaned. The chair of Management Board knew he was about to be minister of Health as well.

As it turned out, Wright took more than two months to file his report. The day he filed it, Wilson returned to his old job. As Wright reported, the Specialist Retention Initiative Program encourages specialists to set up in underserviced areas by exempting them from their $404,000 billing cap. The names of the doctors in the program are a matter of public record, though the actual amount earned by each specialist is confidential. James had seen the list of exempted specialists, which included Hughes' name, and that formed the basis of his remarks. Wright concluded that, even though the record was public, James had violated Hughes' right to privacy, but that Wilson was blameless.

The one-day strike went ahead December 13, though many doctors around the province refused to participate. And the event was overshadowed by word that the doctors and the government had finally reached a deal. It came the next day. In essence, the agreement reworked the rejected earlier deal, by raising the ceiling on billing for family physicians, and slightly lowering it for specialists. Instead of having to practice without billing numbers, new doctors in overserviced areas would receive only 70 per cent of what they would otherwise be entitled to in their first year. That would go up each year; by the fourth year it would disappear completely. And, as before, the clawback on incomes went down from 10 per cent to 2.9. In effect, the doctors received a 7 per cent increase in pay. And the agreement was only an interim one; in the new year, talks resumed for a permanent solution to the doctors' gripes. Meanwhile, a chastened Jim Wilson, back at the helm, watched what he said around reporters.

Six months later, on May 31, 1997, the armistice became a treaty. The OMA ratified a three-year contract that eliminated all clawbacks and offered doctors a yearly 1.5 per cent increase in total billings. The doctors proclaimed victory; they had forced the government not only to abandon plans to increase clawbacks on their incomes, but had eliminated the clawbacks altogether. Wilson said only that it was a good deal for everyone.

In the premier's office, there was guarded relief. They estimated the deal would cost the taxpayers only about $300 million. (Critics put the potential cost as high as $1 billion.) The incentives to get doctors into underserviced areas remained. A trickle, at least, of doctors were expressing interest in a new capitation-based pilot project. The hospital closures were going ahead. And the medical profession was at peace.

The fight with the doctors represented another case of the government having to give in to more powerful interests. As long as health care in the province is socialized, and as long as health care in any other part of the developed world isn't, the market will continue to exert pressure on the province's health-care system. The Tories were accused, once again, of sticking it to the poor and infirm, while bowing to pressure from the powerful. The accusations are true. "The public will not tolerate a protracted doctors' strike or lawyers' strike," one senior adviser quietly acknowledged after it was all over.

Politics is a schoolyard at recess. The doctors were simply the bigger bullies.

CHAPTER 9

Labour Pains

On December 9, 1996, forty representatives of the public- and private-sector membership in the Ontario Federation of Labour gathered in a conference room of a suburban Toronto hotel to assess the effectiveness of the October Days of Action protest that had partially paralyzed Toronto, and to plot strategy against the Harris government for the coming year. At least, that was the ostensible reason for the conclave. In reality, the meeting was the latest, critical step in the struggle between the public- and private-sector unions for control of the province's labour movement— and it quickly descended into a shouting match.

Federation president Gord Wilson pleaded for greater unity in the fight against the Harris government. "If we leave this room without having taken steps that are meaningful, then . . . this federation will start to fall apart," he warned the union heads. Already, the next Days of Action work stoppage, scheduled for Sudbury in February 1997, had been postponed because the local labour council had refused to support the action. Now Wilson listened as leaders of the Steelworkers, Communications, Energy and Paperworkers, and Food and Commercial Workers berated both the Days of Action strategy and the labour federation itself. "If the Federation of Labor isn't going to perform its function any more, let's get rid of it," fumed Tom Collins, Canadian director of the Steelworkers' Retail and Wholesale Division. "Maybe it would be better if we had two movements of the world [sic], two kinds of federation."

The meeting ended with some paper agreements: for example, a committee would explore ways to promote greater labour unity. But a bitter Wilson told the members that, after ten years as leader, he wanted out. "I may not even be here at the end of the term," he warned.

"We're immolating ourselves," one leader groaned.

Nineteen-ninety-six had been a good year for Mike Harris and his government. The early missteps of some rookie ministers had been largely forgotten. Most of the cabinet had performed ably; some—Dave Johnson and Ernie Eves in particular—had done admirably. And the Common Sense Revolution agenda that had helped catapult Harris to the premiership was within sight of completion. There had been a few bad patches in the previous months—two ugly confrontations at the legislature; the bitter public-service strike; the cave-in over the doctors; and the embarrassment of Jim Wilson's temporary resignation—but overall when Mike Harris surveyed the year past, he could take satisfaction in where he stood and how far he had come. And he could take particular pleasure in the discord and disarray within the various enemy camps.

Most potential sources of trouble had proved remarkably ineffectual. Welfare recipients, natives, women's groups, the Toronto intelligentsia—all these opponents of the government made lots of noise but were having no discernible impact on the Tories' agenda. And the political opposition had proven hardly more effective. Both the Liberals and the NDP had been hamstrung by lame-duck leaderships and internal dissent through much of 1996. In June, Rainy River MPP Howard Hampton had won the NDP leadership in a surprise upset over Toronto MPP Frances Lankin, the clear choice of the party leadership. Her support drew heavily on the Toronto Mafia that traditionally dominates the party—the powerful Lewis family and the union leadership, including Steelworkers leader Harry Hynds. Hampton had only his northern Ontario riding as a base of support.

But, though both Lankin and Hampton had served in Bob Rae's cabinet, Lankin was viewed as the one closer to the former leader in outlook, and her close association with the party leadership only strengthened that impression. The rank and file had not forgiven Bob Rae and his government for betraying so many of the party's principles, in what turned out be a losing cause. Throughout the convention and the final voting, strength steadily bled to Hampton. Renegade MPP Peter Kormos, who cordially detested Lankin, threw his support behind the MPP for Rainy River. Third-place candidate Tony Silipo did likewise. And union delegates defied their leadership and voted for Hampton, finally handing him the prize.

Though Hampton brought a tougher, more aggressive leadership style to the opposition benches, the NDP continued to be plagued by its tendency to worry its own wounds. A purge by Hampton of Lankin supporters left many in caucus sullen, and the resentments caused by the rift with the public-sector unions still festered. As 1996 waned, the NDP appeared to be hanging half-heartedly to organized labour's coattails in its campaign against the government.

Meanwhile, the Liberals were, if possible, even more ineffectual, waiting to no discernible advantage until November to choose a new leader. It hardly seemed worth the delay. The major feature of the drawn-out race had been the reluctance of prominent candidates to run. Veteran MPP Sean Conway, having toured the provincial riding associations, had announced back in January that a life of church-basement meetings was not for him, and that he wasn't available. Finance critic Gerry Phillips entered the race in March, then was forced to drop out almost immediately, when his doctor advised him that it might not be good for his heart. Former Peterson cabinet minister Murray Elston was wooed but demurred. In the end, six MPPs with no serious record in government fought for the prize. This might not have been such a bad thing. After losing two elections in which they set out with 50 per cent of the vote, the Liberal leadership had little to be proud of. All the candidates shared the implied slogan: "We Had Nothing to Do With It."

Newcomer Gerard Kennedy had the most strength coming into the November convention. Best known as the executive director of Toronto's Daily Bread food bank, Kennedy had used his reputation for progressive politics to fight and win the May 1996 by-election in York South, Bob Rae's old riding. Young, handsome, earnest, articulate, Kennedy represented a highly attractive alternative to stolid Harris. The party leadership, including the *Toronto Star*, certainly thought so. But the convention delegates were not so sure. Kennedy was bound to represent a distinct shift to the left for the party. Former food bank directors are more at home talking social policy than deficit reduction. Many Liberals were convinced the electoral centre of gravity had shifted to the right, that the population was permanently more conservative than in the previous decade. Moving the party to the left ran the risk of marginalizing it.

And Kennedy was a newcomer in a party that had been out of power for forty-seven of the past fifty-two years. He lacked any network of grassroots support in the riding associations, the long-term Liberals who had been with the party through thick and thin. Kennedy was seen as a parachute candidate brought in by the party elites and was resented for it.

Dalton McGuinty, on the other hand, had been patiently wooing the party faithful from the day after the election, endlessly travelling the province, meeting supporters, forming bonds. In walk and talk, he appeared solid, pragmatic, dependable. He would push the Liberals as close to the Tories ideologically as the party could get without disappearing up the Tory platform. This, for many Liberals, seemed the safest place to be. After an excruciating convention marred by unparalleled incompetence—it took six and a half hours to conduct the first ballot, and the fifth and final ballot concluded at 4:30 in the morning—McGuinty emerged the winner.

With the Liberals consumed in a protracted leadership campaign, and the NDP estranged from its own allies, the Conservatives could count on little effective opposition through 1996 from the other side of the House. The counteroffensives that mattered were coming from labour, the only force in the province with the potential to disrupt the economy and confront the Tories with anything like equal power. Labour in the 1990s remained a more potent factor in the Canadian economy than in its American counterpart. While the unions in the United States had declined from 20 per cent of the total work force in 1983 to 14.5 per cent in 1996, union membership in Ontario had remained steady, at about 32 per cent.

But Ontario labour's power was far from absolute. A series of recessions followed by uncertain recoveries and stubbornly high rates of unemployment had left workers increasingly willing to make concessions to employers who said they needed to cut costs to survive. Many union members themselves had become suspicious of the power of labour. In the 1995 election, the Tories had racked up some of their largest wins in auto-industry towns such as Oshawa and Oakville.

Compounding labour's malaise was its demoralizing experience under Ontario's first NDP government. The party of labour had not only led the province's first successful assault on the contracts of public servants, it had opened a fissure between those unions and their private-sector counterparts. During the confrontations with the conservatives, that fissure had widened and deepened. In the summer and fall of 1996, Mike Harris and his supporters were able to watch, almost passively, as the labour movement tore itself apart in the act of confronting the government.

Although most provincial public servants belong to OPSEU, most indirectly employed government workers—teachers, municipal workers, hospital employees, power workers—belong either to a teachers' union or to the Canadian Union of Public Employees. Most large-scale manufacturing or industrial workers belong to one of the big private-sector unions, such as the Canadian Auto Workers, the Steelworkers of America, the Communications, Energy and Paperworkers Union of Canada, or the United Food and Commercial Workers. A concerted, province-wide action by labour in defiance of the Harris government could have crippled the province and forced a crisis severe enough to require either a compromise or an election. Such action is not unprecedented in western democracies. Labour militancy brought down the British Conservative government of Edward Heath in the 1970s. Labour protests in France have repeatedly forced governments to post-pone economic reforms. And although labour opposition to Bob Rae's Social Contract did not force the government to back down, the ensuing labour boycott of the party during the 1995 election certainly helped consign it to a distant third place.

Bob Rae's Social Contract represented the largest-ever con-frontation between an Ontario government and its public service, a confrontation that presented the public-sector unions with a choice between lost wages and lost jobs. They chose neither. Their denunciation of their former NDP friends was long and bitter. In the fight against the Social Contract, the public-sector unions were joined by the Canadian Auto Workers, whose president, Buzz Hargrove, maintained that any labour government that asked for concessions from labour, especially by reneging on a collective agreement, was a Judas to the movement. In the after-math, the Ontario Federation of Labour, which represents both the private-sector and public-sector unions, withdrew its support for the Rae government. But the OFL's decision was by no means unanimous. Most of the private-sector unions, including the Steelworkers, Communications, Energy and Paperworkers and United Food and Commercial Workers, opposed the split with Rae. Their members had already endured the painful restructur-ing of the Ontario economy, and it was high time, they felt, that the public-sector unions shared some of the pain. During the Social Contract furor, about twenty unions expressed their dis-agreement in a manifesto printed on pink paper; they became known as the pink-paper unions.

With the election of the Harris government, labour found itself confronted, almost refreshingly, with a real enemy. And just in case there was any doubt, one of the Tories' first legislative acts had been to roll back all of labour's gains under the NDP: the ban on replacement workers during a strike, the new rules making it easier to organize, the new right to organize agricultural workers. But labour's opposition to the Harris government was based on more than simply the repeal of the NDP's labour law. A large part of the Common Sense Revolution was an affront to unionism.

Take, for example, the new government's job-creation strategy, which boiled down to one word: deregulation. The Tories did not expect the tax cut to lead to a net increase in jobs, at least initially. Its purpose was to offset the economic drag caused by laying off thousands of public servants and other public-sector workers. (Only in the weeks before the first budget did Harris and Eves begin to promise the tax cut itself would stimulate new job growth.) Rather, Harris and his brain trust believed that increased investment was the key to job creation, and that investment was being driven out of the province through a welter of excess labour, safety, and environmental regulations. Thus their systematic and wholesale attack on those regulations.

In the spring of 1996, Labour Minister Elizabeth Witmer had announced changes to the Employment Standards Act that set new rules for unionized workplaces. Employers would be exempted from regulations requiring pay for vacation, statutory holidays, and overtime, provided the unions agreed with the changes and overall benefits were not reduced. The move allowed employers to put this demand on the contract-negotiation table, an extra bargaining chip for their side. The changes also reduced the options of employees who might complain their rights under the act had been violated. Then Consumer and Corporate Affairs Minister Norm Sterling followed with new rules that let car dealerships, travel agencies, real estate companies, and cemeteries regulate their own industries. Although the province would continue to set standards, the industries would henceforth be responsible for enforcing them. Elevators, amusement-park rides, heating-plant boilers, and other potential hazards would now be inspected by independent agencies. The Environment ministry scythed half of all existing regulations and controls from its books, while Natural Resources dispensed with many of the existing controls on the development of shoreline and other environmentally sensitive areas, leaving it to the municipalities to provide their own regulations, if they chose.

The economic and environmental impact of all these loosened rules won't be known for years, but they did have one unmistakable short-term effect: they made Ontario union leaders even more angry. Deregulated industries, they maintained, were both less safe and employed fewer unionized workers. The Tory assault on red tape, combined with the stripping of union rights from labour legislation, convinced many in the leadership that they had to try to bring down the Tories through massive protests, possibly even a general strike. But first the public- and private-sector unions would have to patch up their differences.

The tensions created by the Social Contract, which ran deeper than anyone was prepared to admit, played themselves out during the summer and fall of 1995, during meetings of the Ontario Federation of Labour, which was charged with co-ordinating labour's response to the Tories' anti-union legislation. During this period, longtime president Gord Wilson, a former auto worker, confronted a difficult dilemma. The pink-paper unions wanted to return labour to the fold of the NDP, arguing that by financially and publicly endorsing the party, labour could help strengthen it to take on the Tories in the next election. But the public-sector unions weren't prepared to wait until then, believing the Harris government needed to be stopped now, before tens of thousands of unionized public-sector jobs disappeared. And the public-sector unions were permanently disillusioned with Rae's party. For Sid Ryan, leader of the Ontario wing of the Canadian Union of Public Employees, OPSEU's Leah Casselman, and their allies, the newly elected legislature held no friends of labour; its real friends were out on the street, among the anti-poverty, women's, and other social-action groups who were also victims of the Harris cuts. Ryan, in particular, believed labour needed to forge the largest possible coalition of opposition to Harris and confront the government at every opportunity.

Finally, in early November 1995, the OFL leadership hit upon a solution everyone could support. Together, the public- and private-sector unions would stage a series of rotating one-day strikes in cities across the province. The strikes would demonstrate labour's power to shut down the economy, while avoiding an all-out confrontation with the new government. The pink-paper unions, in particular, were anxious to avoid that confrontation, since many of their members had just voted Tory. Besides, some leaders of unions representing workers in large industries weren't that concerned about the Tories' plans to permit replacement workers during strikes or lockouts. Large-industry unions didn't need to worry about scabs. There was no way Stelco would be able to operate the mills if the Steelworkers walked off the job. Rotating strikes would flex some traditional muscle, while providing the social-action groups that Sid Ryan and the other public-sector unionists had become so fond of a forum to show their solidarity. And it promised to be great theatre.

London was picked as the first target, and a date was set of December 11. It proved an auspicious moment: the opposition parties had just completed their successful filibuster of the omnibus bill, a rare moment of effective political resistance to the Tory steamroller. And when the results of labour's first Days of Action protest were tallied, they looked impressive. Public transit and the post office had been shut down, some schools closed, Labatt and Kellogg's closed their plants, and the auto workers successfully shut down the GM diesel-engine plant, the Cami Automotive plant at Ingersoll, and Ford's Talbotville assembly plant. Ford forfeited $36 million in lost production, that day, and 2,800 workers ate a day's pay. The economic news wasn't all bad, however; with the day off, many workers went shopping. By noon, the parking lot at the White Oaks mall was jammed.

But even during the London protest cracks were visible. Over at Kaiser Aluminum, the United Steelworkers of America agreed to take Friday off and work Saturday, showing solidarity with the movement while ensuring the employer wasn't inconvenienced. Accuride Canada let its members book the day off as a holiday; it prepared for the lost production by beefing up earlier shipments. And the public-sector unions, who organized the day, outraged the

private-sector unions by not permitting any provincial NDP leaders to speak at the rally, though federal leader Alexa McDonough
took to the mike. However, the tensions within the movement
were not yet publicly visible. The London Days of Action protest
was proclaimed a success, and Hamilton was announced as the
next target. The second protest would coincide with a Tory policy convention scheduled for late February. As it turned out, it
would also coincide with the launching of the province's first
strike by its public servants.

Hamilton, the last Saturday in February, was a circus. Police
estimated 100,000 demonstrators packed the streets, to protest
just about everything to do with the Harris government.[1] Inside
the Hamilton Convention Centre, which was protected by a
ring of police in full riot gear, Harris greeted an enthusiastic
crowd of a thousand loyal supporters to the strains of Bruce
Springsteen's "The Promised Land," perhaps unaware the song
is a working man's lament against "lies that leave you nothing
but lost and brokenhearted." He joked about the police protection. "The local managers of Tim Horton's tell me they've never
had it so good." To thunderous cheers he vowed, "We promised
to deliver the Common Sense Revolution. No special-interest
group or lobby will stop us. No union-leader-led demonstration
will deter us."

The day before, union protesters had shut down Hamilton's
public transit, garbage collection, and libraries—but not the steel
mills. The Steelworkers were having none of it. And many of the
bigger unions were becoming increasingly resentful of resistance
by the public-sector unions to the idea of donating to the NDP a
portion of the funds raised for the Days of Action. With the
Hamilton Days of Action, it became clear within the movement

---

[1] It should be noted that estimating crowd sizes is a notoriously difficult practice, and
police are little better at it than others who are interested in the size of a turnout. When
scientific studies of crowd sizes have been undertaken, such as the study of the pro-unity
rally in Montreal before the October 1995 referendum, the numbers have generally been
found to be much lower than organizers, the media, or police estimated.

that the rotating protests were hurting union solidarity as much as they were inconveniencing the cities they afflicted.

Nonetheless, the protests continued: in Kitchener in April, where perhaps 15,000 or perhaps 40,000 protesters congregated, depending on whether you believed police or protester estimates; and in Peterborough in June, where both the city and the crowds were smaller. A pattern emerged. Government services, from postal delivery to garbage collection to public transit, suffered. But while many private-sector firms closed for the day, employers and employees quietly agreed to make up the lost time by working extra shifts, creating merely a chimera of solidarity. And each shutdown was followed by ever-more-divisive post-mortem shouting matches between public- and private-sector unions at the Ontario Federation of Labour headquarters.

The question now was: how far would labour go? Would it attempt a one-day province-wide shutdown? Ryan and his one private-sector ally, Buzz Hargrove of the Canadian Auto Workers, repeatedly predicted a province-wide strike to be inevitable. As one Days of Action protest succeeded another, it certainly appeared they were becoming an effective focus of anti-government sentiment. But no one was certain how far the strikes could be pushed. And behind the scenes, labour leaders were wondering how much longer the facade of union unity could be maintained.

The protest scheduled for Toronto for the last weekend of October 1996 was the big test. If labour could shut down the country's largest city, then maybe Mike Harris would be forced to listen. As D-Day neared, unionists warned repeatedly that the Toronto Days of Action protest would be something big. Public transit might be shut down; so might Pearson International Airport. The bank towers would probably be picketed, causing chaos in the financial markets. The major factories would stand idle. And the city would witness the biggest march and demonstration in its history. As the autumn days cooled and tempers rose, the media warned that the city was on the brink of labour chaos.

Faced with impending disruption, governments and private-sector employers adopted various approaches. Toronto city council voted to support the protest and promised employees they would not be punished for failing to show up for work. (Mayor Barbara Hall's support for the demonstration infuriated Harris. It was an act of defiance for which she would later pay.) Metro government, however, was less supportive, refusing to give its workers the unpaid day off. The Toronto Transit Commission management tried, unsuccessfully, to have pickets banned at subway stations and work sites. The management at Pearson International Airport also failed to get pickets banned. Yet when the day of action finally came, it turned out that the warnings had been too effective by half. Most workers stayed home, having no intention of facing traffic jams and picket lines on their way to work. At eight o'clock in the morning, you could take the 401 all the way from Pearson to the Don Valley Parkway at 120 kilometers per hour. It must have been decades since such a rush-hour feat was possible. It may never be possible again.

Although illegal picketing succeeded in shutting down the TTC, the roads remained empty, almost ghostlike, throughout the day. As in many other cities, employers had negotiated deals with workers to take the day off in exchange for extra work later to make up for lost time. The banks and other financial institutions had put up their essential workers in downtown hotels the night before. (The hotels were connected to the towers as part of the network of passageways and shopping malls that links the downtown core.) Hotels have bars, and if the Friday action in the trading rooms of Bay Street was muted, Tylenol was as much responsible as pickets. The GO trains were running, but there weren't many riders. Most schools cancelled classes, as did universities and colleges. Hospitals cancelled elective procedures. Provincial government offices were open, municipal ones largely closed. Mail delivery, once again, was halted. At Pearson, passengers who showed up for flights half a day early found the airport serene.

The largest single act of defiance against the provincial government in Ontario's history, for all its size and clamour, represented an ambiguous victory for the labour movement. If the goal was to shut down the city, then the goal was largely achieved, but only because most Torontonians took the day off. Fortunately, it was a pleasant day. The labour movement gave Toronto an involuntary long weekend.

The next day, tens of thousands of protesters marched from the Canadian National Exhibition, past the Metro Convention Centre, where the Tories were holding yet another policy convention, to Queen's Park. How many tens of thousands were in that march became a matter of hot dispute. Organizers had promised that as many as 250,000 workers, social activists, and their supporters would descend on the legislature. But despite the organizers' claims that that many or more participated, Metro Police put the figure at a paltry 40,000, revised upward to 80,000 after union cries of protest poured in. The teachers caused part of the confusion. As many as half of the protesters in the parade marched behind teachers' federation signs. But as soon as the parade reached Queen's Park, many of them headed straight for the rows of buses waiting to take them home. Perhaps as many as half of those who participated in the march failed to stay for the demonstration.

Inside the Metro Convention Centre, Harris and his supporters watched as the demonstrators marched by. One aide turned to the premier and observed that associations representing Iranians and Iraqis were in the parade. The words stuck in the leader's head, and he later told a reporter about seeing "the banners going by from some of the Communist parties . . . and I guess [from] the Iraqi group [and the] Iranian group." Even more telling, at a closed-door meeting with delegates Sunday morning, Harris derided the protesters who had succeeded in partially shutting down Canada's largest city and staging one of the largest rallies in memory. "If you took away all the government employees, the other four or five had a point to make," he joked. The party faithful roared. After the remarks were reported in the press, Harris apologized. But "Iranians and Iraqis" along with the "candy" and the soon-to-come "hula hoops" quotes would be offered as proof of the true contempt the premier felt for those who didn't share his vision of the province.

The Toronto Days of Action protest represented the zenith of the labour movement's campaign against the Harris government. Yet even the thousands who marched and rallied that Saturday could not disguise the growing crisis in the labour movement. There was room on the program for songs from Bruce Cockburn and Billy Bragg, but provincial and federal NDP leaders Howard Hampton and Alexa McDonough were permitted only to wave. While teachers and government workers clogged University Avenue, Steelworkers and Teamsters were stuck in the rear. Gord Wilson, who had attempted to paper over the holes in the federation's solidarity, but who was also mistrusted by the public-sector unions as a pawn of the pink-paper brigade, proved them right by not even showing up for the Saturday demo.

And so, by the December 9, 1996 meeting in the Toronto hotel, with the Sudbury Days of Action protest cancelled because the local pink-paper unions wouldn't go along, the internal dispute went public. The feuding union representatives spilled into the hallways and their feud spilled onto the pages of the daily newspapers. CUPE's Sid Ryan and his supporters wanted to move the Days of Action protest forward to culminate in a province-wide general strike. But the private-sector unions were fed up with the whole thing and wanted the protests scrapped. And the leaders wrangled over who owed money to what, with the private-sector unions refusing to help fund the Days of Action campaign, and the pro-protest faction withholding donations to the NDP.

At the root of the disagreement were the social-action groups allied with the public-sector unions. Ryan saw the alliance between labour and social activists as the cornerstone of an extra-parliamentary coalition that could ultimately bring down the Harris government. But the blue-collar unions were uncomfortable sharing power with environmentalists, child-care supporters, and minority-rights activists. "They say they're not going to let a bunch of lesbians tell them when to shut down the mills," sneered one public-sector union leader. But the December 9 meeting, while it surprised some outside observers, only exposed what the labour movement in Ontario had become. "We'd been beside ourselves for the last year and a half," Ryan later acknowledged. "Every single meeting we went to was exactly the same kind of thing."

Labour's self-immolation flamed higher the following week, when Power Workers' Union leader John Murphy pulled his members out of CUPE Ontario. The Power Workers' Union represents about 15,000 employees at Ontario Hydro and some local utilities and was the largest local among CUPE Ontario's 115,000 members. Murphy and Ryan had once been friends and allies. Both sons of Ireland, they had started out together as co-workers and union organizers at the Pickering nuclear generating station. But time and circumstance had pushed them apart, and the Power Workers increasingly sided with the pink-paper unions, in opposition to CUPE Ontario. With pink-paper support, Murphy had ousted Ryan as CUPE's representative on the OFL executive during a bitter fight in 1995. His union also withheld dues to CUPE Ontario and the national union, claiming it needed the money to fight the Tories' privatization plans. But the real fight between the two was over the Days of Action strategy. "The idea that you can just go in and shut down a city is silly, if you're not evaluating whether you're getting more or less public support for what you're doing," Murphy maintained. With the rift growing, he decided to sever his ties with Ryan completely.

By the beginning of 1997, Ontario labour's voice had become increasingly muted. Ryan and Hargrove quietly abandoned hope of organizing a province-wide protest, while the focus of opposition to the Harris government shifted to the fight against its urban amalgamation plans. Union members had a vital stake in that debate. Amalgamated cities would mean lost jobs for CUPE members. And Education Minister John Snobelen's plans to downsize and amalgamate school boards promised grave consequences for CUPE workers in the education sector. But when about a dozen CUPE executives staged a one-day sit-in at Snobelen's office in April, their gesture was largely ignored by the media. The spotlight had shifted to the Citizens for Local Democracy's campaign to stop the unification of Toronto, a campaign that was attracting a level of popular support not seen since the days of the fight to stop the Spadina Expressway, two decades before. And in the legislature itself, Ryan's despised NDP were showing new life in their fight to stop the megacity. Mike Harris could no longer feel secure in his enemies' disarray. For though labour's mighty voice had become a murmur, it was drowned in the cacophony of the latest and boldest challenge to the Common Sense Revolution.

CHAPTER 10

The Disentanglement
Web

$The Common Sense Revolution$ takes up twenty-one pages. It
deals with tax cuts, spending cuts, deficit reduction, welfare
reform, eliminating red tape, eliminating public servants, and
much else besides. Yet in all those words, among all those promises, the issue of restructuring municipal powers occupies only one
sentence. "We will sit down with municipalities to discuss ways
of reducing government entanglement and bureaucracy with an
eye to eliminating waste and duplication as well as unfair downloading by the province."[1] If the government had failed to live up
to this promise, it is unlikely anyone would have noticed. But
Mike Harris kept that commitment with a vengeance. In the second year of his government's mandate, he launched a restructuring of the roles and responsibilities of the provincial and municipal governments so massive and so controversial that it seemed,
at times, it might overwhelm his regime. Municipal restructuring
sidetracked other issues that much of the government's own constituency felt were more important, paralyzed the legislature, and
pushed many former Tory supporters into opposition.

The question is why. Why did the Tories become so obsessed
with the process known as disentanglement? Why were they prepared to risk so much, expend so much political capital, defer so
much of the rest of their agenda? The answer is education. "In the
NDP government," mused one bureaucrat, "there were five

[1] $The Common Sense Revolution$, p. 17.

ministers of the Environment on any given day. In this government there are five Education ministers." And each brought what he or she considered to be expert opinions to the education debate. In addition to Education Minister John Snobelen, there were Labour Minister Elizabeth Witmer, former chair of the Waterloo Board of Education; Intergovernmental Affairs Minister Dianne Cunningham, once chair of the London board; Minister Without Portfolio Cam Jackson, who had sat as a trustee on the Halton board; and finally the premier himself, a former board trustee and chair, and once head of the northern association of trustees.

All five were convinced Ontario's education system was rotten and regarded transforming education as a mission as important as cutting taxes or slaying the deficit. All agreed that any truly fundamental change to the education system required simplifying a jurisdiction where power and responsibility were hopelessly divided between local and provincial authorities. They were determined, not to reform the system, but to dismantle and recreate it, which made Snobelen's off-the-cuff musings about the need to "invent a crisis" in education so silly. In education, the Tories *were* the crisis.

The education system in Ontario does not inspire confidence. Prior to 1995, both in absolute terms and on a per-student basis, Ontario matched or exceeded every other province in spending. At the elementary-school level, the 1994–95 education budget represented an expenditure of $7,556 for every student. British Columbia, by comparison, spent $6,955, Alberta spent $6,222, Newfoundland spent $5,794. Only Quebec matched Ontario's outlay, at $7,557. These high levels of spending were driven by a system of 129 major school boards that combined a maximum of authority with a minimum of accountability. In the Ottawa area, there were no fewer than six school boards with eighty-eight trustees, representing city of Ottawa students, suburban students, Protestant students, Catholic students, Anglophone students, and Francophone students, all for a population of 730,000. To supplement provincial grants, the boards raised funds through residential and commercial property taxes. Half of the typical property-tax bill went to support local education. The boards spent most of that money—generally about 80 per cent—on salaries, mostly for teachers. About a third of electors regularly voted for school board trustees in municipal elections. The typical elector had little idea who the candidates were or what they stood for.

The teachers were represented by a variety of unions, representing public school, separate school, elementary, and secondary teachers. (There was even, until recently, a union of women teachers.) It was widely believed that the unions had employed a leap-frog strategy to improve salaries and benefits; if the settlement at one board was particularly generous, it became the precedent for other boards. In truth, teachers salaries had kept pace with the increase in the cost of living and no more; in the ten years prior to 1996, both had risen by 40 per cent. But cutbacks in provincial funding had forced boards to impose ever-higher tax increases. During the same period, total education property taxes rose by 133 per cent. Meanwhile, the student population increased by only 20 per cent.

Yet, despite Ontario's lavish spending on education, student performance wallowed in mediocrity. Some examples: A 1992 science test conducted by the International Assessment of Education Progress (IAEP) testing service found Canadian thirteen-year-olds ranked ninth out of fifteen countries. Worse, while Canada as a whole rated slightly below average (behind, among others, Korea, Switzerland, the Soviet Union, and Israel), Ontario ranked well below the Canadian norm. Thirteen-year-olds in Alberta, British Columbia, Quebec, Saskatchewan, Nova Scotia, and Manitoba all surpassed their typical Ontario counterparts. (The very worst scores in the country were reported by French-language Ontario students.) In a 1996 international math test of Grade 8 students, Ontario placed at the bottom, tied with New Brunswick and behind Newfoundland. In science, the province was all alone in last place. A further study, released in June 1997, revealed similar results. The tests served as statistical confirmation of what anecdotal evidence had long suggested: despite its enormous cost and elaborate bureaucracy, Ontario's education system offered only a second-rate education to its clientele. Most alarming of all, the gap between Ontario's performance and those of the top-ranked provinces (Alberta and British Columbia) appeared to be widening.[2]

Harris and his four education-minded ministers were convinced Ontario's substandard performance could be traced to the symbiotic relationship between the boards and the teachers' unions. Teachers could, and often did, go on lengthy strikes against school boards for better wages. A Ministry of Education office, called the Education Relations Commission, could intervene if it felt the strike was placing the students' school year in jeopardy, ordering the teachers back to work and sending the dispute to binding arbitration. More often, the teachers and the board settled before the commission intervened on terms not far from what an arbitrator might have been expected to impose. Though strident and disruptive, teachers' strikes served both the unions' and the boards' interests. The teachers believed they won better terms for their members by taking on the employer one board at a time, while the boards demonstrated their importance as the taxpayers' representative in the struggle to keep teachers' salaries under control.

This tacit collaboration between board and union extended beyond the bargaining table into the world of curriculum. Ontario was one of the few remaining jurisdictions in the world whose curriculum was based on a relatively unmodified application of what is called "child-centred learning." Both teachers and administrators had resisted calls for its reform, defending the system's obvious strengths. Child-centred learning seeks to bring

---

[2] The newly created Education Quality and Accountability Office notes, "Earth science is a consistently weak area for Ontario with the gap between Ontario and the highest-scoring provinces widening over time." (An internal Education ministry memorandum of November 17, 1996.)

each student along at his or her own pace, imparting new skills in the various disciplines only after the student has mastered the previous set of skills.

But though the child-centred approach lessens the stigma that can be attached to students who learn more slowly, it also makes it difficult to compare what an individual student knows to what the typical student of that age ought to know. Students in Ontario schools were advanced to the next grade even if they hadn't mastered everything from the previous grade. Report cards were often marvels of obfuscation; curriculum "benchmarks" were deliberately left vague; comprehensive and comparative testing was discouraged. Unlike other jurisdictions, curriculum was often developed at the board level by teachers in collaboration with local bureaucrats, with jurisdictions such as Toronto and Ottawa creating their own, independent curricula that shared nothing in common except their adherence to equally vague provincial standards.

All of this, while further enhancing the power of the boards and the teachers, made it virtually impossible to compare the performance of students across the province, or to compare the effectiveness of a teacher in one classroom with those in others. When international tests showed Ontario students lagging behind many of their counterparts, many trustees and union leaders argued Ontario should stop participating in the tests. The final result was that employers and post-secondary teachers complained that they saw students who, while filled with confidence and creativity, couldn't read, write or calculate.

Previous administrations had recognized the problem but done little to correct it. Although both the Liberal and NDP governments commissioned studies on education reform, the Liberals ignored George Radwanski's report calling for back to-basics changes to education, while the NDP's Royal Commission on Education report arrived too close to the 1995 election for any meaningful action. And although that report contained many worthwhile suggestions—such as emphasizing early-childhood education and regularly testing teachers for competence—it failed to address fundamental questions of governance and curriculum.

This was the sorry situation John Snobelen inherited as Harris's surprise choice of Education minister in 1995. Like Harris, Snobelen is the son of a tough-as-nails father. Ross Snobelen dropped out of school in Grade 8, drove trucks, joined the RCMP, started up his own trucking firm. "Oh, he was tough, hard-working," Snobelen once reminisced. "Great sense of humour. Not given much to praise." His son followed in his father's footsteps, dropping out of high school and helping run the family trucking business. Ross, who had a serious drinking problem, turned the business over to John and his wife, Frieda, when John was only twenty. Ross went to law school. (Snobelen remembered his dad "drank a quart a day through law school, drank two quarts a day through bar ad, never cracked a book." But he graduated.) Snobelen and his wife converted Ross's trucking business into a waste-haulage business. John Snobelen become rich.

With wealth came expensive hobbies. Snobelen became interested in quarter horses, getting deeply involved in the sport known as reining (a means of forcing a horse to perform complicated maneuvers), even helping to standardize its rules. He also became interested in management consulting, in Jimmy Carter's anti-hunger projects—meeting and travelling with the former president—and in the Progressive Conservative Party of Ontario. In the 1990 election, Snobelen ran and lost. In the lead-up to the 1995 election, he was the only candidate to file his nomination papers before *The Common Sense Revolution* was published. Snobelen talks and dresses like a personal-power infomercial, combines great charm with baffling psychobabble, and is so slick he deliberately messes up his syntax to sound down-home. Harris picked him for Education because he knew Snobelen was loyal, talked the change-management talk, and, as a rookie politician, would take direction.

The problems in education facing Snobelen were threefold: cost, governance, and curriculum. Of course, Tories being Tories, cost came first. The government wanted to excise $1.4 billion from the $12.3-billion school system, which would bring provincial education spending down to the national average. The question was how the province could impose such deep cuts without further lowering educational standards. Snobelen, who believes no problem exists that can't be solved by managerial reform and entrepreneurial spirit, dove into his task with gusto.

Shortly after he was sworn in, the new Conservative Education minister met with former Liberal cabinet minister John Sweeney, who chaired an NDP-created task force on whether and how to reduce the number of school boards in the province. In the course of the conversation, Sweeney told Snobelen that in his opinion simply reducing the number of school boards wasn't the answer. The provincial government's share of education spending was steadily declining as boards relied more and more on property taxes to supplement their budgets, a situation that only produced greater inequality across the province. Catholic boards had weaker property-tax bases than public boards; rural and northern boards had weaker tax bases than southern, urban boards. The quality of a student's education (at least to the extent money could determine it) was increasingly dependent on where he or she lived. The real challenge, said Sweeney, would be to create a uniform system of funding that gave each student equal access to education.

Furthermore, Sweeney maintained, far too much education spending was being wasted on infrastructure and administration. This fit hand-in-glove with Snobelen's own thinking. A school classroom, he later said, was "one of the few places where, if you fell asleep fifty years ago and woke up today, you'd recognize where you where." Yet schools deal primarily with information, the engine of the late twentieth century's technological revolution. This could only prove, Snobelen argued, that imparting information had taken a back seat to preserving institutions. Sweeney had come to the meeting assuming he was about to be fired and his task force disbanded. Instead, Snobelen told him to complete his report and not to hesitate to mention the funding concerns.

But the government didn't have time to wait for task-force reports. As part of the November 1995 economic statement,

Snobelen had announced cuts of $400 million in funding to school boards. He knew these cuts were patently unfair. Assessment-poor boards, which relied on the province for most of their money, would be hit harder than assessment-rich boards, which funded more of their budgets from the property tax. The wealthy Toronto and Ottawa boards received no provincial grants at all and were left virtually unscathed. But the government didn't have the leisure to be fair: the tax and deficit-cutting agenda brooked no delay.

School boards weren't alone, of course, in taking hits. In the November economic statement, municipalities and hospitals were also victims. But the Health Care Restructuring Commission was in place to help hospitals cope with their cuts (whether they wanted the help or not) through closures and amalgamations. Municipalities had been granted powers to charge user fees and issue licences under Bill 26. But in the omnibus bill the school boards got nothing.

After the $400-million cuts were announced, Snobelen promised the boards a "toolkit" of reforms to help them reduce costs without affecting classroom quality. When he asked board representatives what they wanted in that toolkit, they urged him to re-open the collective agreements with their teachers to unilaterally remove benefits from teachers' contracts. For instance, teachers have the right to accumulate a portion of unused sick leave throughout their career, using the saved days to retire up to half a year early. In 1995, the school boards were carrying an unfunded liability for accumulated sick leave of a billion dollars. The contracts also provided compensation for hours of "class-preparation" time. If the province took those benefits away from the teachers, the trustees said, they could absorb the cuts.

This idea fit with the government's own thinking. Snobelen had been encouraged by the staff in the premier's office not to shy away from tough choices. Going after the perks in teachers' contracts would save the system money and demonstrate the Education minister's resolve. Of course, it could also lead to job action by the teachers, but Snobelen believed that anything the teachers did to protect their benefits would only translate into increased support for the government from the rest of the population. In February 1996, Snobelen went to the Priorities and Planning Committee with his toolkit, which included most of the trustees' recommendations. There he met a brick wall by the name of Elizabeth Witmer.

Witmer opposed having the province do the boards' dirty work for them. The boards had negotiated those contracts, she argued; let the boards force the teachers to surrender the benefits. The NDP had been prepared, under the Social Contract, to abrogate collective agreements. Witmer was not. And when the toolkit came before Priorities and Planning and then cabinet in February, others around the cabinet table echoed Witmer's concerns.

To Snobelen's surprise, so did Harris. The premier saw no political advantage in having the province, which didn't negotiate with teachers, attack teachers' contracts. The Tories would be blamed for taking away benefits that the boards had granted in the first place. Besides, in the winter of 1996, the Tories were in the middle of their fight with the public servants, and even Mike Harris was reluctant to conduct labour wars on two fronts at once. Harris vetoed Snobelen's toolkit, choosing instead to soften the impact of the government's previous announcement: there would be a moratorium on capital construction, but there would be more money for operating costs. The province had already told school boards they could drop junior kindergarten programs if they wished; about half of them planned to. The boards were given new freedom to reduce benefits in teachers' collective agreements, if they wished. In essence, the boards were being given a year to put their houses in order.

The reversal was a clear rebuff to the Education minister. "I had colleagues who were not in favour of taking on all the unions," Snobelen later acknowledged. "I was less reluctant." But he said he accepted the interference by his cabinet colleagues in his portfolio philosophically. "Everyone has an opinion about education, because everyone has been to school." Other observers, however, say Snobelen was angry and humiliated by the emptying of his toolkit by Harris and Witmer. "Elizabeth Witmer was a Chamberlainesque appeaser when it came to the education system," one angry Education staffer later complained, adding, "Snobelen was left hung out to dry" by Harris's cave-in on the toolkit. Some Education insiders think Witmer undermined Snobelen in cabinet because she wasn't minister of Education and wanted to be. Witmer is a powerful minister, and widely thought to be considering a leadership bid when Harris steps down. Whatever her motives, Snobelen's supporters still haven't forgiven Witmer's performance at cabinet over the toolkit.

When the much-ballyhooed toolkit was publicly revealed in March 1996 and no one could find anything inside, many observers assumed Snobelen had failed to deliver on a key Tory promise of education reform, and his days were numbered. But Harris didn't believe his Education minister should be held accountable for taking a tough line at the urging of the premier's own staff, only to have the premier change his mind. Snobelen got to keep his job. But he was determined not to let himself be humiliated again.

Meanwhile, a permanent solution to the question of education financing had to be found, and the boards proceeded to provide it. While hospitals absorbed the cuts of the November 1995 economic statement, and municipalities absorbed theirs, 78 per cent of the boards—even though the cuts had been partially clawed back—raised property taxes yet again. Old spending habits didn't just die hard; they didn't die at all. From that moment on, the days of the boards were numbered. They had demonstrated their unwillingness to co-operate with Queen's Park and their inability to handle cuts in funding. In the spring of 1996, Snobelen set out on a new mission: to reconstruct the relationship between the boards and the province. And he quickly became convinced of a simple truth: the solution to the education conundrums of funding, governance, and curriculum was simply to abolish the boards.

The arguments for such a bold step were powerful. First and foremost, abolishing the boards would solve the financing question by putting control over both taxing and spending squarely in provincial hands. Abolishing the boards would also give the minister of Education direct, total, central control of the elementary and secondary school curriculum. No longer would local school boards create their own programs and set their own standards within broad provincial guidelines. From now on, one provincial curriculum would apply, with one report card and with regular, province-wide tests to measure how students—and their teachers—were performing.

And, of course, abolishing the boards would solve the governance problem outright. The real power to shape education would belong to the minister of Education. Fortunately for Snobelen, the Rae government had left him with the perfect vehicle for maintaining some local participation in school affairs. At the suggestion of the Royal Commission on Education, the NDP had directed each school to create a parents' council, in which local citizens would be consulted for advice on how to administer school programs. By abolishing the boards and strengthening the councils, Snobelen could ensure parental influence in education, while keeping the real power in his own hands.

If Snobelen had been blocked by Harris and other cabinet ministers at his first attempt to take direct control of education funding, this new plan was right up the premier's alley. The boards had committed the cardinal sin of passing on cuts from the provincial level in the form of increased property taxes. There could be no greater crime, as far as Harris was concerned. Just as bad, the most affluent cities in the province, Toronto and Ottawa, which didn't qualify for provincial grants, had been able to escape the funding cuts entirely. Abolishing the power of boards would eliminate a barrier between provincial aspirations for education and the classrooms where those aspirations would be carried out, while punishing the rebellious and impudent trustees.

Initially, Snobelen wanted to eliminate the existing boards entirely, turning each school into its own board, the system that existed in the nineteenth century. By doing so he would get around a tricky constitutional problem: in Ontario, Roman

Catholic citizens could choose whether to have their education taxes dedicated to public or separate schools. Creating single-school boards would protect that right. As late as autumn 1996, Snobelen was still arguing in favour of single-school boards. But the premier's staff were skeptical. Creating such a system would be horribly complicated and would bring with it considerable potential for chaos. What's more, without district boards of some sort, parents who were unhappy with the education Rita or Paul were receiving at school would take their complaint directly to Queen's Park, which was not something Queen's Park wanted.

A compromise emerged. Strip the boards of all their powers, including their power to tax and to impose curriculum. Instead, fund education entirely at the provincial level, with a uniform per-pupil spending level. (Extra funding would be available for students with special needs, and for rural and remote boards.) Reduce the number of boards and the number of trustees on the boards. Take away most of their salaries, so that only volunteers would want to serve. Leave them limited power to organize busing, school construction, and administration. Let them serve as liaison between the parents' councils and Queen's Park. This was the solution arrived at by October 1996, a solution shared by all five would-be ministers of Education.

But all solutions pose problems, and the problem posed by the education solution was a whopper. Taking education financing away from the school boards—and off the property tax— and handing it over to the province instead would increase the size of the provincial budget by $5.4 billion. Yet *The Common Sense Revolution* had pledged to reduce, not increase, provincial expenditures. Raising taxes to pay for the new provincial responsibility would be political suicide. Sure, property taxes would go down by an equal amount, but who could expect taxpayers to make the connection? Furthermore, Snobelen had not been working in a vacuum. Janet Ecker, over at Community and Social Services, had problems of her own, problems that could interfere with his proposed solution.

Over the decades, an enormously complex relationship has developed between the province and its towns and cities. Not only in education, but in welfare, housing, long-term health care, policing, water and sewers, public transportation, libraries, and on and on, the province and the municipalities have increasingly shared responsibility for funding and administration. Just as the federal government after the Second World War had intervened in areas for which it traditionally had no responsibility, in order to promote new programs and standards, so too the provinces—Ontario especially—had become more and more intricately involved in the lives of the towns and cities through incentives and shared-cost programs. But the federal government under the Mulroney Conservatives and Chrétien Liberals had steadily been cutting back its involvement in social policy, by reducing transfer payments. In Ontario, all parties agreed it was also time for the province and the municipalities to decide who does what and who pays for it. The technical term is disentanglement.

If there was one social policy promise in *The Common Sense Revolution* that overrode all others, it was the promise of workfare. The Tories had committed to finding work or training for every man and woman on welfare in the province. Those who were offered work or training and refused it would be cut off. Anti-poverty groups damned the program—it condemned those on social assistance to menial and stigmatizing jobs. Worse, it re-reinforced the noxious notion of the deserving and undeserving poor, of those who, though of limited resources, worked hard for their income and their dignity, and those who sat around doing nothing. People on welfare were there because they couldn't find work, their advocates argued. Either work wasn't available in their community or their personal resources made it impossible for them to land and hold a job. Workfare would only increase the stigma against those who were already struggling to overcome the barriers before them.

These arguments, however compelling, failed in two respects. They didn't quell a growing conviction among the middle classes that their taxes were being diverted to sustain those who preferred to live on the dole rather than contribute. Conservative Party polls consistently showed workfare had the support of a majority of the population. And the fact remained that other jurisdictions that toughened welfare requirements and reduced benefits found their welfare roles declining over time. In Ralph Klein's Alberta, the number of people on welfare declined by 58 per cent in the four years after rates were cut and workfare introduced. Cutting benefits and imposing workfare were two sure-fire ways to get people off social assistance, though why they left and where they went remains a matter of debate. But even though the Tories wanted to impose workfare, and the population supported it, creating the program was another thing. By August 1996, when Ecker assumed the portfolio, only two pilot projects were under way in the province.

The problem was the municipalities. Ontario's welfare system, like so many other shared-cost programs, was senselessly complex. There were two main programs: General Welfare Assistance (GWA), for able-bodied people temporarily on welfare, and Family Benefits Assistance (FBA), for long-term cases. About half of all welfare cases fell under GWA, a program administered by the municipalities but funded 20 per cent by the municipalities (through their property tax) and 80 per cent by the province. FBA was both funded and administered entirely by the province.

Because workfare would be targeted mainly to people on GWA, the province needed municipal co-operation to implement its job-training and make-work programs. But many municipalities either opposed workfare or feared its consequences. Public-sector unions, afraid that welfare recipients would supplant union jobs, threatened job action. (Sid Ryan's CUPE threatened to boycott the United Way if donations from his members went to agencies that employed people on workfare.) Anti-poverty and other social activists promised to make life uncomfortable for any councillors who supported the scheme. The Tories were as stymied in their attempts at launching welfare reform by the municipalities as they were at reforming education by the school boards.

The NDP had attempted a disentanglement exercise when they were in power. Responsibility for welfare was to have become entirely a provincial responsibility. In exchange, municipalities were to have taken over responsibility for such services as local highways and public transit. The idea was to make each level of government entirely responsible for its own area of responsibility, reducing both waste and confusion. The agreement was mortally undermined when the Association of Municipalities of Ontario, which brokered the deal on behalf of the municipalities, was unable to get many of its members to go along. Bad blood between the province and municipalities over the imposition of the Social Contract nailed the coffin shut. But to many social-policy analysts, some of them Tories, the NDP idea remained a good one. If the province took over responsibility for welfare, then it wouldn't need to haggle with the municipalities over how to implement workfare. Maybe some version of the old NDP swap could be revived. Only this time the Tories wouldn't worry about getting municipal agreement. They'd just do it.

There was one problem. It would cost something like $5 billion for the Tories to take over full responsibility for welfare. Fortuitously, Solicitor General Bob Runciman and Transportation Minister Al Palladini were already looking at offloading provincial responsibility for funding local policing and secondary highways. With the co-operation of a few more ministries, perhaps a revenue-neutral swap would be possible—except that John Snobelen was already proposing that the province upload more than $5 billion in education funding and responsibility from the boards. There wasn't enough downloading potential in the rest of the government to come close to matching the $10-billion cost of uploading both welfare and education. Something had to give.

As far back as the spring of 1996, while Snobelen was still wrestling with the school-board question, the internal debate within the government over disentanglement had got underway. At a meeting with the editorial board of the *Ottawa Citizen* in April 1996, Harris publicly revealed his government's intention to re-order its relations with school boards and municipalities. "I don't want to have to go through another year under the current system," he growled at the startled editors. A special panel would be created, he announced, to look at the issues of municipal taxation and the division of powers between municipalities and the province.

The chair of the Who Does What panel, announced in May, was David Crombie, the former "tiny perfect" mayor of Toronto, the tiny imperfect cabinet minister in the Mulroney government (he was too much the Red Tory for Mulroney's team), and, more recently, the czar overseeing the redevelopment of Toronto's waterfront. Fifteen other members filled out the panel, including Mississauga mayor Hazel McCallion, Hamilton-Wentworth regional chair Terry Cooke, and Linda Rydholm, chair of the Lakehead Board of Education.

The panel was intended as an exercise in co-option. The Tories knew that the government's final proposals, whatever they might be, would be greeted by a surge of outrage from trustees and mayors, along with the usual union and social-activist suspects. Harris and his advisers figured that by creating a board of credible yet generally sympathetic municipal experts—Hazel McCallion, for example, though a known enthusiast for the Harris regime, was also a respected and independent-minded politician—and by feeding them the same statistics that Tories were themselves grappling with, the panel could be gently coaxed into endorsing the Tory recommendations, which the Tories could use to counter protests from groups such as the Association of Municipalities of Ontario. And who knows? Maybe the panel would even come up with an idea or two of its own.

The problem was, the answer to the disentanglement dilemma was anything but clear, as the Tories themselves were finding out. Snobelen was determined to wrest control of education financing away from the school board, but what to do about welfare? Ecker was determined to streamline welfare programs and enforce workfare policies. To do this, her ministry would need to retain its control over spend. It might even need to increase that control. "It was something ComSoc [Community and Social

Services] wanted to do, and it made sense," she later acknowledged. But even as Ecker was trying to convince her cabinet colleagues and the advisers in the premier's office that control over welfare mattered as much as control over education, Al Leach was leading a charge in the opposite direction. He wanted to see welfare downloaded entirely onto the municipalities, which he felt were better able to monitor the program and to detect fraud. "Everyone agreed that the best level of government to deliver and administer the [welfare] services was the municipalities," he maintains. "So my argument was, if they can deliver it and administer it, let 'em pay for it." Since the province's financial obligation on welfare was almost exactly equal to the financial obligation on education, the swap would be almost perfectly revenue-neutral.

Ecker fought tooth-and-nail against Leach's initiative. For one thing, she argued, the government would lose the power to ensure province-wide standards of delivery: that which you don't finance, you can't control. Getting the municipalities to implement workfare would become a virtual impossibility. For another thing, municipalities hated paying for welfare. Their main source of revenue is the property tax, and property-tax revenues invariably decline during times of recession, as businesses close their doors and factories sit idle. Thus welfare costs would skyrocket just as the money to finance them dwindled. Of course, revenue from provincial income taxes also declines in a recession, but it has become a mantra that income-redistribution programs, such as welfare, should be funded from income taxes, just as infrastructure should be funded by the properties they service. The property tax was already an inherently flawed means of raising revenue—many people are land-rich but money-poor—downloading all costs of social assistance onto it would only make things worse.

Throughout the summer and early autumn of 1996, cabinet ministers, political staff, and bureaucrats argued long and loudly as they struggled to find a compromise they could accept and then sell to the voters. More than once, a tentative solution fell apart amid inter-ministerial bickering. Meanwhile, the Who

Does What panel was wrestling with the same problems, but instead of faithfully parroting the Tory line—in part because the Tories didn't yet have one—the Crombie team began coming to its own conclusions. Though its deliberations were secret, its recommendations were there for all to see. In a series of public letters to Leach, Crombie's task force recommended that the province take over funding for both education *and* welfare. This was in keeping with the panel's principal assumption: that municipalities should be responsible for "hard" services—roads, sewers, public transit, and the like—while the province should be responsible for "soft" services, such as education, social services, and public health.

But, as far as the province was concerned, such a solution was simply not on. Assuming responsibilities for both education and welfare, even while downloading every other possible service, would add at least another $7.5 billion dollars to the province's $56-billion budget. Either the Tories' commitment to deficit reduction would have to be postponed or the cherished tax cut reversed, both politically unthinkable. Even if municipal taxes declined by as much as provincial taxes went up, most voters were likely to conclude that the Tories had forsaken the promises of their Common Sense Revolution.

The debate was more than simply philosophical; it was also a contest for political power. Snobelen was not a strong minister; he lacked the insider's clout of Ernie Eves, the authority of Dave Johnson, the reputation for effectiveness of Elizabeth Witmer. But he was in the right portfolio. For Harris and the other ministers of Education, controlling the school system took priority over controlling the welfare system. It was more important both to them and to their supporters. Everyone goes to school; few go on welfare. Ecker was even more junior than Snobelen, and she was arguing the province should retain full responsibility for a program many voters wished would go away. The newly appointed minister simply hadn't the heft to sway Harris, his advisers, or her cabinet colleagues.

In the end, says Snobelen, "they put their case forward and I put my case forward." His case won. Education would be exclusively financed by the province. The boards would be reduced in number, their powers curtailed, and their ability to tax eliminated. In exchange for taking education off the property tax, welfare would become an entirely municipally administered program, with the family benefits and general welfare divisions merged. The financial responsibility for funding welfare would be increased from 20 per cent of general welfare and zero per cent of family benefits to 50 per cent of everything. As well, municipalities would assume responsibility for public transit, water and sewers, some highways, long-term care facilities, public health units, and subsidized housing. To cushion the impact, a $1-billion reserve fund would be created to assist municipalities who were seriously affected by the download.

The compromise violated the Tories' own values. The municipalities would be entirely administering welfare, even though they paid for only half of it: a clear abandonment of the who-does-what principle. This Harris understood. It was simply necessary, to make possible the higher priority: provincial control of education. Taking responsibility for education away from regional boards also appeared to contradict the Tories' commitment to keeping government small and close to the people. But Harris shrugged this criticism off. The net amount of government, he believed, would be reduced, as would its net cost.

Ecker describes the final disentanglement package as a carefully worked-out compromise in which all sides surrendered something. "If we had planned it on our own, in isolation, I don't think any of us would have come up with what each of us now has," she says. Certainly it wasn't what ComSoc would have come up with. But in the end, the major compromises had been wrung from her ministry, not Snobelen's.

When the members of the Crombie panel got word of the government's intentions, they panicked. Downloading more responsibility for welfare to the municipalities violated the first principle of keeping soft services off the property tax. They sent a final letter to Leach in December, backing off their original recommendations and urging that, if the whole thing had to be revenue-neutral, education should stay on the property tax, but the rates be determined by the province. But it was too late. The Tories had made their decision.

As Christmas 1996 approached, Leach, Ecker, Snobelen, and other cabinet ministers readied their disentanglement package for its January rollout. The Tories knew their plans were rough-hewn. Not everything had been thought out, and resistance would be fierce. "We knew this was going to be a dog's breakfast," Leach agrees. But they weren't worried; no doubt there would be amendments, perhaps even a few minor concessions. But the gist of the solution would remain intact. The Tories had been down this path before, more than once.

But even the most sanguine advisers in the premier's office might have reconsidered had they fully understood what lay just beyond the horizon. Simultaneously, the Tories had decided to make some changes to the way Metropolitan Toronto was governed. Resistance to those changes was coalescing like an emerging hurricane. The Conservatives were about to be engulfed by the Mistake That Ate the Agenda.[3]

---

[3] The author of the phrase is John Duffy, Liberal strategist and business partner to Leslie Noble.

CHAPTER 11

Megachutzpah

Before becoming premier, Mike Harris had not travelled wide-ly. Florida for golf; Atlantic Canada on vacation with the Eveses; a fact-finding trip to the New Jersey of tax-cutting gover-nor Christine Whitman—that sort of thing. He is a parochial man, generally happiest inside his native province, and not especially curious about the world outside. But Mike Harris also believes that the premier of Canada's industrial heartland should be a trav-elling salesman to the world, promoting the new wide-open-for-business philosophy of the Common Sense Revolution, and so in the first two years of his mandate the premier travelled extensive-ly, hanging out the sign that Ontario was once again welcoming customers. As part of the Team Canada trade missions, Harris has travelled to India, Korea, Thailand, and other points in Asia. He complemented those trips with separate visits to Japan, Hong Kong, and Switzerland. A premier travelling on official business sees a much different world from a student hiking the globe, but it is a world, nonetheless. And travelling the world, he made a dis-covery. "He discovered nobody knows about Ontario," David Lindsay relates, "but everyone knows about Toronto." Harris had stumbled into the modern world of city-states, of economic zones dominated less by national governments—and far less by provin-cial or state administrations—than by conurbations, a world econ-omy realized through great urban hubs: Tokyo, Hong Kong, Singapore, Los Angeles, New York, London, Paris, and, among the foothills of this landscape, Toronto.

As premier, the boy from North Bay had discovered the importance of large, powerful cities as engines of the late twentieth-century economy. The stronger, healthier, and more livable those cities, the greater the competitive edge of the political region they inhabited. Harris also realized, says Lindsay, that "for Toronto to compete on this world stage—well, who ever heard of Scarborough or Etobicoke? Maybe what we needed to do is make it bigger, stronger, bolder, so it can compete with the Tokyos and the Parises and the Londons and the New Yorks." And so the plan to amalgamate the cities of Metropolitan Toronto was born.

But there were other forces shaping Mike Harris's attitude to Canada's largest metropolis. One observer close to the premier's office maintains that Harris was driven to amalgamation by his frustrations over the administration of the City of Toronto, the urban heart of Metropolitan Toronto. Toronto city council was emphatically anti-Harris and anti-everything Harris stood for. The majority of its members believed that Harris's cuts to welfare, his general reduction of support to social services, his gradual elimination of rent control, his emphasis on promoting business over protecting the community, threatened the well-being of the inner city. Toronto's Board of Health went so far as to urge a boycott of the Harvey's hamburger chain because its corporate owners supported the Harris government.[1]

Two actions of Toronto council particularly annoyed Harris. The first had been council's decision in October 1996 to ban smoking in restaurants and bars, except for those with sealed, separately ventilated smoking sections. (The most punitive anti-smoking bylaw on the continent was to go into effect March 1, 1997, and would last a mere six weeks, before enraged restaurant owners convinced council the law was driving them out of business.) When Harris heard about council's decision to impose the smoking ban, he was incredulous at what he considered their

---

[1] The reasoning was that the Conservatives' cuts were a menace to public health, and therefore those who supported them . . . and so on. The board eventually backed down, under protests it had strayed rather far from its mandate.

stupidity. How was Toronto, which prided itself on its night life, to attract conventions and other business with such Draconian restrictions? Shortly after the Tories took power, Consumer and Commercial Relations Minister Norm Sterling had extended the province's legal drinking hours from one to two a.m. Now the city of Toronto wanted to move in the opposite direction.

The second action that infuriated Harris was spearheaded by Mayor Barbara Hall, who made an implacable enemy of the premier when she endorsed a motion to let city employees take a day off work to join in the October 1996 Toronto Days of Action protest. If there was any residual reluctance on Harris's part to abolish the city (and there probably wasn't), Hall's determination to let Toronto government employees go on strike against the provincial government eliminated it. Harris believed there were good economic reasons for amalgamating the communities of Metro Toronto into one city. Hall made sure there were good personal reasons, as well.

But the need to reform the governance of Toronto predated Mike Harris's Damascene experience on the road to Seoul. For years, urban observers had shaken their heads at the jurisdictional mess of the Greater Toronto Area (GTA), as it was increasingly being called. Toronto was more than just a city of 650,000 people, it was more than a metropolitan city of 2.4 million people. It was a conurbation of some 4.6 million souls, wrapped around the western end of Lake Ontario, from the fabricated town of Clarington (east of Oshawa) in the east to the dormitory community of Burlington in the southwest. And other cities, once proudly independent but increasingly satellites of the GTA, clustered around this amorphous mass. Hamilton, Guelph, Barrie, and Cobourg were increasingly being transformed into commuter towns.

Yet, except for the provincial government itself, there was no co-ordination of this great, diffuse, urban conglomerate. Metropolitan Toronto, the core, comprised a lower tier consisting of five cities and one borough, and an upper-tier metropolitan level that oversaw such shared services as police and public transit. The outer cities—including Mississauga, Oakville, Burlington, Vaughan, Ajax, Pickering, Whitby, Oshawa, which inhabited the regions of Peel, Halton, York, and Durham—were generally thriving, attracting housing and businesses with their cheap, available land and unseemly disregard for long-term planning. Meanwhile, Metro Toronto, short of land, bedevilled by high property taxes and a patchwork assessment scheme, found its population and tax base draining into the hinterlands.

The Peterson government had acknowledged the problem but largely ignored it. The Rae government, as usual, confronted the crisis by creating a task force, which would, also as usual, not report until it was too late for the government to do anything. The Tories themselves had been vague during the 1995 election; Harris generally mumbled that the fewer politicians there were, the better, and the closer government got to the people, the better as well. It never occurred to anyone to ask how having fewer politicians got government closer to the people. His most specific commitment, during a debate on the future of the region, was to promise that, one way or another, the metropolitan level of government in Toronto had to go. But all three political parties used the task force, chaired by Anne Golden, president of the United Way, as a way to duck the issue. They promised to read carefully whatever she presented.

Golden's report, which arrived in January 1996 in the midst of the public hearings on the omnibus bill, contained potent and sweeping recommendations. It urged eliminating the regional governments entirely, including the metro level of Toronto, and giving the individual municipalities greater powers. But upper-tier government wouldn't disappear completely: a region-wide Greater Toronto Council would co-ordinate infrastructure, transportation, and economic planning throughout the entire region. The task force also recommended widespread property-tax reform.

All communities in the GTA, and in Ontario, employed a property-tax assessment system known as Market Value Assessment (MVA). In theory, under this regime, a property was assessed for what it would fetch if sold on the open market, and the owner was taxed at a percentage of that assessed value. True MVA involves regular reassessment; as neighbourhoods go up or down in desirability, or as improvements or deterioration make a home more or less valuable, taxes go up or down. But different communities had updated their assessments at different times, and in the GTA a wide disparity in assessment values had grown up. Some communities delayed updating the assessment roles to avoid punishing property owners who improved their homes and therefore increased their property values. Prior to 1997, Metro Toronto hadn't been reassessed since 1950. Oshawa and Whitby were using assessments from the fifties and sixties. Taxes, of course, went up during these years, through inflation and across-the-board tax hikes, but no one had reassessed the communities to discover where relative values had declined or increased. Some residents were paying far too much tax so that others might pay far too little. Yet there was justified fear that reassessment would send property taxes skyrocketing in once dilapidated but now fashionable neighbourhoods. Poorer residents in these communities wouldn't be able to afford the new, higher taxes. The neighbourhoods themselves could go into decline.

That the proposed reassessment was revenue neutral, once all the disparities were eliminated, had little impact on local politicians, who fought implacably to keep their communities from being reassessed. Opposition to reassessment had been the *cause célèbre* of downtown Toronto for years. Golden's report recommended that the entire region be placed on Actual Value Assessment, a form of Market Value Assessment that uses a computerized data base to regularly reassess all properties and smooth out hikes and drops in values fuelled by market speculation. Golden also recommended regional pooling of education taxes paid by business. The idea was to distribute property-tax dollars evenly throughout the region, taking money from assessment-rich cities and disbursing it to poorer areas. The goal was, in essence, to reverse taxes bleeding out of Metro into the edge cities, to prevent Toronto from being "hollowed out."

At the press conference on January 16 where Golden publicly released the report, Municipal Affairs Minister Al Leach waxed visibly enthusiastic, praising her recommendations and promising prompt action. For Leach the longtime bureaucrat, Golden's exhaustive research and consultation had doubtless produced a well-crafted blueprint for the best of all possible worlds. But Leach the politician, a much more recent incarnation, had lessons to learn. No sooner was the Golden Report public than municipal politicians from all locales heaped abuse on it from great heights. The 905 belt was happy and prosperous; why should it see its regional-government structure, which had been in place only twenty years, abolished? Why should the school taxes of its citizens and businesses be diverted to profligate Toronto?

Toronto was also not amused. Politicians on Metro council objected to being dispensed with, while downtown councillors raged that Actual Value Assessment would turn Forest Hill into a slum. No one could see the good in the report: lower property taxes in suburban Pickering, help for schools in troubled Toronto neighbourhoods. Leach, chastened, created a committee to gather public input into the task force's recommendations. It reported back in April that no one agreed on anything and no one was prepared to compromise. Local politicians everywhere had reached a zenith of inflexibility.

At this stage, previous governments that had tried similar exercises shelved reform, citing the lack of consensus as the reason for inaction. But the Tories weren't interested in consensus. Mike Harris had decided that Toronto needed to simplify its local government, so that it could compete in the cities market. The Tories meant to tackle the problem, regardless of whom they offended. As it turned out, they offended just about everyone.

With the Golden Report on hold, it fell to Leach to craft an alternative. The more he studied the report, the unhappier he became with its conclusions. Golden wanted to abolish the Metro and regional governments. But wouldn't that mean downloading police, ambulance, and sewer and water services onto the local municipalities? No, the report replied, such services could be co-ordinated through inter-jurisdictional agreements. To Leach, that meant abolishing the upper tier, only to recreate it. "All of a sudden the light came on and we said, 'We're going in the wrong direction here,'" Leach remembers. Instead of eliminating the upper tier, why not eliminate the lower tier? "It makes a hell of a lot more sense." Leach increasingly became convinced the solution was not to eliminate Metro, but to amalgamate the cities within it: to create, in other words, one city of Toronto. Now Leach had a plan. All he had to do was sell the scheme to the premier.

Mike Harris could be expected to instinctively oppose amalgamation. His philosophy leaned towards smaller, not larger, government. Local citizens should, as much as possible, have control of the political process. How could abolishing the city governments and creating one large bureaucracy for the entire city accomplish either of those two goals? Leach's relationship with Harris has often been tumultuous. "If there are any fights in the cabinet, it's usually him and me," the minister confesses. Leach had the confidence of a career bureaucrat; Harris the confidence of a career politician. Both are stubborn men. "He encourages people to speak out," says Leach, "but the manner in which he does that is often to attack your proposal. I sense that he criticizes sometimes because he's waiting to see how strongly you come back."

On amalgamation, Leach came back strongly. And he had a more receptive audience than he might have expected. Leach's solution appealed to Harris's conviction that Toronto needed to be politically more coherent and competitive. A unified Toronto would boast a population of 2.4 million people—hardly Tokyo, but respectable. And the new council would temper the hot-headed socialism of the downtown with the suburban pragmatism of the boroughs. There'd be no more smoking bans, Harvey's boycotts, or sympathy strikes. The inner cities had rejected Harris in the provincial election. They had been the loci of opposition to the government from its first day. They were, in the premier's mind, selfish, impractical, and unpleasant political entities. Though Mike Harris would never admit it, perhaps not even to himself, amalgamation offered revenge.

Though the Tories are wont to govern as they see fit, they do try to avoid proposing ideas that are anathema to their own constituency. Harris ordered the political staff to look into the potential fallout from the proposal. After ordering up a couple of quick polls, they concluded that public support for amalgamation would be high, though the political heat from the municipalities would be intense. The more the government studied the matter, the more amalgamation appeared worth the political risk. Golden's report would have created a skein of municipalities under the wing of a Greater Toronto Council, responsible for almost half the province's population, with a chair almost as powerful as the premier. No premier was going to warm to such a notion. And the regional opposition to Golden's recommendations came from the communities that had elected much of the Tory caucus. As Leach and the premier's staff debated, the 905 MPPs made it clear their constituents opposed both political reform and regional tax pooling. Reforming Metro Toronto while leaving the outer regions alone would be politically less risky for the government.

By the end of October 1996, the Tories were ready to make their move. Harris's staff leaked the government's "preferred option" to the media, and Harris confirmed that his government was leaning towards a single-city option: a *Toronto Star* headline dubbed it "megacity."[2] The six local mayors, faced with extinction, held an emergency meeting even as Leach and Harris briefed the Toronto members of caucus on the government's plans. In a mere two days of meetings, the mayors came up with a Goldenesque alternative: cut the number of local politicians and gut most but not all of the powers of Metro. They pleaded for thirty days before the legislation was introduced to work out their alternative. Reluctantly, the Tories gave it to them.

With hindsight, Leach believes that granting the mayors the thirty-day reprieve was a mistake. Had the government proceeded directly with megacity legislation, the opposition forces

---

[2] "Harris favors plan for megacity." *Toronto Star*, October 30, 1996, p. A1. The term "megacity," however, meaning a sprawling conurbation, has been in use for years.

wouldn't have had time to coalesce. "I didn't think they would be able to mount a sustainable attack, as much as they have," he now says. The amalgamation legislation could have been passed before Christmas. Granting the reprieve meant the bill had to be postponed until the new year, when it ran smack into the disentanglement plans.

The mayors' joint report arrived at the end of November. It called for the elimination of the Metro level of government, strengthened city governments, and a "Municipal Co-ordinating Board" to handle services such as police, transit, water, and sewers—in other words, most of the Metro responsibilities. It also called for a referendum on any proposed changes to local government. Leach dismissed the plan and the referendum proposal out of hand. A week later, David Crombie's Who Does What panel, which up until now had confined itself to disentanglement issues, waded in with its two cents' worth. The panel recommended amalgamating some of the cities in Metro, maybe all, depending on the recommendations of a fact-finder. But it also urged that the regional governments outside Metro be abolished, and a GTA-wide Greater Toronto Services Board be appointed to co-ordinate services throughout the area. For Crombie, as for Golden, the solution had to focus on the entire region, not simply on Metro.

By now the number of recommendations and scenarios had become mind-numbing. Metro to be abolished; Metro to be preserved; six cities to become four; six cities to become one; regional governments to go, regional governments to stay. Leach closed down all options but his own on December 17, with the introduction of Bill 103.

The bill, considering the reports and studies that had preceded it, was remarkably simple—simplistic, its opponents claimed. The six cities and one regional government of Metropolitan Toronto would be dissolved into a single city, called Toronto. Council would consist of forty-four members, two from each ward, the new wards corresponding to the federal ridings in the city, plus a mayor. Community councils, composed of city councillors, would look after local concerns, advised by various neighbourhood committees. The GTA regions outside Toronto would be left untouched, but a Greater Toronto Services Board, with unnamed powers, would co-ordinate services, also-unnamed, within the region. During the months leading up to the creation of the new city, due to be born January 1, 1998, a provincially appointed committee would watch over the transition and veto any municipal expenditures it considered unreasonable. The idea was to keep municipalities from raiding their reserves for last-minute schemes or gold-plated severances.

The Tories believed they had worked the problem through to a solution. They believed they had calculated, and could contain, the expected opposition. On all counts, they were wrong. On the day Bill 103 was introduced in the legislature, Leach outlined the details of the new city at a breakfast meeting of the Toronto Board of Trade. John Sewell was there, in his capacity as a columnist for NOW magazine. As Leach unfolded his plan, Sewell, apoplectic, cried out, "Shame! Shame!" He spoke for thousands.

With their amalgamation legislation, the Tories awakened what had until now been a dispirited urban opposition. Shortly after Harris took power, John Sewell had launched the Together Movement, a band of several dozen intellectuals and activists who met periodically to discuss how to revive the disintegrating sense of community in the city and, implicitly, how to counteract the forces of neo-conservatism. The movement petered out after a few months, when their application for a provincial grant was refused. Meanwhile the Tories had blithely wielded their axe, including chops to the planning act Sewell had so lovingly crafted for the late NDP regime. (Its environmental safeguards were so weakened that Sewell and his allies believed they amounted to a virtual invitation to developers to send in the bulldozers.) But Bill 103 energized Sewell and his followers as no grant ever could have. It gave those who love traditional cities and the downtowns that anchor them a cause on which to found a crusade—a crusade to eject the barbarians who would dismantle their communities and subvert their local democracy.

Sewell detests the urban world created after the Second World War. As he wrote in his 1993 book *The Shape of the City*, Sewell believes that "urban areas are divided into two distinct parts: one part has straight streets and short blocks, with dense development and little green space, and with housing and commercial uses mixed together, whether as corner stores or as shopping strips with apartments over stores; the other part of the city is more open, streets more often than not are curvy, development is much less intense, and there is a clear distinction between shopping areas (shopping centres), work areas, and residential areas."

This "other part"—the modern suburb first brought to Toronto in the community of Don Mills and now dominating the Greater Toronto Area—was designed to be different from the Victorian-era inner cities, "although the reasons underlying the plans are often weak, flimsy, or downright unsubstantiated. The new style of city building, one might conclude, seems to have emerged from half-baked ideas and has led to the rise of many urban problems."

Sewell, following in the footsteps of Jane Jacobs and other anti-modern urban theorists, blames the shapeless suburbs for many of our modern urban ills. Low-density development leads to a thin tax base; more built-up areas are drained of resources as they subsidize the transit and infrastructure needs of the suburbs. High-rise apartment buildings and sterile public-housing tracts, set back from the street and surrounded by "green space," cut residents off from the community and each other. The vast tracts of land required for all this diffused development sprawls the city into the hinterland, absorbing farmland, towns, and villages and zombifying them into commuter edge cities.

In essence, John Sewell is one of the last great Ontario Tories, fighting to protect the privileges of the urban community from attacks by the hinterlands. He celebrates the enrichment that comes from having a great many people of diverse backgrounds living close together, producing the energy and cohesiveness of the downtown neighbourhood. He mourns that communities constructed in the past fifty years have turned their backs on the old urban form and surrendered community living for sterile, fenced-in isolation within homogeneous suburban wastelands. Like all Tories, from Edmund Burke to Dalton Camp, he views modern history as one of general decline and disintegration. And he views the absorption of the city of Toronto—his city, the city he lives in, the city he has written about, the city he once governed—into a largely suburban conglomerate as an act of legislative rape. He and his friends set out to stop it.

Fortunately for them, the six Metro mayors handed them a means to rally the opposition. In giving the mayors thirty days to provide an alternative plan, Leach also gave them time to consider how best to fight amalgamation. The mayors' response was to propose a spring referendum, or more accurately, a series of local plebiscites,[3] to give the residents of the proposed megacity a say in their future.

Harris dismissed the plebiscite proposal, saying the government would not be bound by the results, and that the bill might well be passed before the vote was held. But the mayors forged ahead. And they were about to be aided, inadvertently, by the government itself. The Tories realized that by pushing through the Metro amalgamation bill at the same time as the disentanglement legislation, they were imposing a serpentine mess of complex issues on the public all at once. They hoped, as they had hoped with Bill 26, that the issues would be so many, so large, and so sudden that they would overwhelm the opposition. Instead, in the first few months of 1997, the Tories found themselves in the fight of their political lives.

During December 1996, the Tories refined their strategy. Bill 103, the Toronto amalgamation bill, had already been introduced. In early January, the government would recall the legislature for a

---

[3] Generally speaking, a referendum asks voters to approve or reject a specific proposal. Its results are legally binding on the government. A plebiscite is similar, except that the results are non-binding.

special sitting. For one week, in a series of daily announcements, the government would lay out its grand plan for disentanglement, detailing the coming uploads and downloads in education, welfare, social housing, transportation, highways, libraries, et al.

The government knew the reaction would be tempestuous, but felt confident it could survive the storm. Besides, there was no real alternative. The Tories' opponents, inside and outside the legislature, "were going to look at amalgamation and downloading and service deliveries and they were going to tie the whole thing together," says Leach, in retrospect. "What could we do about it? Not a whole lot, because if we didn't roll out the whole agenda pretty quickly, we wouldn't get the agenda done." Everything had to be in place in time for the municipal elections, to be held in the fall of 1997, or else delayed until 2000, by which time the Tories might no longer be in power. But Leach figured the payoff would be worth the heat—at least until Harris pulled him aside, one day in mid-December. "The premier said, 'I'm going to be out of the country [on the latest Team Canada trade mission], and you, Leach, are going to carry this.' All of a sudden I didn't think it was such a good idea."

Such absences were becoming a trend. As with Bill 26, Harris would conveniently find himself on a different continent when a battle was joined. The timing was not a coincidence. In office, Harris has adopted a consistent strategy of being out of town when the fight over his government's agenda is at its peak, particularly when the arena of conflict is the Ontario legislature. For majority governments the legislature is a no-win institution, a forum where critics and the media come together to scrutinize and criticize its agenda. Sweating cabinet ministers, surrounded by cameras and microphones, are shown on television fending off barbed questions from hostile reporters. The possibilities of positive spin for the government are minimal.

Given these circumstances, most governments prefer to restrict House sittings to the minimum required by law and their legislative agenda, governing as much as possible through decrees and press conferences. But the Common Sense

Revolution required the mother of all legislative agendas. Not only did the legislature have to sit throughout its regular fall and spring sittings, the government was regularly required to convene special sittings. In doing so, it made itself all the more vulnerable to attack.

Cagily, Harris chose simply to disappear when the heat was most intense, to let his cabinet ministers absorb the opposition barrage. If, in the end, they fell in the line of duty—well, there were plenty of backbenchers who could replace them in the next cabinet shuffle. But no one could replace the premier. And so Harris and his staff husbanded his resources.

The Tories, however, were not the only ones making plans that December. The first Monday of the month, Toronto mayor Barbara Hall invited interested parties to present briefs in support of the city's campaign against the megacity at the city's council chambers. One of those presenting briefs was John Sewell. He urged Hall to form a citizens' committee that could serve as a focus of grass-roots opposition to the Tory plan. Hall ignored him. The next Monday, at a similar meeting, she refused to let him speak. "Politicians just don't like citizens' groups," Sewell later shrugged. Another speaker ceded her place so that Sewell could take to the mike. Though Hall tried and failed to block him, Sewell urged everyone interested in forming a citizens' committee to meet again next Monday at city hall. Then he phoned everyone who had submitted a brief at the two meetings. On Monday December 16, 200 people arrived at the council chamber, and Citizens for Local Democracy, C4LD, was born. The next Monday, 300 appeared. The next Monday, 400. The week after that they moved to a church. The week after that, they moved to a larger church. The crowd had surpassed a thousand.

In the fight against disentanglement and the amalgamation of Toronto, the contest between Tory and neo-conservative Ontario reached its apogee. A government that existed to serve an assertive suburban majority, resentful of the influence of downtown elites, resentful of ongoing demands for transfers and subsidies, had enacted broad and brutal measures to please its constituency. The old Tory coalition—downtown-based, community-driven, strident in its demands that the suburbs follow the city's lead—fought back against the erosion of its ancient liberties and against the now-misnamed Tory party with all its declining might.

Megaweek began on Monday January 12, when Education Minister John Snobelen arrived at the historic Enoch Turner schoolhouse to launch the first of four days of shattering announcements re-ordering the roles and powers of government in Ontario. Snobelen's particular bombshell was Bill 104, the Fewer School Boards Act, which slashed the province's 129 major school boards to sixty-six, and the number of trustees from about 1,900 to 700. Trustees' salaries would decline from a maximum $49,500 (the salary at the Toronto board) to a ceiling of $5,000. But that was reasonable—there'd be almost nothing for them to do, for accompanying announcements promised to strip the boards of virtually all their powers. Education taxes were to be abolished; education would now be paid for entirely by provincial revenues. A new province-wide curriculum would shortly be revealed by the ministry. Report cards were to be standardized. In short, the entire education system constructed by a previous Education minister named Bill Davis was about to be demolished and built anew.

The next thunderbolt came Tuesday, with Janet Ecker's announcement of changes to social-services funding. The province made the municipalities entirely responsible for administering welfare and for funding half of it. Though Ecker had been forced to cede some of her ministry's sovereignty, that surrender wasn't total. The province could still influence programs and services, and Ecker took comfort in the hope that, once they were responsible for administering welfare, municipalities would become more responsive to the workfare option. If they weren't, well, Ecker was not above a little political hardball. It's a game she'd already played with the municipalities. "I said to a couple of municipal politicians, 'If you really want to go into the next municipal elections firmly opposed to workfare, I can help the voters understand that that's your position,'" she confides. "They look at you for a minute, then they go out and test the waters, and they discover workfare is an extremely publicly supported program."

There were other downloads in the Ecker package. From an 80–20 provincial-municipal split, local subsidized day care would now be funded 50–50. More significantly, the municipalities were required to take over responsibility for social housing and for all public-health programs. These big-ticket items caused the local mayors to blanch.

There was more to come. On Wednesday, Transportation Minister Al Palladini waded in with his own download, requiring municipalities to take over the cost of public transit, thousands of kilometres of secondary highways, and the GO commuter train service. Bob Runciman, Marilyn Mushinski, and Jim Wilson piped in to announce that provincial subsidies for community police forces were abolished, as were grants for libraries, and the provincial share of long-term health-care services was reduced to 50 per cent. Finally, Thursday was Ernie's turn. The Finance minister announced the official launch, province-wide, of Actual Value Assessment. "The people who have been getting a free ride are not going to get a free ride any longer," the Finance minister vowed. From now on, everyone would pay property taxes based on the same assessment. Toronto mayor Barbara Hall predicted an urban exodus from her city.

If the December unveiling of Bill 103, amalgamating the cities of Toronto, seemed a direct assault on the city's downtown, then the hammer-blows of megaweek could only be compared to rape. The move to Actual Value Assessment would double or triple property taxes in gentrified inner-city neighbourhoods. The downloading of welfare would punish everyone in Metro, which has 22 per cent of Ontario's population, but 27 per cent of its welfare cases.

The province assured citizens the entire disentanglement operation was revenue neutral. In total, the province was taking on $6.4 billion in added responsibility (the education upload plus a $1-billion reserve fund to aid municipalities that lost in the equation), while downloading almost exactly the same amount. In the long term, the Tories assured the mayors, municipalities would benefit. After all, welfare rates were declining, while education costs were climbing. Over time, the municipalities should come out ahead.

Affluent communities with low welfare case loads, a relatively small percentage of subsidized housing, and little reliance on public transit stood to gain from the deal. In such jurisdictions, the elimination of the education portion of the property tax could cause municipal taxes to actually decline. But in communities with high percentages of people on welfare, sophisticated public-transit systems, and great demand for subsidized housing and day care, the costs threatened to go through the roof. Metro chair Alan Tonks warned that the city would be out $378 million, requiring an 8 per cent increase in property taxes. The announcements simply fed the convictions of downtowners opposed to amalgamation that the Harris government saw them as the enemy and was deliberately punishing them by gutting their neighbourhoods.

By the time megaweek rolled out, Citizens for Local Democracy was putting 1,500 people into the pews of local churches, where the faithful listened to heartening speeches, reports of resistance from other cities—such as Hamilton— facing amalgamation, songs and skits, and impassioned oratory by actor Eric Petersen in the role of William Lyon Mackenzie, Toronto's first mayor and the leader of the Rebellion of 1837.

One of the Monday rallies was at St. James' Cathedral, once a bastion of Tory power in Upper Canada, and these were unmistakably Tory gatherings, collections of mostly white, mostly well-educated, politically active inner-city residents, enraged at what they saw as an assault on their communities, fighting to protect their rights and privileges. Though the rants of Eric Peterson were as inspiring as they were eloquent, the old Reformer rebel's true heir was not the Tory John Sewell but the populist radical Mike Harris, and the real spiritual leader for C4LD was Family Compact founder John Strachan, on whose bones in the cathedral Peterson literally danced. But if the heirs of

Strachan led the charge against the Harris interlopers, riding close behind were the opposition parties, whose new leaders had finally found a cause to revive their demoralized troops. And they found an unexpected ally on the field of battle in the form of the Speaker of the legislature, Chris Stockwell.

In the autumn of 1996, David Lindsay had convened one of his regular sessions of the Bradgate Group, to brief the party's informal advisers on the impending agenda: restructuring of government roles and responsibilities; major changes to the powers of school boards; amalgamation of Toronto. For the first time, Tom Long, Leslie Noble, Alister Campbell, John Mykytyshyn, and George Boddington were worried. That big an agenda was bound to have a serious impact on the government's popularity, which up until now had held up remarkably well despite the massive controversies that had beset the government. (Various pollsters put the Tories either in first place or in a close second with the Liberals, with the NDP forever languishing a distant third.) As they discussed it, someone suggested that maybe this was the time for an advertising campaign. Harris had always argued that political parties should spend money on promoting their message between elections. Before the 1995 campaign, the Tories had effectively promoted the launch of their Common Sense Revolution. Now, the inner circle of advisers suggested, was another time. Go over the heads of the media and the opposition and sell the disentanglement agenda directly to the people.

Being in government offered an additional advantage. Part of the money for an advertising campaign could come from the ministry budgets, under the heading of government advertising to explain new initiatives. The Tories started out with an ad of their own: an $800,000 pure-propaganda spot in which the premier, perched on a bench in a hockey arena, reminded the voters he had made a bunch of promises in his Common Sense Revolution, and he was keeping them. Other ads, paid for by $2.5 million in taxpayer money, showed Harris standing beside a fuse box or in a classroom or an empty hospital ward, explaining the rationale behind the government's disentanglement policies. The difference was supposed to be that the hockey-rink ads were Conservative justification of election promises; the others, government justification for proposed legislation. To the average television viewer, the distinction was meaningless. And it is debatable how effective they were. Harris remains a wooden speaker, uncomfortable delivering a prepared text. He was no less stilted and wooden in these advertising spots than he had been in others.

The government also distributed a pamphlet to every home in Metro Toronto, at a cost of $300,000, explaining and defending its amalgamation plans. The opposition parties, understandably furious at the advertising campaign, complained in the legislature that the advertisements and the literature violated the privileges of the House by selling, as a *fait accompli*, a legislative package that hadn't been passed yet. Stockwell agreed to look into the complaint. On January 22, the Speaker stunned the government and enthralled the opposition by ruling that one portion of the campaign placed Municipal Affairs Minister Al Leach in contempt of the legislature. The pamphlet, he found, failed to state that the changes advertised would take place only if the proposed legislation were passed. Instead, it assumed the changes were law. The remainder of the advertising campaign was not in contempt, Stockwell ruled, but it personally offended him. And, speaking from the chair, he went on to berate the Tories for their advertising. "Personally, I would find it offensive if taxpayer dollars were being used to convey a political or partisan message," he intoned.

Never in memory had a member been found in contempt of the legislature. Never had a Speaker taken it upon himself to personally chastise the government for its communications policy. Never in its wildest nightmares had the Bradgate Group anticipated such a blindside. Leach rose immediately to apologize, saying he "would never knowingly commit an offence against the authority or the dignity of this Parliament." Shortly afterward, the embattled minister of Municipal Affairs met with media adviser Paul Rhodes, David Lindsay, and Ernie Eves in an anteroom off the legislature and offered to resign. Leach was despondent, but he knew that if the opposition was able to transform the contempt citation into a serious crisis, the government would have yet another obstacle in its path to restructuring. Leach asked Eves, who was on his way over to Harris's office, to communicate Leach's offer of resignation. "If it looks like it's the right thing to do, it should be done today," Leach told Eves. "The message came back, 'Forget it. Not a big deal.'"

Government insiders remain convinced Stockwell was simply exacting revenge on Harris for being kept out of cabinet. "Chris Stockwell thought he should be the minister of Municipal Affairs," one adviser bitterly confided. "If you can't get the big guy, you get him through his ministers." Although probably sour grapes—the pamphlet was, after all, improperly worded—there is no doubt Speaker Stockwell felt less reluctance to rub the government's face in it than a more loyal Tory MPP might have displayed. Watching him, it was difficult not to suspect the Speaker was having fun.

Opposition from city activists and the other parties could have been expected. But what truly set the Tories back on their heels was opposition from within their own ranks. The very day after the Stockwell ruling, George Fierheller, president of the Board of Trade of Metropolitan Toronto, called a press conference to denounce the disentanglement legislation. The downloading of welfare and other social services, Fierheller warned, would undermine the city's tax base and cost the average home owner an extra $350 annually in property taxes. He urged that the costs of social services be pooled across the entire Greater Toronto region, another way of coercing the edge cities to help pay for Toronto's welfare costs.

The government's opponents were delighted. The Metro board of trade had been one of Harris's most staunch allies, supporting his pro-business labour legislation and tax cuts. Now even it had lashed out against the megamess. As a *coup de grâce*, David Crombie then waded in, adding his voice to the chorus against welfare downloading. Speaking to the King Township council, the head of the Who Does What panel called downloading welfare onto the municipalities "wrong in principle and devastating in practice." He warned he would fight publicly to get the decision reversed. Neither Crombie nor Fierheller was arguing against the amalgamation of Toronto, but that no longer mattered. Though separate issues, urban amalgamation and disentanglement of services had become inextricably linked in the public mind. Megaweek and megacity were one and the same. Each issue had contaminated the other, and to criticize one was to criticize all.

The chorus of opposition from friends and enemies alike was beyond anything the Tories had expected, far surpassing Bill 26 or the Days of Action. If business leaders were joining the opposition ranks, then the very coalition of interests that had swept the Tories into office and supported their radical remaking of the province was threatened. David Lindsay found himself lying awake at night, staring at the ceiling, wondering what the government had got itself into.

As with their other great legislative offensive, Bill 26, the Tories had once again failed to construct a communications strategy, to craft a long-term approach to selling the government's agenda, as the party had done so successfully with the Common Sense Revolution. In the wake of the debacle of Bill 26, the Tories had tried to fill the hole left by Jamie Watt's premature departure with Ed Arundell, a former adviser to Brian Mulroney. But Arundell failed to gel with the premier's staff. He had left at the end of his contract, and media adviser Paul Rhodes had left with him, to pursue a new life as a consultant.

The Tories had completely lost control of the agenda and there was no one to tell them how to get it back. The municipal politicians and community leaders dominated the news. The plebiscites set for March 3, rather than being dismissed as a meaningless exercise of the politically powerless, were increasingly being touted as a crucial test of the government's popularity. But since Harris and Leach had dismissed the plebiscites in advance, they couldn't campaign to bring out the Yes vote. In retrospect, perhaps nothing could have blunted the rage of the activists, but nothing could have been worse than doing nothing, and nothing was what the Tories did.

Throughout February, the opposition to megacity and megaweek mounted. The city of Toronto contributed $150,000 to fight amalgamation, The Citizens for Local Democracy troops created a Web site, printed posters and buttons, and turned their Monday rallies into not-so-amateur theatricals. Yellow became the anti-mega colour, and yellow ribbons festooned trees and windows and doors throughout the city. But though John Sewell and the leadership of C4LD threw their weight behind the campaign for a No vote, privately they were less enthusiastic. For Sewell, local politicians were simply small-scale versions of provincial politicians. It was his inability to work with and forge consensus among city councillors that had doomed him to one term as mayor in the late seventies. The latest mayor, Barbara Hall, seemed to him more interested in promoting the NDP's opposition to the bill than in allying herself with the citizen activists of his own campaign. Sewell wanted to focus opposition to Bill 103 at the public hearings on the bill. His supporters successfully packed those hearings, overwhelming the MPPs on the committee with their complaints and objections. The hope was that, more than any plebiscite, the groundswell of opposition to the bill at the hearings would frighten the Metro Tory MPPs into demanding the leadership back down. Nonetheless, as it became clear the March 3 vote was going to be a major humiliation for the government, C4LD took the cause on as its own.

In a fitting end to February for the beleaguered Tories, Mr. Justice Lloyd Brennan of the Ontario Court's General Division ruled the government had broken the law by appointing trustees to oversee amalgamation before the legislation was passed. Fine, said Leach, the government would appoint the trustees after the bill was passed and make their powers retroactive. But it was one more piece of bad news the government didn't need.

On March 3, the citizens of Metro Toronto voted with unexpected force and in surprising numbers against amalgamation. Toronto, Scarborough, East York, and York mailed out ballots, asking voters to send them back in. Etobicoke asked people to come to the polls; North York conducted a phone-in vote. The question was simple, if loaded: "Are you in favour of eliminating [then came the city or borough name] and all other existing municipalities in Metropolitan Toronto and amalgamating them into a Megacity?" The answer was no, at an average 76 per cent.

East York was most opposed, with an 81 per cent rejection rate, Etobicoke the least, with only 70 per cent voting No. The results were far from authoritative—Scarborough distributed its ballots in a newspaper and got a 17 per cent response rate as a result; some cities mailed ballots based on obsolete voters lists— but the 36 per cent overall response rate, better than a typical municipal election, remained impressive. And the latest polls indicated that a slim majority of residents were opposed to amalgamation, a sharp shift from the previous autumn, when the Tories' own polls had shown majority support. Now even Tory caucus members were privately complaining that their ridings were becoming unwinnable.

The assault on the government seemed to be coming from all sides, and the strain was beginning to tell. Shortly after the megacity plebiscite, the Health Care Restructuring Commission announced that ten hospitals across Metro would have to be closed, including Women's College Hospital, a leader in health-care services for women, and Wellesley Hospital, which specialized in AIDS treatment and health care for the homeless. Harris, never at his best in public during a crisis, tossed off another one of his regrettable off-the-cuff lines in a scrum, remarking that hospital workers about to lose their jobs weren't really any different from those who once made hula hoops. "Just as hula hoops went out and those workers had to have a factory and a company that would manufacture something else that's in, it's the same in government." After the predictable howls, he apologized.

Next to being corrupt, the worst label a government can be tagged with is incompetent, as Bob Rae had discovered to his sorrow. The swirling opposition to the Tories' many initiatives threatened to coalesce into that most damning indictment: Mike Harris didn't know what he was doing—closing the wrong hospitals; downloading the wrong services; merging municipalities against their will. If the growing impression of boneheadedness were at all to persist, a public conviction could emerge that the government either didn't know or didn't care about the consequences of its actions. Arrogance, of course, is the third-worst sin.

Although the Tories intended to keep their hands off hospital restructuring in Toronto, they decided they had to do something about the groundswell of opposition to the megacity, especially among their own friends. In late March, Al Leach announced a package of minor reforms, geared to win back some of the megacity's wavering supporters. To offset complaints of diminished representation, the number of councillors in the new city would rise from forty-four to fifty-six. The community councils would have their roles strengthened, would be coterminous with the old cities, and would have powers defined by the megacity council, though they still wouldn't have budgetary powers. Leach also revoked a strange clause in the megacity bill that had made the trustees overseeing the amalgamation immune to court action. Meanwhile the Tories moved to get their former friends back onside on the disentanglement front. Terry Mundell, of the Association of Municipalities of Ontario, was invited to put together a team to help with the implementation of the offloading of social services. The municipalities were also told that, if they had any other ideas for a services swap that (a) was revenue neutral and (b) kept education financing in provincial hands, the government was happy to hear it.

On the eve of the vote on Bill 103 in the legislature, Leach and Sewell had a memorable face-to-face confrontation. The Saturday afternoon of the Easter weekend, as Leach was coming in from the garden of his Moore Park home, the doorbell rang. When he opened the door, there was John Sewell.

"How are you, John?" Leach asked in surprise.

"I want an interview," he recalls Sewell defiantly responding. "Your amendments are disgraceful, you should be ashamed of yourself, your government is destroying our city, and I want to talk to you about it." Leach invited him into the living room, where they sat on chairs opposite each other. Sewell brought out a list of questions about the amendments. Leach attempted to answer each charge.

Suddenly, after about half an hour, Sewell jumped up. "That's all I have," he said abruptly and walked out the door. For Sewell, the meeting had been a waste of time. As far as he could tell, Leach didn't even comprehend the objections to the bill. "It was like talking to a crazy person," he recalled.

As they watched Sewell drive away, Leach's wife remarked, "That guy's a wingnut."

Everyone at Queen's Park knew the forces of opposition were prepared to go to the wall to delay the passage of Bill 103. The bill was scheduled to pass during a special session of the legislature, called for the first week of April. (The legislature had been dormant since March 6.) In anticipation, Queen's Park security had even checked the red alarm buttons located under each MPP's desk, in case some crazed opponent of megacity threatened an honourable member. The opposition parties, however, could be expected to use more effective tactics. The opportunity to filibuster—delay legislation by having members speak endlessly, until time for passage of the bill has expired—had been curtailed by rule changes imposed by the NDP when they were in government. One tactic, however, was open to both the NDP and the Liberals. Before third and final reading, the House would sit in committee of the whole to vote on any proposed amendments. Typically, this is a fairly efficient process; both the government and opposition present amendments to the proposed legislation, with the government using its majority to pass its amendments and defeat the opposition's. This time there were rumours the opposition would try to present so many amendments that it would take more than a week to vote them all down, delaying passage of the bill until the House resumed its regular spring sitting in the last week of April.

In fact, the NDP had been working for weeks on just such a strategy. Brian Charlton, Howard Hampton's executive assistant and a former cabinet minister in the Rae government, had come up with a scheme to introduce thousands of amendments, each requiring that implementation of the bill be delayed until the residents of such-and-such a street had been consulted. At first, a staffer had typed each street name separately into the appropriate space in the master form. Then someone introduced the NDP to the miracle of data bases. With a few keystrokes and a ten-minute wait, the NDP was in possession of 10,000 individual motions, requiring that the opinions of the residents of each street, avenue, laneway, and cul-de-sac in Metro be canvassed before Bill 103 was passed.

On Wednesday April 2, the House moved into committee of the whole. NDP Leader Hampton wheeled into the chamber a furniture cart filled with a dozen boxes containing the 10,000 proposed amendments. The Liberals threw in about 1,000 amendments of their own. House Leader Dave Johnson tried to block the amendments, arguing they were vexatious and identical, but Hampton figured "we had about a 70 per cent chance" that their motion would be in order. Sure enough, Stockwell blackened the government's eye yet again, by ruling the amendments were in order. The House began to vote on the motions, one at a time.

Now the chairs of the committee of the whole House—deputy speaker Gilles Morin (a Liberal), first deputy chair Marilyn Churley (of the NDP) and deputy chair Bert Johnson (a Progressive Conservative)—proceeded to read each motion, one after the other, each identical but for the name of the street, into the record, where it was voted on and defeated by the Tory majority. The House was in constant session, twenty-four hours a day, staffed by weary teams of MPPs. As the voting dragged on, it became clear that, even sitting day and night, it could take two months or more to read all the amendments. No one knew whether the MPPs could survive such a marathon. Ultimately, the opposition would be tested more sorely than the government, since the NDP and Liberals had fewer MPPs.

The Liberals were almost as vexed by the filibuster as the Tories; it was far more clever than their own, limited scheme. Dalton McGuinty had reportedly been for compromising with the Tories, but in a session with his caucus, he was talked into sticking with the NDP. Day after day, the legislature sat round the clock. As the television lights heated up the chamber, a pungent odour reminiscent of fish guts filled the space, perhaps contributed to by the cleaning fluids used on the carpets and by the socks of the honourable members. Meetings between the House leaders went nowhere—the NDP wanted the bill withdrawn; the Liberals wanted it delayed one year; the government hung tough. The Tories put their members on twelve-hour shifts; the other parties used shorter shifts and more rotations.

Inevitably, the filibuster reached farcical proportions, when one team of Tory MPPs nodded off and forgot to vote down one motion. The good citizens of Cafton Court, a tiny cul-de-sac in Etobicoke, now had to be consulted and could request public hearings before regulations under the act were imposed. Instantly, teams of journalists descended on the quiet street, to grill the at first bemused and then increasingly annoyed home owners on their views on amalgamation.

Though members of Citizens for Local Democracy came to the legislature with coffee and muffins to bolster the opposition MPPs' spirits, behind the scenes there was a growing rift between the parties and the people. John Sewell had urged the NDP to employ a different strategy to confront the government. Rather than introduce motions of amendment, he wanted the opposition to argue that the government's own amendments were out of order, since they were not based on the representations of those who spoke at the public hearings. By bringing in their filibuster amendments and causing Stockwell to rule all the motions were in order, the NDP had legitimized the government amendments. "It made me quite furious," Sewell later said. Hampton had defied the citizens' movement that had ignited the opposition to Bill 103. Hampton, in reply, maintains there was little chance Stockwell would ever have ruled a government amendment out of order.

On Sunday April 6, Stockwell gave the MPPs a break. He agreed to a government suggestion that the entire motion did not need to be read each time; the street name alone would suffice.

Hampton's crew breathed a quiet sigh of relief. They had been counting on Stockwell to find in favour of some government motion to end the stalemate, but they themselves had no idea what it would be. The NDPers were getting very, very tired. With Sunday's ruling, it became clear the filibuster would end early in the week. Since the House had already sat past Friday and would not reconvene until the end of April, the opposition had succeeded in delaying the passage of Bill 103. Any time now spent in the legislature was time wasted.

But there was another problem. Once amendments are voted on in committee of the whole, the House must reconvene for a recorded vote. During that time, the doors of the legislature are locked and no one can go in or out, including to use the bathroom. Nor is there food. Recorded voting on the amendments would take days, and some older MPPs might expire before it was all completed. The physical state that the legislature would be in did not bear contemplation. The parties compromised by agreeing to let the MPPs vote in shifts, and by expanding the defined area of the legislature to include washrooms. At 9:23 p.m. Friday April 11, the filibuster ended. The MPPs went home for their first good night's sleep in over a week. The NDP congratulated themselves on having made the Tories suffer for their noxious bill. Cafton Court returned to obscurity when the government voted down the entire section of the bill including that passed amendment. (The other portions of the section were introduced and passed later.)

Two weeks after the filibuster, all options exhausted, Bill 103 passed final reading. As dozens of spectators hurled insults at the Tories from the gallery, the NDP and Liberal members rose and offered their extra-parliamentary allies a standing ovation. John Sewell rose to his feet in response, though in his heart he believed the NDP had betrayed him. Now his only hope lay in a court challenge. In a July hearing before Mr. Justice Stephen Borins, lawyers for the citizens' movement argued that amalgamation violated their Charter rights to freedom of association and freedom from unreasonable search and seizure of property. More realistically, lawyers representing the Toronto cities argued there was an implied constitutional right of municipalities to be consulted before their boundaries or powers were changed.

These legal strategies were naught. In his July 24 ruling, though Borins strongly criticized the Conservatives, agreeing that the government failed to perform "the type of public consultation which should have preceded the introduction of the legislation," and though the judge believed "the government displayed megachutzpah in proceeding as it did, and in believing that the inhabitants of Metro Toronto would submit to the imposition of the megacity without being given an opportunity to have a real say in how they were to live and be governed," he nonetheless concluded "the charter does not guarantee an individual the right to live his or her life free from government chutzpah or imperiousness." Nor could he find any implied constitutional rights of consultation for municipalities. The cause was lost.

There is a recurring irony to the Tories' legislative adventures. As the opposition rallies to oppose one government initiative, it surrenders on another. On April 23, Bill 104 passed. The legislation amalgamating and eviscerating school boards became law. The government sidestepped opposition attempts at another amendments filibuster by voting the legislation in without amendments. The members opposite complained but complied. In its reordering of the number and powers of school boards across the province, Bill 104 was profoundly more revolutionary than the amalgamation of Toronto. That it received comparatively little attention, while Mike Harris's opponents exhausted themselves fighting the megacity, revealed the upside, at least for the government, of the Tories attacking on all fronts at once, paying whatever the political price.

In any other day, with any other government, Bill 104 would have been the most contentious act in the mandate. There would have been province-wide protests, demonstrations by teachers, endless meetings and debates. Instead, Bill 104 whimpered its way onto the books. The Tories' massive overhaul of the education system was safely launched. Another stronghold had fallen to the Mike Harris revolution.

CHAPTER 12

Promises,
Promises . . .

In early May 1997, the Mike Harris government appeared to have found a final way out of its disentanglement imbroglio, a path that yet again proved to the inner circle the efficacy of their ongoing strategy: threaten cataclysm to obtain substantial change. But once again, before achieving its goal, the government had to backtrack and regroup. To many observers it appeared that, rather than achieving a strategic victory, Mike Harris had finally been forced to blink.

In a tactical retreat, the government accepted a proposal worked out by the Association of Municipalities of Ontario (AMO), headed by Terry Mundell. The AMO proposed to modify the education-for-welfare swap that the Tories had announced with such bravado in January's megaweek by rejigging the planned upload in education funding. Instead of money for education being taken entirely off the property tax, 50 per cent (about $2.5 billion-worth) would remain. However, the province, not the school boards, would set the rate and receive the funds. In exchange, the municipalities would be required to pay only 20 per cent of the costs of the new unified welfare system, instead of the originally mandated 50 per cent. (Welfare administrative costs would be shared fifty-fifty, but the administration itself would be an entirely municipal responsibility.) At the same time, the province agreed to resume its responsibility for long-term health care. And it offered to ease the transfer of social-housing responsibilities to the municipalities with a one-time grant of $200 million to upgrade housing stock. Finally, the government would once again assume its 80 per cent responsibility for funding day care, rather than reducing that responsibility to 50 per cent, as proposed during megaweek.[1]

Opponents of the government labelled the compromise a flip flop, and indeed the government had reversed several previously stated commitments. But the real significance of the disentanglement deal lay in the area of taxation. Traditionally the province has raised revenues principally from two sources: income taxes and sales taxes. Municipalities, on the other hand, have relied principally on property taxes. Under the AMO compromise, the province has in fact further intruded into the municipal jurisdiction, by adding property taxes as a revenue source. The compromise, in other words, simply allows the province to get its education money from what used to be a municipal tax.

The question is: why didn't the province think of it first? In all the months of discussion and wrangling inside the government and its bureaucracy, why did no one propose a solution that AMO executives were able to hammer out in a matter of weeks, a solution in many ways better for the government than its own proposal? The AMO compromise goes farther in meeting Community and Social Services Minister Janet Ecker's goal of preserving control of welfare at the provincial level, while still allowing Education Minister John Snobelen to retain control of education financing. Surely it is a compromise the province should have been pushing from the beginning.

---

[1] The May announcement was not, however, the end of the Tory tinkering. On August 6, the government bowed to widespread criticism that disentanglement would force Metropolitan Toronto to bear a disproportionate share of welfare and other social costs (since the city contains half the region's population, but three-quarters of its welfare caseload and subsidized-housing stock). The August announcement compelled the entire Greater Toronto region to share the costs of welfare, child care, social housing, and GO Transit. An enraged Mississauga Mayor Hazel McCallion accused the Conservatives, uniquely, of "socialism." Harris, characteristically, was out of the province when Al Leach made the announcement.

Senior advisers in the premier's office maintain the AMO solution was one they had considered but rejected, because they feared that the Roman Catholic school boards would challenge it in court on constitutional grounds. Provincial pooling of education property taxes—in effect, the AMO compromise—appeared to violate the constitutionally guaranteed right of Roman Catholic taxpayers in Ontario to dedicate their property taxes to separate-school boards, if they so choose. When the association representing the Catholic boards readily agreed to the AMO compromise and promised not to challenge it, the Harris government's only potential objection was removed.

Nonetheless, the premier and his inner circle could argue that their January megaweek juggernaut had forced the various stakeholders to accept—in fact, propose themselves—a solution they otherwise would have fiercely resisted. That the Tories' strategy threw the province into months of agonized debate and uncertainty, and that the government once again took a public-relations hit, seemed not to matter.

And indeed, by the end of June, polls showed that the Harris government, having dipped to second place behind the Liberals during the megaweek and megacity debates, was back on top, albeit by the narrowest of margins. According to a poll conducted by Angus Reid, the Tories now enjoyed the support of 38 per cent of Ontario voters, up three points from the month before, while the Liberals had dropped to 36 per cent, down from 39 per cent. (The results are considered accurate to within three percentage points, nineteen times out of twenty.) More significant still, Harris's personal popularity had climbed to 56 per cent, up ten points, while six out of ten Ontarians agreed with the statement that the government was "on the right track."

As well as the megaweek compromise, the month of May also saw Ernie Eves deliver his second budget, an annual document that was becoming one of the government's least interesting publications. As widely anticipated, the deficit numbers were declining steadily—the projected deficit for 1997–98 was down to $6.6 billion—the tax cut was on track, and it appeared the Tories would be able to back off on much or all of their final $3 billion in expenditure cuts, thanks to robust economic growth. The savings were principally funnelled back into education and health care.

The government claimed, of course, that its own supply-side policies were responsible for this boom. Economists, however, pointed out that Ontario, like most of Canada, was enjoying a prolonged period of economic growth, buoyed by healthy international markets and the new wave of fiscal prudence by governments across the country. Ontario contributed to that return to sound financing, but neither as early nor as emphatically as the federal and most other provincial governments. Ontario, under the Tories, will still be one of the last jurisdictions to eliminate its deficit.

And the budget contained one damning number that no amount of spinning could charm away: the Ontario economy had created only 107,000 net new jobs since the Harris government took office, far from the goal of 725,000 new jobs promised during the life of his mandate. Mike Harris had vowed to resign if he failed to keep any of the promises of the Common Sense Revolution. Tory insiders say that, with the target unlikely to be met, in two years' time the premier will finesse the promise by saying, "We promised to reduce taxes, eliminate the deficit, and create 725,000 new jobs. We have met the first two promises, but the third is not yet fulfilled. And in keeping with my commitment to resign if I could not fulfill all of the promises of the Common Sense Revolution, ladies and gentlemen, I today asked the lieutenant governor to dissolve the legislature and call a general election."

With the arrival of June, and the approaching end of the spring 1997 legislative session, many observers predicted that the most militant phase of the Common Sense Revolution was drawing to a close. Virtually all of its initiatives were underway, from reducing the deficit and cutting taxes to reforming welfare and transforming education. Indeed, the Harris government had gone well beyond its original mandate in ramming through the amalgamation of Toronto and approximately fifty other municipalities across the province, though it backed off amalgamation plans for Ottawa and Hamilton. Conventional punditry dictated that the Tories would now seek to present a kinder face to the electorate. First would come a cabinet shuffle to shift or replace some of the more embattled ministers and put more conciliatory faces on the front benches. Then would come a change in public tone: "reinvestments" in education and health care that would outpace cuts. The government emphasis would be on managing change, or on bringing people together, or on whatever variant the spin-doctors came up with. With an election as little as two years away, so the argument went, the Tories needed to soften their image.

Fat chance. On June 3, Labour Minister Elizabeth Witmer introduced Bill 136, a legislative number destined to rank up there with 26 (the omnibus bill) and 103 (the megacity legislation). Witmer insisted the legislation was mere housekeeping, a means of smoothing potential conflict during the dislocations and re-alignments produced by disentanglement and municipal amalgamation. In fact, the bill promises to cross the one line the Tories had vowed never to violate: the principle of collective bargaining.

Back in 1996, when Witmer, with the support of Harris and his advisers, emptied John Snobelen's toolkit of educational reforms, the argument was that the province should not be re-opening collective agreements signed between the school boards and the teachers. The socialists under Rae might be willing to pry open a contract, went the reasoning, but for us a deal is a deal, and the boards will have to negotiate away those benefits during the next rounds of talks. Similarly, when the public servants went on strike, the government resisted using the legislative hammer to force them back to work. Dave Johnson, who as Management Board chair spearheaded the negotiations, maintained that the government wanted to end the strike through collective bargaining, not with an arbitrated settlement.

Bill 136 rudely revokes those previous positions. It mandates, in essence, that when workers from different unions and under different contracts find themselves thrown together as a result of restructuring, they will be treated as if they are seeking a first contract with their employer (most likely a municipal government). In the event of a dispute over which union should represent the newly amalgamated employees, a government commission will arbitrate. More controversially, in the event a union and an employer are unable to reach a new contract, either side can appeal the matter to another new commission, with members appointed by the government, which will have the power to simply impose a contract, temporarily eliminating the right to lock out or strike. Although teachers' unions are not included within the legislation, Education Minister John Snobelen promised similar legislation for teachers would follow in August. When Snobelen was asked in late June whether he believed teachers should even have the right to strike, after a very long pause, he shook his head and replied, "No."

The Tories cite two grounds that have forced them to interfere in the collective-bargaining process. First, permitting a bargaining free-for-all could have led to a wave of strikes and mass confusion as the new municipal and education regimes came into place in 1998. The disruptions would no doubt be blamed on the provincial government, which had initiated the changes in the first place. Second, the Harris government's advisers detest the Ontario Labour Relations Board, the traditional forum for resolving such disputes, maintaining that it is hopelessly biased on the side of labour—as they believed it was during the public servants' strike. By creating a new commission and giving it instructions to take into account the costs to the taxpayer of its decisions, the Tories hope to bypass all existing tribunals and ensure rulings more favourable to their cause.

They may in the process have finally provided the catalyst that draws Ontario's fractured labour movement together. In May 1997, CUPE's Sid Ryan quietly acknowledged that province-wide labour action against the Tories was impossible in light of the breach between the public- and private-sector unions. But even though Bill 136 does not directly affect private-sector workers, it alarms even the most conservative unionists. The bill violates the collective-bargaining process for public-sector workers, removing their right to strike and, worst of all, deliberately skewing (as labour sees it) the arbitration process, dealing a triple blow to labour relations. On July 28, more than two thousand union delegates met in emergency session and vowed to go to any extreme to force the Tories to rewrite Bill 136. Private-sector union leaders offered strong support. The prospect of a general public-sector strike, that would close schools and hospitals, leave garbage uncollected and potholes unfilled, that might even affect police and fire service, loomed as a clear and imminent danger.

In this book I have attempted to chronicle the life of the first two years of the Mike Harris government and its Common Sense Revolution. It is by necessity a report on a government in progress, an attempt to understand events whose significance continues to unfold. Inevitably, it is also an incomplete record. The pressures of time and space have forced me to neglect several themes that cry out for analysis.

For example, we need a thorough assessment of the Harris government's environmental policy. In everything from lifting the ban on incinerating garbage to transferring responsibility for the Niagara Escarpment to the Ministry of Natural Resources, the Tories have reshaped and relaxed the controls on environmental protection. And because they have eliminated so much staff at Environment and at Energy and at Natural Resources, it is no longer certain the province is able to adequately monitor and enforce those regulations that remain. To some extent, these changes may represent a necessary loosening of what were turning into excessive limitations on development. But a balanced and thorough assessment of Conservative environmental policy—and its likely long-term effect— remains to be carried out.

Also beyond the scope of this book is an assessment of Conservative agriculture and transportation policies—the former now virtually ignored by the mainstream media, the latter the subject of too many stories on flying truck wheels and too few on crumbling infrastructure—or an assessment of the impact of cuts at the Ministry of Citizenship, Culture, and Recreation on the province's vital entertainment industries, or of the efficacy of the move towards super-jails and boot camps by the Solicitor General's ministry, or of the clogging of the courts and the Attorney General's efforts to unclog them.

I have covered the birth of workfare, but only time will tell whether it is failing or succeeding at providing people living on public assistance with new skills that enable them to find jobs. And no one has been able to satisfactorily explain why welfare rates are falling. Since Ernie Eves' first financial statement in July 1995, which announced a 22 per cent reduction in welfare payments, the number of people on welfare in Ontario has notably declined. Actually, the drop had begun the month before, after a decade of continually rising numbers. But the major declines came after the cut in benefits kicked in in October. In that one month, there was a 3 per cent drop in caseloads. Six months later, welfare numbers had gone down by another 3 per cent; six months after that they were 6 per cent lower still. By June 1997, two years after the Tories came to power, the number of people on welfare had declined by 15 per cent.

The relationship between the minimum wage, the guaranteed minimum annual income (which is what welfare, in fact, is), and employment levels is complex and controversial. We know that if the minimum wage is pushed higher, some employers will find it unproductive to hire workers, which can lead to higher unemployment. Similarly, if welfare rates rise beyond a certain level, a worker loses the incentive to take a job at the minimum wage, since the benefits of that wage may be less than those of staying on welfare. This can be especially true if the worker must pay for child care, or if the worker, by taking the job, is deprived of under-the-table income.

Numerous explanations have been put forward to account for the recent decline in welfare rates. Some people may have left the province in search of other jurisdictions with better rates, although this is unlikely, since Alberta and British Columbia, the other "have" provinces, have both tightened welfare eligibility. Others might have given up on welfare altogether and taken to living, and earning a living, on the streets. One highly disputed study commissioned by the Harris government suggested that many of those who dropped off welfare did so because it was now in their financial interest to take a minimum-wage job. Only a dispassionate investigation of the causes of the drop in welfare numbers and the effectiveness of workfare in creating jobs will answer many of the rhetorical questions flying about on the subject.

While I have concentrated on the role played by education-finance reform in the disentanglement controversy, I have neglected the equally important subject of curriculum reform. John Snobelen arrived at Education with a mandate to revolutionize the province's curriculum as well as the way its schools were financed and governed, to make Ontario students achieve as much as their Alberta and British Columbia counterparts. But the Education ministry, as one former deputy minister put it, is a place where you push a button and nothing happens. Orders from Snobelen's office for new proposals and guidelines went unanswered. Demands for specific benchmarks for academic performance, grade by grade, resulted simply in reworded formulations of old documents.

"There is absolutely no doubt, they (the bureaucrats) dragged their heels," says a former senior official in the government. Ministry staff went so far as to withhold information from Snobelen that would help his cause. British Columbia, Alberta, and Saskatchewan, for example, were already at work on a common curriculum that met most of the goals Snobelen had set. "No one in the minister's office was told about what the West was doing," another ministry source said. Nor were they told that the Atlantic provinces had launched a similar project of their own. When asked why these developments had not even been mentioned, the bureaucrats explained that there was nothing the other provinces were up to that could possibly be relevant to Ontario.

The minister himself was also part of the problem. Snobelen was more interested, say staff, in the nuts and bolts of administrative reform than in the arcane subject of curriculum. A minister who had dropped out of high school and become a businessman and management consultant was more into structure than content. The price of distraction was delay.

Snobelen's 1995 announcement that Grade 13 would be eliminated in time for the 1997–98 school year turned out to be a fantasy. In July 1996 he announced that it would be set back to the 1998–99 school year. In June 1997 he announced it would be delayed until 1999–2000. Gradually, however, Snobelen and his staff gained ground. Outside advisers were imported to assist in developing the new curriculum—an accountant for the math panel, for example, and a nurse for the panel developing the science curriculum. On orders from the minister's office, the Western and Atlantic curriculum projects were raided, along with a pan-Canadian study of science curriculum that was also under way. At one point, the minister's staff threatened simply to adopt, province-wide, the highly-praised curriculum created by the North York Board of Education. And Snobelen's staff, though devoid of pedagogical training, went so far as to start writing guidelines themselves. The situation further eased as senior staff more sympathetic to the Tories' philosophy gradually replaced their more obstructionist predecessors.

In June 1997, the Education ministry introduced a new curriculum in reading, writing, and math for pupils in Grades 1 through 8. A new elementary science and technology curriculum was expected for November. The completed revised curriculum is to be in place for the beginning of the 1999–2000 school year.

Early reviews of the new educational standards have met with high praise. But the tougher requirements are bound to leave some students behind, as others flourish. How the education system will accommodate those unable to cope with the rigour of the new Tory schools remains an unanswered question.

Nor have I adequately evaluated the Tory commitment to privatization, much of which has been delayed, quite possibly until a second mandate. So far, Mike Harris has resisted the privatization of such large assets as Ontario Hydro, the Liquor Control Board, and TVOntario. During the Bill 103 filibuster, one Conservative MPP who thought the entire amalgamation initiative was a waste of government time bitterly complained, "How many operations could we have privatized by now, instead of going through this?" But the premier has adopted a pragmatic approach to converting public to private ownership. The onus is on advocates to prove to him that selling off assets would save the consumer money. As of yet, say advisers, he remains unconvinced.

Early in Al Leach's tenure, the Municipal Affairs minister diluted the province's planning laws, making it even easier for shapeless suburbs to creep across and absorb rural southern Ontario. Ironically, this continuing sprawl must ultimately erase many of the last vestiges of the settler culture on which the Harris government's political philosophy is founded. But there is no stopping this march of suburbia. The first, inviolate principle of the settler culture is that a property owner has the right to sell his land, whatever the consequences to the larger community. In strengthening that right, the Harris government is simply assisting a culture's suicide.

And I have ignored most of the petty scandals and controversies that have occasionally marred the first half of the mandate, from the revelations that Harris let the Progressive Conservative Party pay for his tuxedo rental to the premier's sacking of several parliamentary assistants who defied his authority. Such matters must await a more encyclopedic accounting of the Harris years in office.

One of the more fascinating unexplored areas of Mike Harris's first two years in office is his relationship with his federal and provincial cousins, a case in point being the conflict over post-secondary education, an area of shared provincial and federal interest. (Although tuition subsidies are a provincial responsibility, student loans are jointly funded by the province and the feds.) The Tories' determination to reform Ontario's student-aid system has been partially stymied by Ottawa's intransigence.

There is good reason for abolishing subsidized tuition, which permits the better off in society to send their children to university with the financial help of all taxpayers, while the parents of poorer students must undergo means testing to determine whether their children are entitled to government loans. A fairer solution would see tuition subsidies gradually eliminated. Those who could afford to pay the entire cost would do so. Those who needed assistance would receive grants and income-contingent loans. These loans would finance the cost of a student's tuition, with the cost deducted from the graduate's income, as with income tax, until the loan and interest were paid off. Although the income-contingent system has its own drawbacks—a $40,000 loan is both practically and psychologically much more daunting for a poorer student majoring, bravely, in the humanities, than for an affluent student at a professional school—it nonetheless continues to make university accessible to all, while depriving the affluent students, and their parents, of the gift of unneeded tuition subsidies.

From the time John Snobelen took on the Education portfolio, he was committed to replacing Ontario's existing system for providing financial aid to post-secondary students, and he immediately moved to phase in market-value tuitions. But to replace student loan programs with an income-contingent loan system required Ottawa's co-operation. And this has not been forthcoming. Thus Ontario post-secondary students find themselves living in the worst of all possible worlds: escalating tuition fees, without innovative solutions to help those with lower incomes cope.

Student loan programs are not the only area in which the Mike Harris and Jean Chrétien governments have failed to find common ground. Relations between the provincial and federal regimes have been strained since the autumn 1995 referendum. Three days after that hair-raising result, Prime Minister Chrétien came to Toronto to urge Premier Harris to join his initiative to grant Quebec distinct-society status and a veto over constitutional changes. Harris flatly refused, saying this was not the time for hurried concessions. Chrétien went away disappointed and angry. When the details of the meeting appeared in *Maclean's* magazine in October 1996, in the form of an excerpt from the book *Double Vision* by reporters Edward Greenspon and Anthony Wilson-

Smith, the Tories—who vehemently insist the leak came from the feds—were furious. As far as they were concerned, the incident demonstrated that nothing said between Chrétien and Harris could ever be considered confidential.

The provincial-federal ill will extends to their respective ministries of Finance. Ontario angered Ottawa by refusing to harmonize the provincial sales tax with the Goods and Services Tax, which Ernie Eves maintained would result in an overall tax hike. Ottawa, on the other hand, has ignored Ontario's complaint that, by contributing the single greatest share of unemployment insurance premiums, the province is subsidizing federal deficit reduction. (The fund is in surplus, with the extra money going to general revenues.) At a personal level, Ernie Eves and federal Finance Minister Paul Martin simply dislike each other. At one point, federal fixer Eddie Goldenberg even paid Eves a visit, in hopes of ironing out the differences between the two strong-willed men. It was to no avail.

By contrast, Harris has cultivated a surprisingly friendly relationship with Quebec Premier Lucien Bouchard. The Ontario and Quebec premiers spent much time in each other's company during the winter 1997 Team Canada trade mission—and even their wives seem to get along. In one sense, this public amicability represents little more than political posturing. Harris hopes to use his cordial relations with Bouchard to improve his credentials in Quebec in the event of another referendum on sovereignty. But at another level, the two men share a remarkably common vision of the country. Neither believes that granting Quebec distinct-society status will solve Canada's ills. Both believe that any future confederation will involve loose co-operation among much more powerful provinces. The only real difference is that Bouchard is seeking the powerfully symbolic trappings of a sovereign nation for Quebec, while Harris has no such goals for Ontario and would resist granting sovereignty to Quebec as inimical to Ontario's interests.

In his own way, Mike Harris has done as much to undermine the federalist cause as has his Quebec counterpart. Unlike previous Ontario premiers who have participated actively in the ongoing constitutional question, Harris spends as little time as possible on the issue, and when he does speak, it is to insist that (a) all provinces need to be recognized as more powerful entities, and (b) no province should be granted a status different from any other. Neither position sits well with a federal government striving to strengthen its waning influence while seeking an accommodation with Quebec.

But Mike Harris's greatest wound to federalism has been simply to ignore the government in Ottawa. While other provinces have berated the feds for cutting this or imposing that, Harris prefers to act as though Ontario is sovereign in its economic and social affairs. Cuts to federal transfers are rarely mentioned. Proposals for joint initiatives in tax reform and child care have been rebuffed. By moving so emphatically in so many areas of crucial concern, and by simply not mentioning the declining importance of the federal government in the debate, Harris has successfully created the impression that his government is the only one that matters in Ontario. The province, under Mike Harris, is evolving into an entity only a *soupçon* less sovereign than Premier Lucien Bouchard would like Quebec to be.

Editors regularly vex journalists with the question: What does all this mean to the reader? Many of the readers of this book hardly need to be told what the Common Sense Revolution means to them. The Harris government has already profoundly affected millions of lives. If you receive welfare, you are in the second year of living on an income 22 per cent lower than it was before October 1995. If you are a provincial or municipal worker, you have either been laid off, are working harder for less money, or are facing the prospect of no work or more work come January 1, 1998, when the post-disentanglement regime arrives.

For others, the effects have been more subtle or are yet to be felt. It will be several years before Ontarians start to see the impact of a new, tougher curriculum in their classrooms and of sole provincial funding of their schools. It will be at least as long before we can measure the ramifications on health care of fewer hospitals but more resources directed to people treated at home. It may take a decade or more before the impact of recent changes to Ontario labour laws and environmental standards becomes apparent.

Unquestionably, however, the Common Sense Revolution has affected the civil discourse of Canada's most populous province. A society that governed itself by seeking to accommodate conflicting interests has been transformed into one where interests hurl themselves against each other until the more powerful prevails. Such a confrontational method has made possible enormous changes that, in many cases, were arguably long overdue. It has also left the citizenry raw and bruised and surly towards one another. And there is no end in sight to the prevailing public distemper.

Only the brashest of prognosticators would dare predict what verdict the voters will pass on Mike Harris's revolution come the next election. In recent times, governments in Canada and around the world that have eliminated deficits, cut government spending, and stabilized or lowered the tax burden have usually been re-elected. By that measure, the Ontario Conservatives should be confident of a second victory. But the Ontario electorate is cagey and volatile. The Liberal Party under leader Dalton McGuinty promises to consolidate the Conservative reforms while lowering the level of political tension. Voters weary of confrontation and crisis might find such an offer tempting. And many of those who abandoned the NDP in 1995 may return to it once it is purified by the absence of any real prospect of power.

Meanwhile, the Tories confront a dilemma. Revolutions evolve in one of two directions. Either they institutionalize themselves, with the vanguard simply replacing the elite it overthrew, or they escalate, seeking ever greater heights of ideological purity. Either path looks dangerous for the Harris Conservatives. If they settle into the comfortable role of establishment government, they risk alienating the ideologues in their midst who brought the party to power and remain its most devoted supporters. If Tom Long and Alister Campbell and their comrades ever conclude that the Mike Harris government has become complacent, they may well seek allies among the more Reform-minded members of the government caucus. Then the split that has bedevilled the federal Right will be recreated within the provincial party.

If, however, the Tories remain true to their revolution, then they must pursue it to its logical conclusion. There must be yet more tax cuts, yet more deregulation, much, much more privatization. Ultimately, if the revolution continues, the party risks pushing itself into an ideological region remote from most of the people who elected it, who will turn to a party with a more sensible agenda and a more sensitive approach.

John Sewell believes the Harris government is "truly the most revolutionary regime this province has ever seen. And like all true revolutionaries, they are prepared to go to any lengths, no matter how many they may harm, in pursuit of their ideological ideal. They are even willing, if they must, to destroy themselves."

Recently, Harris's loyal principal secretary David Lindsay has launched yet another of his beloved visioning exercises. He is canvassing party supporters across the province, asking them to describe what they think Ontario should look like in the next millennium, and what government can and should do to help get us there. Project 21 (for twenty-first century), as this exercise is called, may serve as the basis for the campaign platform on which the Conservative government will enter its re-election campaign. If so, it must first find a solid middle way between the diverging paths of consolidation and perpetual militancy.

There remains, finally, the enigma of the man in the middle of it all. Mike Harris is, ultimately, no better known today than he was in 1990, when he arrived as leader on the provincial scene. Deeply private, intensely competitive, powerfully intuitive, and utterly committed to reshaping the province, he is still, in the minds of many, a slow-thinking front man for his smart young advisers. As usual, this perception is ultimately to the premier's advantage: Mike Harris has always surprised those who underestimated him.

Harris's old friend Peter Minogue likes to describe the summer Mike decided to run the 440-yard track event in under sixty seconds, at the time considered something of a feat in local sports circles. Though Harris was never keen on track and field, he simply got it into his head that he wanted to match that pace. At the Wasi Falls resort, which Harris helped manage with his father and brother, he had to repeatedly walk up and down a 200-yard path. So, rather than walking, he simply started to run this path. Finally, Harris went with Minogue to the high-school track and asked his friend to time him.

The future premier ran the 440 in under sixty seconds. "I don't think he's ever run it since," Minogue says.

When will Mike Harris decide that he has run to the end of his revolution?

Index